BR

PROFIT MAPPING

PROFIT MAPPING

A Tool for Aligning Operations with Future Profit and Performance

ANIL MENAWAT AND ADAM GARFEIN

McGraw-Hill

New York   Chicago   San Francisco   Lisbon   London   Madrid
Mexico City   Milan   New Delhi   San Juan   Seoul
Singapore   Sydney   Toronto

Copyright © 2006 by Anil Menawat and Adam Garfein. All rights reserved. Printed in the United States of America. Except as permitted under the United States Copyright Act of 1976, no part of this publication may be reproduced or distributed in any form or by any means, or stored in a data base or retrieval system, without the prior written permission of the publisher.

1 2 3 4 5 6 7 8 9 0   DOC/DOC   0 9 8 7 6

ISBN 0-07-147228-2

McGraw-Hill books are available at special quantity discounts to use as premiums and sales promotions, or for use in corporate training programs. For more information, please write to the Director of Special Sales, McGraw-Hill Professional, Two Penn Plaza, New York, NY 10121-2298. Or contact your local bookstore.

ProFIT-MAP and the ProFIT-MAP triangle are trademarks of Menawat and Co.

This book is printed on recycled, acid-free paper containing a minimum of 50% recycled, de-inked fiber.

Library of Congress Cataloging-in-Publication Data

Menawat, Anil.
  Profit mapping : a tool for aligning operations with future profit and performance / by Anil Menawat & Adam Garfein.
    p. cm.
  ISBN 0-07-147228-2 (alk. paper)
  1. Industrial management.   2. Organizational effectiveness.   3. Business.
  4. Corporate profits.   5. Corporations—Finance.   6. Cost control.   I. Garfein,
  Adam.   II. Title.
HD31.M3968   2007
658.4'03—dc22

                                                            2006005498

Contents

A. M.

Vibha—my love, my life, my eternity
Dhruv and Radhika—my joy and delight
My parents, Govind and Sushila—my revered sages and gurus

A. G.

To Gina, my soulmate
To Shane and Devin, my sunshine

Acknowledgments

THIS BOOK IS ABOUT perspectives—identifying, understanding, and balancing them to accomplish a common objective. Profit mapping is about looking at a problem from various viewpoints and finding a solution in a systematic way. It is not about creating a pie-in-the-sky vision. It is about taking action and building a roadmap to create your own future with full cognizance of your capabilities and constraints.

Profit mapping is an expression of wisdom passed on to us by philosophers, thinkers, and doers who came before us and left enduring imprints upon us. They taught us to live in the future with an awareness of the past and present. They persuaded us to get out of our comfort zone of data mining the past and challenged us to confront our own reality gap in creating the future. We are eternally thankful.

A. M.: The roadmap to profit mapping began in the spring of 1978 in the engineering economics class taught by Prof. Wilburn Schroder of the University of Maryland. As a young engineer I was enthralled by the possibilities that were later reinforced during my days at Union Carbide. Looking at a problem from multiple perspectives had become a habit. From early childhood my grandfather encouraged me to think about the future holistically. My parents perpetuated the same ideas with examples from Hindu scriptures and daily living. They explained how decisions in their lives would have affected all of us if they had not considered the future and the holistic view. But, it was not until much later that Prof. Raj Mutharasan (my Ph.D. dissertation advisor) made the two distinct lines of thinking—multiple perspectives and holistic analysis—one whole concept in my mind. The systems theory was the thread that tied the two together. There are far too many people who have played a role in shaping these ideas. S. P. Srinivas, my office-mate in graduate school, helped me understand the nuances of systems theory. My former students from Tulane University—in particular Jay Manouchehri, James Gomes, Mohammed Hindawi, and J. B. Phillips—and I debated each afternoon endlessly until we ran out of coffee. Dr. John Morano, my boss at Aeroquip, challenged me to apply these concepts to real-life situations. The ideas were just a beginning. Transforming the raw ideas into a successful methodology took a lot of support from my wife, Vibha, whose relentless encouragement and endless belief in my capabilities keeps me going. My brothers, Arun and Sunil, believed I was onto something remarkable and encouraged me to continue my pursuit. My good friend Ashok Varma helped me in refining the message and in understanding the challenges. I am forever grateful to all.

A. G.: My profit mapping odyssey crystallized in graduate school at The Pennsylvania State University. As a budding gerontologist I developed an appreciation for the challenges of researching complex dynamic systems (i.e., people) and the holistic insight that comes from investigating multiple perspectives. I would like to single out several faculty members in particular—Michael A. Smyer, John R. Nesselroade, Steven H. Zarit, K. Warner Schaie, and Sherry L. Willis—who instilled the importance of theory (strategy) and methodology (systematic thinking and doing). They helped me develop an appreciation for individual differences (resulting from unique capabilities and constraints) in performance. Later on, I extended these concepts into the business world as a strategy and e-business consultant and educator. Listening to clients, I recognized the commonality in their concerns, although they expressed them differently depending on their roles in the organization. Numerous individuals, too many to name here, greatly influenced my way of thinking about rapidly changing, complex, and interconnected business systems. I would like to thank my wife, Gina Jay, for being a partner in this journey and for her unwavering support and encouragement since the day we first met in graduate school. I also want to thank my mother, Jamee Henson-Hammer, for encouraging me to pursue my dreams.

The process of writing this book has been a remarkable journey for both of us. While our ultimate destination was clear at the outset, the challenge of communicating our perspective and associated bias was greatly smoothed by the invaluable support and feedback received from several individuals. We would like to thank Gina Jay, our independent editor. Her gentle diplomacy and eye for detail constantly challenged us to more clearly articulate our thoughts and ideas, and vastly improved our message. We are greatly indebted to Jeanne Glasser, our senior editor at McGraw-Hill Professional. She believed in us from the outset and provided invaluable advice along the way, for which we are very appreciative. We would also like to thank Janice Race and Alice Manning for their linguistic art.

Profit Mapping—Get the Latest News and Information

See www.profitmapping.com for the latest news and information about the ProFIT-MAP methodology. Be sure to sign up to get on the mailing list.—A. M. and A. G.

You've got to be careful if you don't know where you're going, because you might not get there.

—Yogi Berra

It's not the strongest who survive, nor the most intelligent, but the ones most responsive to change.

—Charles Darwin

PROFIT MAPPING

Introduction

Driving Operational Excellence through Profit Mapping

Not to see the forest for the trees is a serious failing. But it is an equally serious failing not to see the trees for the forest. One can only plant and cut down individual trees. Yet the forest is the "ecology," the environment without which individual trees would never grow.

—Peter Drucker, *Post-Capitalist Society*

EFFECTIVE MANAGERS instinctively know what to do. They labor over facts to understand the current situation, and they try to create mental pictures of the future and what it should look like. They are like artists who focus on the whole painting, but who understand that it is the details that convey their story. Nowadays managers have the benefit of enormous amounts of data collected throughout the organization, residing in massive enterprise databases. They can assess the current situation rapidly. Until now, however, they have lacked methods and management tools that can peer into their desired future and then look back to determine how to get there from where they are today.

This book is about operational decision making in both manufacturing and business services environments. It is not about building a "pie in the sky" future or yet another strategic approach, improvement framework, measurement system, or method of developing good managers. A good strategy coupled with the right people with appropriate knowledge and skills is not sufficient for success. Success comes only with operational excellence that is properly aligned with strategy. The challenge is knowing what actions to take and when and where they should be taken.

This book is about equipping managers with what they most want and need if they are to achieve this—relevant, forward-looking information to holistically compare their operational options on an equal basis. A vision—no matter how timely, insightful, or bold—is hollow if its viability and a path to realizing it cannot be assessed. Even an experienced tour guide with an incorrect or incomplete roadmap can get lost. Navigating without the means to determine the impact that a given set of actions will have on the bottom line is risky.

PROFIT MAPPING—
A GPS NAVIGATION SYSTEM FOR OPERATIONS

ProFIT-MAP™ is a forward-looking management decision methodology that allows you to navigate the forest and trees of business strategy and execution proactively. It is a systematic approach to decision making with six well-defined, intuitive steps. It helps you compare your options for process effectiveness, resource requirements, and financials. ProFIT-MAP simultaneously focuses on multiple parameters of business operations, analyzes their dynamic interactions, and evaluates their impact on resources and costs. ProFIT-MAP does this by reconstructing the environment of the future for each of your decision options, based on the requirements of the future business needs—not on your performance in the past.

Profit mapping virtually eliminates decisions that have adverse effects on your business. It is a dynamic, multidisciplinary, and objective approach that is driven by facts and refined through the validation of real-world implementation. It helps you correct your situation immediately and guides you to where you want to go, like a GPS navigation system. Whether you need to make "real-time" decisions or create an operational roadmap, ProFIT-MAP guides you with confidence.

Most companies focus on tracking their past performance and then trend to extrapolate their future operational requirements and capabilities. Unfortunately, your past performance, no matter how successful, was based on different work requirements, demands, customer needs, and market conditions. Things that may have helped you in the past may not produce the desired result in the future because the environment has changed. Current improvement approaches provide only general guidelines; they have no methodology for application specifically to your business. They are unable to provide the necessary insight into the specific actions you need to take for your company. They cannot help you test your ideas in advance to guarantee success.

There are many helpful books written by academics and former CEOs discussing strategy development, people processes, and the importance of having the right person for the right job. The concepts in this book start with the premise that your organization has already invested in strategy, processes, and people. Still, the competition is putting intense pressure on your business and margins. In *The World Is Flat*, Thomas Friedman[1] issues a wake-up call that in a connected world in which political and trade barriers are falling, countries with lower costs of doing business, particularly when it comes to labor, are going to compete more and more fiercely. There is no time to explore and experiment; you have got to know that your strategy is going to succeed before you implement it.

Our focus is on equipping managers with a management tool to enable them to achieve their operational objectives, ensuring that goals are both attainable and synchronized with strategy. Doing so enables you to control your operational destiny and to proactively navigate your response to the global sourcing pressures that surround you.

Corporations spend countless hours developing strategic plans, reorganizing processes, and putting key people in critical places. Equal or greater effort goes into the activities involved in executing the strategy, yet very few companies succeed in fully achieving their goals. Management's dilemma is not about what to do (strategy) or who needs to do it (people); rather, it's about how to do whatever it is they are doing better (execution).

Driving the Organization with ProFIT-MAP

The ProFIT-MAP approach marks a radical, yet intuitive, enhancement to operational decision making that is equally suitable for use from the "top floor to the shop floor." The focus is on the activities performed by people and machines to improve business execution. ProFIT-MAP constructs an activities composition of the process and ties this information to the resource requirements and costs of producing the product or service. As business conditions change (such as changes in demand, product or service delivery capabilities, vendor performance, business strategy, and so on) ProFIT-MAP reassesses the resource requirements and cost/profitability implications of the new activities composition. If your goal is not attainable ProFIT-MAP identifies the gap that cannot be bridged within your current capabilities, constraints, and costs. It can then help redefine your approach based on what is achievable.

Profit mapping does not change the way you run your business. It does not change your ongoing strategy, process improvement initiatives, or measurement frameworks. Rather, it enhances them. For example, if you are not realizing the full potential of your lean, Six Sigma, or continuous improvement initiatives, the problem is not caused by the guidelines provided by these approaches. The problem is that you do not have tools that can assess what it will take to be successful, given the situation at hand. ProFIT-MAP provides insight into which actions will be effective; it helps you avoid decisions that will take the company in the wrong direction. No other methodology can do this!

The ability to redesign activities within operational constraints to achieve the objectives of your strategy is a critical management requirement and sets the stage for winning before taking action. At first glance, this may sound too good to be true; however, the systematic framework, methodology, and case studies presented in this book show that it is real.

We sympathize with managers who struggle with day-to-day strategy execution, knowing that their education and training probably placed greater emphasis on crafting strategy than on making it happen. As Lawrence Hrebiniak[2] aptly observes, "It is obvious that the execution of strategy is not nearly as clear and understood as the formulation of strategy. Much more is known about planning than doing, about strategy making than making strategy work."

Knowing precisely how and what to change to achieve desired results is an age-old management challenge. Larry Bossidy and Ram Charan[3] write: "We talk to many leaders who fall victim to the gap between promises they've made and results their organizations delivered. They frequently tell us they have a problem with accountability—people aren't doing the things they're supposed to do to implement a plan. They desperately want to make changes of some kind, but what do they need to change? They don't know."

Managers are quick to declare how busy the whole organization is at implementing improvement programs and initiatives. They go into great detail about their plans and what they are doing. Yet, when we ask them to explain why they are taking specific actions or how they know whether their efforts will succeed, we typically get blank stares. After some thought, they tell us, "This is the way things are done around here," or "This is the new and improved approach," or (of course our favorite) "Success comes [hopefully] from executing the plan." After reflecting a bit more, they often step back and admit, "There is probably a better way, but we have no way of knowing what it is." Their mantra is that some action is better than none, hence they continue. Doing nothing would be the sure death of a fine career, whereas failure is a mere setback.

Managers therefore forge ahead, typically relying on correlative reasoning, extrapolation of aggregated data about past performances to the future, and rules of thumb about what types of changes are likely to be successful. Companies are realizing, however, that these approaches are not very effective in complex settings where decisions are increasingly "financial-critical" for survival.

Managers also bemoan macro-level concerns that strike at the heart of profitability and competitiveness. Market share is stagnant or decreasing, and never seems to rebound. Health-care costs are astronomical and rising. Labor agreements are chipping away at profitability. Raw materials costs are increasing as a result of global demand and limited supply. Many such examples exist.

Our message, at the risk of being pretentious, in simple terms is—*get over it and let's work with the hand dealt to us*. Managers may not be able to do anything about high fixed costs in the near term, but they can do a lot more operationally to increase effectiveness and quality while striving to reduce cost. In order to overcome changes in demand and financial constraints, organizations must learn to become cost-competitive; price competitiveness is not sufficient. Industry leaders win by focusing on operational execution, cost management, and customers. The devil is in the details, and they understand that success happens only when the plan is grounded in reality, as opposed to invalidated expectations.

THE OPERATIONAL REALITY GAP

Companies are adept at creating strategies and action plans to achieve desired results. Yet, in most organizations, there is some form of disconnection between strategy making and strategy execution. Figure 1-1 illustrates that this disconnection results in a "reality gap" between the expectations of the strategy and the ability of the organization to implement the strategy. The presence of this chasm is in part the result of the lack of convenient and easy-to-use management methods and tools that can foresee the results before implementation, creating a lack of synchronization between those that make the strategy and those that execute it.

The reality gap results from the inaccurate information and analysis that goes into the construction of strategic and operational plans. A disconnection between management's expectations and what can actually be accomplished can occur when operational issues are viewed as "something that can be worried about later" during the strategy-making process. In other words, developing the strategy and then handing it down for execution leads to a reality gap. Other contributors to this gap include incorrect information about markets, customer demands, organizational capabilities, and the framework used to determine expected costs.

A strategic plan is a high-level device to gain excellence—customer, product, and operational. It focuses on taking an organization from its current situation to a new and hopefully better future. Every manager wants the best for his or her company, but when the desire is not in line with the organization's capabilities and constraints, troubles begin. The disconnection creates a false sense of hope and leads to disappointment when things don't work out according to plan. Whether their focus is on gaining market share, improving profitability, improving customer satisfaction, or any other such ideal, strategic plans reflect the vision and the desires of senior management. Well-formulated strategy, carefully communicated throughout the ranks, can inspire the whole organization and lead it into a new competitive mode and greater performance.

Figure 1-1. The Operational Reality Gap

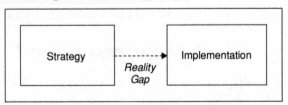

Unfortunately, having a strategic plan and having the right people do not guarantee success. Success comes only from execution of operational plans that achieve the objectives laid out in the strategy. Strategic plans generally do not include roadmaps to achieve their objectives. The responsibility for developing those roadmaps is delegated to middle managers, who create operational and project plans to execute on the strategy. Therein lie two weaknesses leading to reality gaps that frequently spiral into failure: a lack of synchronization between strategic and operational plans, and improper execution of the operational plans.

Operational plans specify how to structure individual process activities and steps within the context of organizational capabilities and resource constraints. They define specific actions that the organization must undertake to advance the strategic goals. Figure 1-2 shows sample strategies and how they are translated into specific projects and programs for execution. Although the specifics may vary, the cycle is fairly consistent in all organizations.

The cycle of meeting corporate objectives is a top-down process. Senior managers define objectives, and middle managers have to figure out how to meet them. Although anecdotal arguments and correlative

Figure 1-2. Translating Strategy into Action

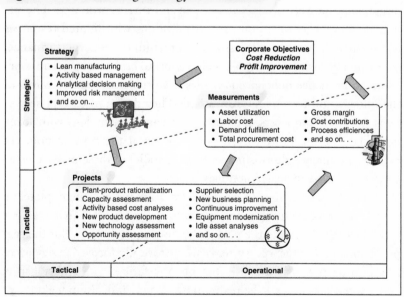

reasons may be communicated to justify the appropriateness of the strategic targets, very little attention is given to detail and full recognition of the organization's capabilities to deliver upon those targets. Despite many discussions about grounding the plan in reality, the setting of objectives essentially happens in a vacuum. That is, the link between the strategy and the specific capabilities that will drive the system to the desired future state is usually absent. Middle managers nevertheless forge ahead, defining and executing the specific projects and programs that implement the strategy. Measures assess their performance, adjustments are made, and the cycle continues.

Central to corporate success is the alignment of operational plans with strategic objectives and their meticulous execution. This is operational excellence. Given this fundamental truth, why is there typically some form of divide between the expectations in the strategy and the actual capabilities of the organization to deliver? The answer has its roots in the traditional management approach shown in Figure 1-3. Corporate strategy is influenced not only by external factors such as product demand, but also by internal factors, including management expectations and the decision framework used to evaluate strategic options. Expectations and decisions are generally based on ad hoc correlative reasoning derived from past performance instead of on a comprehensive analysis of what lies ahead in the future. This creates a discrepancy between what is achievable and what is promised. The situation can quickly turn grave in organizations with limited resources and finances, where there is less built-in margin for underperformance.

In an impressive and commendable effort to bridge the gap and overcome performance deficits, companies have ridden successive waves of the information technology revolution. They deployed enterprise systems, personal computers, and other information technology with abandon. Data were captured from every corner of the organization, yet managers remained dissatisfied with the inability of these massive databases to improve their decision making.

The data were either in an incorrect form for use, incomplete, or void of context for proper interpretation, setting off a management roller coaster of chasing the data and their purposefulness. But the real problem is that enterprise systems are historically focused. They excel at reporting past performance, but not the future. The reality gap is really about the future—the realm of management decision making.

Figure 1-3. Traditional Management Approach

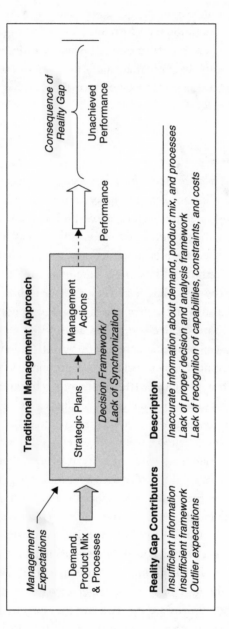

The concept of an operational reality gap is not new, but it has taken on a new prominence in today's global economy. And it is the primary cause of poor operational performance. For most organizations, this is a "black hole" where the truth on the ground is different from the belief. Managers intuitively know that this void exists, but until ProFIT-MAP, they did not have any methods or tools to see what's inside and to do something about it.

The Ground Truth

The term *ground truth* comes from the need to validate remote observation with reality. For instance, cartographers, geographers, and geologists commonly employ satellite imagery, aerial photographs, radar, and existing maps as part of their work. They also visit the actual area being studied to check that the facts are indeed as they appear—to help them interpret and calibrate the remote observations based on the "truth" of what they encounter in the field. The term is also popular with the military. Commanders and troops on the ground are given the authority to make tactical decisions based on the irrefutable ground truth—conditions that may not be perceived at all or in the same way by out-of-theater commanders.

An interesting characteristic of the ground truth in the corporate world is that the "ground" is defined differently by different levels of management, depending on their responsibilities. We illustrate this with a manufacturer, starting with a budgeting example. The budgeting process is based on an aggregated cost model generated from MRP (Manufacturing Resource Planning) data. This form of modeling uses the slowest machine, often called the *bottleneck*, to determine the production rate. Corporate management therefore specifies the budget based on the assumption that production operates at this slowest hourly rate.

The reality at the plant, however, is that it cannot produce collectively at the level of the "slowest" individual machine as assumed by corporate planners. Blockage and starvation dynamics result in a decrease in actual throughput. The plant manager recognizes this and adjusts the production rate downward by reducing the "effectiveness" factor of the machines to account for the ground truth of the blockage and starvation dynamics. Thus, the budget is skewed because it assumes that the plant can operate at a higher rate. The ground truth at the plant is therefore different from the expectations of corporate management.

As we show throughout this book, ProFIT-MAP is designed to bridge this and other operational gaps. Although this example used a manufacturing context, the concepts also apply to business services.

FUNDAMENTAL MANAGEMENT QUESTIONS

Every few years there is a new cycle of management innovation, and, for better or worse, companies jump on the bandwagon. It seems that collectively the more earnest work that is done to improve operations, the more things stay the same. While lots of low-hanging operational improvement fruit has been harvested over the years, fundamental management decision-making challenges remain unchanged. Because of the ever-present reality gap, successfully executing business strategy remains management's Achilles' heel.

Successful execution does not happen by accident; it requires thought and order. Companies cannot approach it ad hoc as something to be improvised later because it is a discipline that requires systematic and continuous application and learning. At a fundamental level, there are three ways to affect business execution performance: change the capabilities (structure of the system), change the constraints (limits on the system), or change the activities composition (the course of the system). When treated as a discipline, business execution helps bridge the reality gap by seeking to provide managers with key information to aid in making operational decisions. This information comes in the form of answers to several critical questions prior to implementing any change:

- Is an objective achievable, and will it ever be profitable?
- Will a proposed change have the intended effects?
- What impact will my proposed change have elsewhere in the organization?
- How do I transform operations from point A to point B? That is, how do I actually get to the desired operational destination (roadmap)?

Obtaining answers to these and other questions prior to undertaking any action can save a great deal of time, money, and resources, and vastly reduce organizational and personal headaches. For the first time, these questions can be answered by using the ProFIT-MAP methodology.

Companies are realizing that the standard "tools" of correlative reasoning, extrapolation from aggregate data, and rules of thumb are of limited value in complex settings. Demand-driven and dynamic operational environments therefore require a new integrated capabilities and cost framework to assist managers in making operational decisions.

PROFIT-MAP HELPS MANAGERS
MAKE BETTER OPERATIONAL DECISIONS

ProFIT-MAP helps companies improve their operational performance by prescribing an integrated and dynamic activities-oriented approach that enables them to understand and test the impact of multiple factors, such as product demand and mix changes, process and technology changes, resource limitations, and so on, at a fundamental activities composition and cost level—prior to taking any action. ProFIT-MAP lets managers look into the future and gather practical insights about a range of potential decisions, allowing them to systematically test the viability and profitability of their ideas in advance. The ProFIT-MAP methodology creates a source of sustainable competitive advantage with its ability to

- Create a roadmap to a company's desired future operational state, the operational equivalent of a GPS navigation system, based on an organization's actual capabilities, constraints, and costs.
- Close the "reality gap" between a strategic objective and an organization's ability to realize that objective.
- Understand the dynamic, integrated, and multidimensional relationship between processes, resources, and financial performance at any current or future point in time.
- Understand the impact of an operational decision across the company's process and product mix.
- Assist managers in synchronizing their actions with corporate and divisional strategy.
- Validate management decisions and make adjustments based on real-world factors that accompany implementation. This helps managers respond to the realities of execution, including any unforeseen events or circumstances that coincide with implementation.
- Facilitate strategy development and adjustment by providing an additional source of input to the strategy-making process.

VSM + ProFIT-MAP Methodologies

✴ Current improvement methodologies describe only the "current" and desired "future" states. The ProFIT-MAP methodology goes a step further by creating a detailed roadmap that can be implemented within the confines of an organization's constraints and capabilities. There is no other performance improvement methodology that actually shows you how to get from point A to point B.

ProFIT-MAP Enhances What You Are Already Doing

The ProFIT-MAP methodology is open and flexible, supporting an organization's current strategy and operational philosophies. It is not a one-size-fits-all solution to all problems. Rather, it adapts to the particular business challenge from multiple perspectives by zeroing in on the dominant factors or parameters. ProFIT-MAP ensures that the activities performed within the confines of the capability and resource constraints of an organization can produce the desired process and financial results. ProFIT-MAP is designed to enhance an organization's strategic initiatives, its operational way of life (e.g., Six Sigma, lean operations), its tactical decision-making process, and its measurement approaches (e.g., Balanced Scorecard). As such, it is a decision-making framework that is agnostic to organizational policies, practices, and politics.

The name ProFIT-MAP is derived from a combination of terms. Process and Finance Integration Technology (ProFIT) reflects the underlying integrated and dynamic framework linking business processes; human, capital, and other resources; and finance in a way that forms an activities-based profile of the organization. "MAP" refers to the use of the methodology to develop a roadmap to the future, complete with the steps and projects required to achieve the desired operational state.

To borrow from the catchy marketing tag line of a particular chemical conglomerate: ProFIT-MAP doesn't make your operational processes, it makes them better. It makes them better by enabling managers to identify and evaluate multiple options and their expected outcomes from an integrated activities-based process, resource, and finance perspective prior to implementation. As you are perhaps painfully aware, once changes are implemented, it can become exponentially more expensive to have to make unanticipated corrections to a process that produces less than desirable results.

The ProFIT-MAP methodology, which we explain and illustrate with checklists and case studies starting in Chapter 6, was developed and refined over years of practical application and incorporates the best ideas from business and thought leaders. The ProFIT-MAP methodology prescribes a six-phase gated process starting with framing the problem, then moving on to incorporating data and conducting the analyses, and finally to validating and refining the implementation.

Multiple Management Perspectives Help Synchronize Business Execution with Strategy

ProFIT-MAP is built around three integrated "perspectives," process, resources, and finance, that collectively characterize the essence of business execution. These perspectives are the "filters" through which managers peer into the inner workings of the business and form perceptions of fact that drive their decision-making process. In many respects these perspectives are obvious—as they should be. However, many managers give them only a cursory glance. A systematic approach for navigating an organization's capabilities, constraints, and costs effectively is needed. Coming up with a strategy is not enough for solving today's operational challenges. The problem is that while the strategy may seem straightforward, translating the strategy into the specific steps and activities that will lead to success is not. Often, the people in charge—such as higher-level managers or out-of-theater military commanders—cannot see the details, and this disconnection leads to a perpetuation of the reality gap.

Benchmarking often confuses the situation. Management might think that because the strategy has been benchmarked against another company, it will be successful—including the transfer of best practices. The problem is that the benchmarking was done against a different company (or division) under different conditions with processes that probably have different circumstances and activities compositions, leading to an apples-to-oranges comparison. This is why best practices rarely deliver the expected results. Benchmarking serves an important function, but managers need to be sensitive to the fact that it is not the best tool for creating their desired future.

ProFIT-MAP is the first methodology, to our knowledge, that works equally well for making strategic, tactical, and operational decisions. In fact, it gives managers a tool that can be used to increase organizational alignment or synchronization. We have identified over 30 unique applications of the ProFIT-MAP methodology for solving business challenges, including current operations, real-time management, plant or site optimization, operations, process design/redesign, business optimization, product planning, and business planning (see Appendix).

Figure 1-4 shows that ProFIT-MAP can assist with making strategy as well as with executing that strategy. Because the ProFIT-MAP methodology can be used across all management levels, it creates a common language that enables people to work together. When organizations use different technologies to do strategic, tactical, and operational analysis, by default a reality gap results.

From ProFIT-MAP's perspective, it doesn't matter which comes first: the strategy or its deployment. Yes, it is imperative that companies have good strategy in place to guide execution; otherwise, they risk doing good things that potentially move them in the wrong direction, wasting valuable resources and opportunities along the way. In reality, companies are already executing strategy every day. The methodology can therefore be applied to improving current operations, planning future operational execution, and influencing corporate and divisional strategy. The specific application and ordering of such efforts is determined uniquely by each organization. Not only does ProFIT-MAP facilitate making proactive decisions, but it also enables companies to systematically validate and refine their actions based on real-world conditions.

Figure 1-4. Synchronizing Strategy and Execution

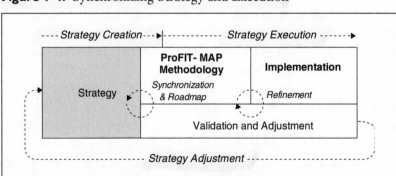

Beyond Allocated Costing

Until you can connect financial performance to process performance, you cannot demonstrate the value of operational change. A strength of the ProFIT-MAP approach is that it advances beyond allocated costs (the de facto costing standard in most organizations) to describe the costs of individual products at the process level based on a dynamic activities-based costing framework. ProFIT-MAP is able to "see" into the future by generating the expected activities composition of processes yet to be executed, or currently executing, based on process and product parameters and their dynamics. The parameters incorporate critical functional knowledge about processes, products, and resources, resulting in an activities-based approach for creating the future, which should not be confused with activities-based costing for accounting purposes.

As shown in Figure 1-5, ProFIT-MAP complements but does not replace traditional forms of measurements and controls. In fact, the ProFIT-MAP approach extends these traditional forms to produce dynamic, forward-looking activities-based cost information grounded in product and process reality. Traditional accounting tools report on historical performance, including costs and profits. They will always be important for financial reporting and auditing requirements. One type of tool is a lagging indicator, quantifying historical performance, while the other approach is a leading indicator used for managing the future. When used together, they help managers make smarter proactive decisions.

In practice, ProFIT-MAP is sensitive to the fact that the activities composition of processes and their associated resources and costs are interconnected and fluctuate differentially over time. The ProFIT-MAP approach does not tell managers how to manage (i.e., what to change or how to change it), nor does it require them to alter the way they make decisions. It is a new management decision tool that strengthens traditional measurement.

As a management decision tool, ProFIT-MAP emphasizes the same kind of information that managers are accustomed to working with. ProFIT-MAP focuses on important process information, such as throughput, work in process, and resource use, and examines the cost and profit of individual products or services. The ProFIT-MAP approach is superior to standard costing approaches in two ways:

Figure 1-5. ProFIT-MAP is a Forward-Looking Management Decision Tool

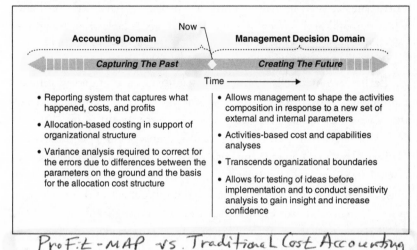

Pro F.t - MAP vs. Traditional Cost Accounting

①• It examines cost and capability for individual products and processes, whereas standard costing approaches are cumulative.

②• It is optimized for dynamic conditions, as it incorporates the changes in underlying activities resulting from changes in the environment instead of extrapolating into the future based on nondynamic aggregated snapshot data.

Having this kind of information enables managers to do a range of things that previously were not possible. For instance, with ProFIT-MAP, managers can test their ideas prior to implementation, increasing their confidence of success. The results are more meaningful because the impact on all aspects of the business, from process to resources and finances, can be seen.

Drowning in Data, Starving for Navigational Guidance

Managers frequently confide their "data" reality to us—that operational data are everywhere, but that the managers don't know how to leverage these data to shape the future. They continue to use extrapolations from past operations and correlative reasoning to justify their next steps. Such approaches lack a holistic focus, perhaps leading to success in isolated areas, but with uncertainty in the overall impact. A common concern is that local optimization or suboptimization of specific processes (i.e., optimization in isolation) does not produce a significant financial return. Furthermore, such narrowly optimized processes have little resilience when demand and process parameters change. A lack of an integrated methodology is the primary cause for disconnects; ProFIT-MAP's integrated approach overcomes these challenges.

Earlier, we mentioned how earth scientists, cartographers, military commanders, and ordinary citizens, among others, benefit from knowing where they are and how to get to where they want to go. Navigating from point A to point B is critical in many pursuits, and tools like GPS systems make navigating easier. A GPS device determines a precise location based on readings from at least three available satellite signals. When combined with navigational intelligence, a GPS navigation system directs the user to the destination of choice. Similarly, ProFIT-MAP provides a form of intelligence that helps managers chart their path from the present to the desired future. The three perspectives of business execution (process, resources, and finance) are analogous to the readings from the three satellites that a GPS device requires in order to triangulate its location and identify each step along the route to the destination.

Like a GPS signal without a map, operational data without a navigational context provides little guidance about how to get to a desired future operational state. Enterprise applications excel at continuously generating operational data, just as the GPS satellites constantly emit signals, but such data alone, without a navigational intelligence, are insufficient. The difference in efficiency between traveling to an altogether new destination with GPS navigation and traveling to that destination without the benefit of a smart guide is a reality gap. There is nothing wrong with using a traditional map, but have you ever been lost in a big city during rush hour when all you have is a printed map? It's not easy to figure out where you are, let alone how to get to where you want to go. A GPS navigation system, on the other hand, always knows your location and quickly recomputes a new route, all without your having to take your eyes off the road. Likewise, if you miss a turn or make a poor operational decision, such smart navigational assistance can quickly point you in the right direction.

Our mission in this book is to take a step forward and present the equivalent of a GPS navigation system for business execution. We provide a better methodology for you to drive your business. Managers continue to make decisions as they always have, but with the distinct advantage of navigational insight developed through the use of the ProFIT-MAP methodology.

Closing the Reality Gap with a Parametric Approach

With ProFIT-MAP, the activities making up the process (the activities composition), including the constraints and cost interdependencies, are all treated as management parameters. ProFIT-MAP's capability to adjust parameters at will offers a natural "what if?" approach to test the sensitivity of the results to parametric changes. Managers no longer have to guess, extrapolate from historical data obtained under different circumstances, or use correlative reasoning, such as rules of thumb or guidelines, to describe what the future may look like. Companies are realizing that these approaches are not effective in complex settings where decisions are increasingly "financial-critical" for survival.

Parametric approaches are not new. For example, the roots of parametric costing can be traced back to the aircraft manufacturing challenges of World War II, when the government needed a better tool for understanding costs. ProFIT-MAP is a natural and intuitive enhancement of parametric costing (as well as financial accounting) that extends the focus to include a parameter-based, activities-oriented future to help managers make proactive operational decisions. This integrated and dynamic extension makes it possible to understand the impact of a myriad of factors, such as product demand and mix changes, process and technology changes, resource limitations, and so on, at the activities composition and cost levels.

The future-looking and dynamic nature of the ProFIT-MAP methodology is able to incorporate management expectations emanating from the strategic plan as a parameter similar to the capabilities and constraints of the organization. With ProFIT-MAP, educated guesses and reliance on rules of thumb go out the window, because managers now have a tool that gives them the answers about expected future performance based on the new activities composition of the process, thereby bridging the reality gap. In other words, ProFIT-MAP enables managers to synchronize business execution with strategy based on a common understanding of what the organization is capable of achieving (see Figure 1-6).

Figure 1-6. ProFIT-MAP Closes the Operational Reality Gap

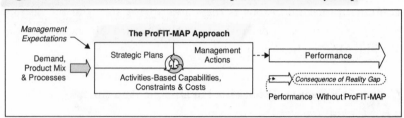

Historically, attempts to understand process efficiency, constraints, and costs have been too difficult, costly, and time-consuming. The end results were usually not of sufficient financial specificity to be of much use to management. Companies frequently confide in us their attempts to optimize their process and cost structures in a given facility or across the portfolio of operations. We hear stories such as, "We took three Ph.D.s and locked them in a room for six months, and they still couldn't figure it out, so we killed the project." In another impressive effort, one company bought a Cray supercomputer, hired a support and modeling staff, and spent five years trying to figure out the process, resource, and cost puzzle. The project was ultimately canceled for lack of results. These well-intended efforts were doomed from the outset because they lacked a structured framework that was designed specifically for business execution.

Fundamentally, ProFIT-MAP enables managers to make better-informed process and product decisions by answering the following questions:

- Can it be done? Is it possible? If not, then what additional capabilities are needed?
- Will it be profitable?
- What is the impact of my particular decision across the product mix and the functional capabilities of the organization?
- How do I get to the desired future (the roadmap)?

Knowing the answers to these questions in advance leads to better execution, enabling companies to reach their operational and product objectives. They address the reality gap head on and help close it, avoiding the surprises and disappointment of unmet objectives—and you don't need a supercomputer to get the answers.

Forests, Trees, and Trail Maps

The ProFIT-MAP message is simple: use the forward-looking, integrated, and dynamic activities-based capabilities, constraints, and costs framework to deliver on your strategic goals. Managers may not be able to do anything about high fixed costs, such as health care or labor agreements, in the near term, but they can influence and control a myriad of other activities to excel at execution.

The ProFIT-MAP methodology helps organizations clearly see the forest as well as the trees. This ecology—the dynamic relationships and interdependencies between the forest and the trees—is a central theme of this book. As in maintaining a healthy forest ecosystem, the health of each individual tree is paramount; organizations can neither ignore strategy and profitability nor ignore their capabilities, constraints, and costs. Leading organizations successfully navigate among and around the opportunities and limitations of their ecosystem.

A forest may be one's destination or a marker along a larger journey. In either case, the weary traveler greatly benefits from a map delineating the best route. Fortunately, this book is not an academic discussion of forests, trees, and trail maps. Rather, this book will enable you to build an operational roadmap at an activities level, so that you can realize your objectives of profitability and operational, product, and customer excellence.

We believe that many of the ideas and practical applications you will encounter in the ensuing chapters will captivate your attention and renew your competitive spirit. Sure, we all have an idea about how to compete successfully in the global economy; it's just that the methods and tools have not kept up with the pace of operational and product innovation. We hope the chapters ahead and the application of the concepts and techniques are enlightening and rewarding for you and your organization. Now, let's get to it!

STRUCTURE AND FUNCTION OF THIS BOOK

The ProFIT-MAP methodology will appeal to all levels of management, from the executive suite to the front lines. Table 1-1 highlights various internal and external audiences and ProFIT-MAP's appeal to each group. The table applies to both manufacturing and business

Table 1-1. ProFIT-MAP's Appeal

<table>
<tr><td colspan="2"></td><td>Organizational Role</td><td>ProFIT-MAP's Appeal</td></tr>
<tr><td rowspan="16">Internal Audiences</td><td rowspan="8"></td><td>Operations manager

Senior analyst</td><td>• Navigating constraints to maximize capabilities.
• Recommending and justifing process level ideas to senior management.
• Refining, implementing, and validating process ideas.
• Prioritizing actions to meet business objectives.</td></tr>
<tr><td>Plant manager

General manager</td><td>• Overcoming specific process / delivery obstacles.
• Planning short-term gains.
• Synchronizing process with cost / profit goals.
• Prioritizing actions to meet business objectives.</td></tr>
<tr><td>Director of operations
Vice president of operations</td><td>• Improving divisional level profit.
• Resolving divisional issues of plant/product/process rationalization.
• Introducing new products/services/technologies/processes/and so on for the greatest performance and profitability.
• Prioritizing actions to meet business objectives.</td></tr>
<tr><td>Director of supply chain

Director of logistics</td><td>• Designing the supply-chain policies (e.g., inventory levels, schedules) in conjunction with constraints and capabilities.</td></tr>
<tr><td>Chief executive officer

Chief financial officer

Executive vice president</td><td>• Articulating quantitatively the potential of the strategy to those who will actually execute it.
• Refining strategy to reflect internal and external changes in the business environment.</td></tr>
<tr><td>External Audiences</td><td>Strategy consultants

(large and boutique firms)</td><td>• Understanding quickly the client's capabilities, constraints, and costs.
• Zooming in on opportunities for improvement.
• Prioritizing actions to meet business objectives.</td></tr>
</table>

Table 1-1. ProFIT-MAP's Appeal (*Continued*)

	Organizational Role	ProFIT-MAP's Appeal
External Audiences	Business execution consultants (large and boutique firms)	• Prioritizing actions to meet business objectives. • Implementing the new process and ensuring that the project objectives are successfully achieved.
	Training consultants (e.g., internal, external, or academic)	• Educating employees about how their actions contribute to the overall business objectives. • Teaching companies to master business execution.
	Academic	• Teaching business execution in manufacturing, operations, and finance courses.

services organizations. The job titles are illustrative and will vary by organization and industry. It is important to understand that although each audience may view ProFIT-MAP from its own particular perspective(s) of interest, all the audiences are in fact trying to drive the organization to a common goal.

CEOs, CFOs, and strategic thinkers will find this book invaluable for helping to shape strategic programs and for managing implementation of corporate strategy over time. For example, are you considering a product or process rationalization strategy, growth-planning options, or capital investments? When applied at a corporate or division level, the ProFIT-MAP methodology enables executives to explore the production, capital investment, and profit implications of major strategic thrusts prior to implementation. Corporate-level executives identify their strategic options, and ProFIT-MAP helps determine the profitability of those options, which can then be prioritized and translated into specific quantifiable projects throughout the various business units.

Tactical-level managers can then run with the strategic initiatives. For example, once a decision is made to rationalize the process and product mix among several capable facilities, a tactical manager takes ownership of the project. In practice, the ensuing project is formulated to address a range of questions pertaining to the optimal way to consolidate the product mix among countless options and limitations. Generally speaking, the majority of tactical improvement efforts may never surface on the corporate-level radar screen—unless, of course, they lead to unintended consequences that capture executive management's attention.

Tactical initiatives may then drive plant or operational-level improvements. Plant or facility managers are typically interested in issues such as line or product profitability, selecting suppliers, budgeting, demand fulfillment planning, and so on. Operations practitioners are keen on issues involving labor planning, inventory planning, and modernizing equipment. Any of these factors are fertile ground for operational improvement. This is not to say that all operational opportunities have tactical or strategic implications, because they don't. As these examples illustrate, strategic, tactical, and operational management challenges and opportunities have implications that can cascade up or down the organization. Irrespective of direction, ProFIT-MAP facilitates communication and collaboration among all management.

The fundamental interests and concerns highlighted here are not exclusive to any particular management entity. Group managers, plant managers, and operational personnel share common interests, such as the profitability of a particular line or facility or a portfolio of facilities. Clearly, corporate-level executives are also interested in profitability. The CEO, for instance, wants to know about profitability across all product lines. The plant manager is most interested in the profitability of his or her facility. An operations person may be interested in only a specific line, or perhaps in several lines spanning multiple facilities. Our message is that ProFIT-MAP is a tool that enables all levels of management to find a common ground and work together on shared organizational priorities, such as profitability and customer service.

Navigating This Book

Parts 1 and 2 of the book present the business and conceptual background of the discipline of business execution and the ProFIT-MAP methodology. Part 3 adopts an applied focus and explains the ProFIT-MAP methodology and its use in detail through examples and case studies. Managers, analysts, and strategic thinkers will find the first five chapters an informative journey through the rationale and operational context of business execution and ProFIT-MAP.

Part I, "Introduction"

The second chapter, "Creating Sustainable Change: The Management Roller Coaster," examines why creating sustainable change is so difficult. It highlights commonalities in operational philosophies, points out how to successfully navigate through organizational constraints and opportunities, and makes the case for how ProFIT-MAP enables sustainable change.

Part 2, "Business and Theoretical Underpinnings"

This section explores the business context and theory behind the ProFIT-MAP approach. Chapter 3, "Business Execution Challenges," discusses what managers should know about their dynamic processes and shows how ProFIT-MAP enables smart decision making. Chapter 4, "Driving the System: A Parametric Framework," describes the theoretical foundation of the ProFIT-MAP methodology. The fifth chapter, "Win Before Taking Action with a Structured Methodology," discusses several key management challenges and establishes the operational requirements for the ProFIT-MAP methodology.

Part 3, "Practical Application and Case Studies"

The third section of the book explores the practical application of the ProFIT-MAP methodology for improving manufacturing and service operations. Chapter 6, "Getting Started with ProFIT-MAP," shows how managers can quickly articulate their strategic challenges and opportunities and help secure support and funding for their improvement effort. Chapters 7 through 9 describe the six phases of the ProFIT-MAP methodology. Chapter 10, "Case Studies," presents detailed case studies illustrating the dynamic nature of the ProFIT-MAP approach and how it provides critical insight into the drivers of operational performance.

Part 4, "Epilogue"

In the last chapter, "Profit Mapping Your Ideal Future," we gaze into our "crystal ball" for planning and managing manufacturing and business services, and we highlight several issues that we look forward to exploring and applying to the discipline of business execution and profit mapping.

REFERENCES

1   Thomas L. Friedman, *The World Is Flat: A Brief History of the Twenty-First Century* (New York: Farrar, Straus and Giroux, 2005).

2   Lawrence G. Hrebiniak, *Making Strategy Work: Leading Effective Execution and Change* (Upper Saddle River, NJ: Wharton School Publishing, 2005), p. 4.

3   Larry Bossidy and Ram Charan, *Execution: The Discipline of Getting Things Done* (New York: Crown Publishing Group, 2002), p. 7.

Creating Sustainable Change: The Management Roller Coaster

Everybody talks about change. In recent years, a small industry of changemeisters has preached revolution, reinvention, quantum change, breakthrough thinking, audacious goals, learning organizations, and the like.

—Larry Bossidy and Ram Charan,
Execution: The Discipline of Getting Things Done

A Change Would Do You Good

—Sheryl Crow

RIDING THE MANAGEMENT ROLLER COASTER

For more than a decade now, there has been a tremendous interest in identifying the factors that create and sustain competitive advantage for corporations. New literature has emerged each year—some more memorable than others. New terminologies have evolved, and a lot of management slogans have appeared. There have been battle cries ranging from "Quality is number one" to "Our people are our most important assets." Collectively, these activities and initiatives set in motion lots of discussion and debate among all levels of management. Corporate visions were drafted that people could recite verbatim. Employee expectations were high, and there was tremendous excitement in the air, with the promise of being the best. Consultants ran everywhere asking questions, coaches were hired, employees were trained, and a lot of data were collected. The cycle was repeated afresh every few years with a new vernacular and renewed vigor.

In each cycle of business discovery, after extensive study and surveys, management and consultants declared that they had identified what was needed for the company to win. They declared that you had to execute better, be more productive, reduce waste, and increase competitiveness by doing a better job than your competition. Yes, they stated the obvious, leaving success to the details of planning and execution, among other things. They constructed lots of charts and developed lots of new processes. New systems were rolled out to manage these processes and collect volumes of operational data. Tremendous energy, not to mention a great deal of money, was expended. Collectively, these cycles formed the peaks and valleys, twists and turns of the management roller coaster.

Managers were excited about the promise of getting the data they needed to make better decisions. In this "new" environment, decisions would be based on facts that would follow from the latest decision-making process. This was going to change the old haggard ways; a new dawn was about to emerge.

Companies collected data like it was going out of style. Huge databases stored data about everything. Manufacturing had Manufacturing Resource Planning systems; sales and marketing had Customer Relationship Management systems; accounting and finance had accounting and financial planning systems; human resources had its systems. Enterprise Resource Planning and Supply-Chain Management systems flourished. Data warehouses were built to consolidate data from multiple systems, and specialized reporting systems emerged.

But the more things changed, the more they stayed the same; the management roller coaster continued on. Collectively, enterprise systems were adept at collecting lots of data about processes (i.e., workflow) and processing technology (e.g., building of product and product quality). Yet, management still complained that it did not have the information it needed to make better decisions. What happened? Although the data existed, they were not in a usable form or in the correct context for decision making. Either disparate systems were not sufficiently integrated or the critical interrelations between data were lost or were not communicated to managers. Thus, managers had difficulty collaborating with their colleagues and synchronizing with corporate objectives because their systems still lacked critical information required for operational decision making.

New technologies emerged that promised to fill the "information gap" by integrating all the relevant management data and creating unified reporting systems. Managers were confident that, with the improved enterprise integration technologies being implemented by their companies, they would be able to get the data they needed, when they needed it. The excitement grew again as the promise of a fresh start with more and better data and information was anticipated.

As a result of the diligent work of the Information Systems group and its business unit "partners," managers were now able to tell what had gone wrong and what had gone right by looking at the historical data and reports. However, business decision makers were still experiencing a gap between these supposedly integrated systems and what they needed on a day-to-day basis. They still lacked forward-looking information to help them make better operational decisions that would lead to improved future business performance. And so, they found themselves still collecting data from multiple functional areas and consolidating and aggregating those data into spreadsheet models for further analysis.

Unfortunately, the spreadsheet-based models were hard to build and maintain, and they often required dedicated experts just to sustain them, let alone enhance them. The models were also limited by two important characteristics: they did not provide contextual information telling managers what to do with the information, and they were inadequate for foretelling the future. Thus, managers were drowning in data and information, but hindered in their ability to use these data in their decision-making thought processes.

WHY CREATING SUSTAINABLE CHANGE IS SO DIFFICULT

Given that so much manual effort by managers was required to account for the complexities inherent in those managers' responsibilities, there was no easy way to link the planning and management of day-to-day operations directly with corporate and divisional strategies. Operational managers didn't know if their decisions were in sync with these strategies. They didn't know if the outcomes of their actions would have tangible benefits that could be evaluated in terms of financial and/or operational measurements. They didn't know how to estimate the impact of their decisions before implementing them.

In the absence of a direct link between the strategy and execution initiatives, managers resort to the same old, and often deficient, methods of correlative reasoning that are more commonly known as "rules of thumb." Such rules tend to be simple and stereotypical, which make full sense only when taken in isolation; combining them with others may lead to unforeseen consequences. Some examples include: "If I improve efficiency, then I should expect to gain financially." "If I reduce inventory, then my overall costs should go down." "Reducing waste should improve my efficiency and thereby my financial performance." "If I make a capital investment in new equipment, throughput will increase and less human labor will be required."

Rules of thumb proliferated as managers attempted to find "simple" principles to help them deal with the vast complexities of organizational performance. And so this reasoning continued and some improvements were realized, but the big questions still loomed. We were still flying in the dark. Despite having all these data, we didn't know how to use them to create the future we desired. Experienced managers could foresee the changes coming into the market, but they didn't have the tools or methodologies to create an appropriate response. The slogans didn't help. The new processes helped somewhat, but they lacked critical functional knowledge about the business.

Unfortunately, such ad hoc attempts usually failed to create long-term, sustainable change. It would be unfair, however, to say that all such efforts have been completely unsuccessful. For example, in the manufacturing industry, the lead time between when orders are received and when orders are fulfilled has been reduced significantly. Overall inventories are down, which has freed up a lot of cash flow. Operations have become leaner, and productivity is up. But, all this has come at a very steep price. Could all the investments made in these areas be justified on sound financial principles? The jury is still out. For example, while successfully reducing inventory, some companies have discovered that unanticipated expedited shipping costs negate the financial promise of lean operations. CFOs understand that the current systems help, but they don't know how to measure the true value of operational changes.

COMMONALITIES IN OPERATIONAL PHILOSOPHIES

Each cycle of business innovation is yet another rung of an evolutionary ladder, where new concepts emerge from attempts to fix the problems that arose from earlier concepts. An exploration across the repeated cycles reveals two commonalities that transcend the way in which organizations operate: (1) an execution philosophy about how work is done, and (2) a dominant principle reflecting a company's excellence proposition.

Management by Processes

Despite various innovation cycles, the execution philosophy has remained unchanged and is characterized by the near unanimous acceptance of a "management by processes" approach. Simply stated, operational processes are at the root of creating and delivering customer value. Companies operate by way of processes, even if some of the processes are not well understood or well documented. In the end, the essence of the execution philosophy has not changed, although some have argued about the forms and significance of individual processes. In *Competing for the Future*, Gary Hamel and C. K. Prahalad[1] forcefully argue in favor of senior managers focusing primarily on core competencies that are at the center of creating competitiveness. They describe a competency as a collection of skills and technologies required to execute. In simple terms, a competency is an adapted view of a process and its interrelationships with other processes that meets three criteria: customer value, competitive differentiation, and extendability. Hamel and Prahalad go so far as to argue that competencies that are not considered core should be candidates for outsourcing.

The concept of management by processes not only has survived the test of time and been maintained through various management cycles, but has further strengthened. In the early days, a process was viewed as the flow of materials in manufacturing or of work in a business or service context. In the heyday of Business Process Reengineering (circa 1980s–1990s), the concept was extended to include the flow of information along with the flow of material and work. The term *value stream*, proposed by James Womack and Daniel Jones in *Lean Thinking: Banish Waste and Create Wealth in Your Corporation*,[2] is a later incarnation of management by processes. It includes a focus on "value-added" steps and on reducing waste in the flow that creates customer value. Other attempts have included the flow of cost through the process to provide insight into financial performance. Through successive waves of business innovation, the concept of management by processes is deepening and becoming more holistic in nature.

Excellence Focus

The other commonality across the various business cycles is a dominant principle—a company's excellence focus that sets it apart from its competition. These principles are divided along some line of distinction—for example, internal (operations, technology, people, and so on) versus external (products, customers, markets, and so on) factors—to create a dominant focus. There are three distinct, identifiable dominant principles on which companies can strive to excel: operations and process technologies, product technologies, and market focus. Each business cycle includes one of these or some variation thereof. The terminology may have changed in the different cycles, but the essence of the content did not. In one way or another, you had to do better at certain things than you were currently doing. In other words, the fault was in the execution, not in the principles. As an example, in their landmark book *The Discipline of Market Leaders*, Michael Treacy and Fred Wiersema[3] justifiably argue that companies cannot be all things to all people and must pick one of the three disciplines at which to excel—operational excellence, product leadership, or customer intimacy. They cite many examples of companies that picked one principle and executed it successfully. The idea is similar to Hamel and Prahalad's concept of focusing on the core competencies.

In recent years, there has been some recognition that a one-dimensional focus is no longer adequate if you want to survive in the market, let alone flourish. You have to strike a balance among the three. Combining this multidimensional idea with the concept that *if you do not measure, you cannot manage* has led to the evolution of a new way of thinking. Robert S. Kaplan and David P. Norton[4] have constructed a Balanced Scorecard tool that in simple terms can be viewed as a weighting of various outcomes and disciplines for managing strategy. They do not restrict their thinking to any of the three main principles, but have a broad construct within which these disciplines can be segmented and selected as needed. And the concept of focusing on the core continues, with one exception, which is to define the core as some judicious combination of various disciplines that are important for the particular function and level of the organization. In other words, the definition of core adapts to the function and the decision level at hand, leaving it for the manager to define what is important and what is not.

OPERATIONAL PHILOSOPHIES ARE OFTEN DISCONNECTED IN PRACTICE

The excellence focus reflects the objectives of a company. It is an expression of the corporate strategy to establish boundaries that define the kinds of things that a company will pursue, as well as the opportunities that it will let pass by. Combining this with the de facto management by processes orientation embeds an implicit assumption about which of the business execution drivers are critical and at the core. The measurement framework is also intimately tied to the operational philosophy.

The disconnection occurs when the particular operational philosophy is applied only to parts of the business objectives, not to all the intentions of the strategy. To state it differently, we tend to execute the business by translating the strategy into individual actions in discrete areas. On the one hand, business strategy is multidimensional in nature, addressing a variety of internally and externally interdependent factors. Business execution, on the other hand, is typically handled as a collection of individual actions that often target single-dimensional business drivers. To cope with the complexities of operations, managers have learned to segment their decisions to increase the likelihood that, despite their interdependence and interference with one another, the individual decisions will produce the desired composite results.

When companies fret over the lack of alignment between their strategy and their operations, they are at least partially alluding to the problems caused by the implicit biases of their operational philosophies. Consider an example of a company that is seeking to enhance profitability, customer satisfaction, competitiveness, or other such objectives by improving business drivers such as operational efficiency, quality, and waste reduction. The thinking, for instance, is typically that "improving throughput should improve on-time delivery and thereby improve customer satisfaction" or "reducing inventory should release working capital and hence improve profitability," for example. Although each approach is well intentioned, there is no guarantee that it will meet the larger business goals. How many times have you witnessed an initiative (e.g., outsourcing a call center or redesigning a manufacturing line) that is deemed to be "successful" by one group of management, only to find that the implementation failed to balance the competing business objectives of customer satisfaction and profitability?

Part of the problem is that we often aren't aware that our favorite operational philosophy or approach has a decision-making bias. This is not to say that biases are inherently bad, just that you can manage more effectively if you are aware of their ramifications. We agree that management by processes is the "correct" approach. However, we do not blindly accept the argument that improving the process will necessarily improve strategic performance, unless the process itself is the sole locus of the strategy. We have been taught to narrow our focus to the process, and this is often done at the expense of other important decision-making dimensions. A process-only focus may lack critical perspective on other important factors that go into executing the strategy, especially if the objectives are broader than the process. How can you really know whether proposed operational changes will result in increased profitability or customer satisfaction? With a process-only focus, you can't; you are operating on a hope and a prayer.

We believe that a process orientation is necessary but not sufficient for achieving the larger business objectives. Decisions often have to take into consideration other factors, such as resource availability and constraints. Are more or fewer people needed to execute the process? What kinds of skills are required? What about the flow of materials in the supply chain? Is there enough? Are the right kinds of materials arriving? Are they arriving at the necessary intervals to keep production running smoothly? Such business issues also have significant financial implications. What if you are considering making capital investments in new technology? What will be the implications for both throughput and profitability?

When decision making is tied to corporate strategy—which we strongly advocate—you quickly find that any decision, no matter how small, has implications across multiple management orientations. Any management framework must be flexible enough to address the objectives of the strategy and support the multidimensional aspects of the business problem at hand. The odds are that when the problem is viewed holistically in the larger context of the strategy, more than one orientation is relevant.

Let's take a look at some important approaches to business execution to highlight how each approach has its own natural bias toward a particular dimension, and hence misses other important perspectives. It is not for us to say that a perspective is indeed missing, just that the business problem, and not the operational philosophy, should dictate the correct combination of perspectives. That is, the objectives of the strategy should define the relevant analysis dimensions of any particular improvement method or measurement framework. Unfortunately, many available frameworks forget that the goal is the prosperity of the enterprise, not the specific bias of the approach.

Process Bias Examples

Lean operations and Six Sigma are immensely popular and useful improvement methods with a distinct process focus. The former helps to increase efficiency and reduce waste. The latter is a quality management program. However, neither method explicitly contains a cost component (i.e., perspective) that would enable managers to understand the profitability implications of their decisions.

The problem with these approaches is that they often lose sight of the overall goal. Delphi's filing for bankruptcy on October 8, 2005, one of the largest such filings in U.S. history, is a prime example. The nation's largest automotive supplier is a poster child for lean implementation in North America. It was an early adopter, spending a great deal of time and money to copy practices from Toyota. While implementing lean was an important objective for Delphi, its problems were of a larger magnitude and lay somewhere else. Lean operations could not possibly provide a sufficient financial boost to overcome the other ills. Delphi made the classic error of investing in local optimization and not looking at the big picture.

Jim Womack, the founder of the lean movement in North America, acknowledged, "One of the hardest things in my line of work is seeing a company make enormous strides in getting lean and yet fail to prosper." [5]

Delphi failed to prosper because it did not properly align its execution with its strategic objective of making profits. It spent too much time on becoming lean and not enough on solving more pressing issues.

We often find that companies become blindsided when going lean. They see lean as a panacea and assume that it is something concrete and easy to do, with great potential to help the organization become more effective. They implicitly assume that lean actions will somehow improve financial performance. The cost surprise arises as a result of the disconnection between their lean actions and their lack of understanding of the associated financial impact. We are proponents of lean, but we see a great deal of misapplication of lean principles because lean, by itself, doesn't close the loop between what is controllable and the business objectives.

Recently some attempts have been made to incorporate additional dimensions, including cost, but they are add-ons and are not integrated into the original philosophies. Lean accounting approaches, for example, are biased toward operational costs. They exclude overhead costs, such as health care, SG&A, and so on, so their estimates of financial performance are inherently biased. If the labor cost is high (direct cost), this will show up in lean accounting. Health-care costs, on the other hand, will not show up because they are overhead. In reality, production facilities generally pay a corporate allocation that pays for the corporate overhead, including such things as the costs of retirees' health care. Even Womack acknowledges that while a process bias is helpful, it is insufficient in practice: "Simply fixing operations may not be sufficient if managers wait too late to start and factor costs (principally wages and healthcare costs these days) [that] are too far out of line."[6]

Resources Bias Examples

Typical approaches for managing the supply chain also contain an implicit bias toward resources—to optimize the flow of materials and information across multiple organizations in order to produce a finished product or service. Two goals for managing the supply chain include driving down costs of supplies and freeing up cash by reducing the inventories on hand. Reducing material costs is presumably a good thing. But paying less for materials may have implications down the line—for example, this practice may result in poorer quality and higher warranty costs. The assumption is that lowering finished and unfinished inventory holding costs increases cash flow. Unintended increases in other costs can, however, offset the gains in cash flow.

Lean principles, when applied to the supply chain, focus on running the system in a way that maximizes throughput and eliminates waste. The implicit assumption is that doing this reduces cost and therefore increases profitability. However, you don't actually know if this relationship indeed exists or in what form when applied to the given situation in your organization. The question is, why not also explicitly drive the system to maximize profitability? Wouldn't you want to know how the new policies and the corresponding cost to maintain the "improved" supply chain affect profitability? This would enable you to make much more fine-grained decisions on a day-to-day basis for optimizing the links among production, the supply chain, and profitability. You could, for example, minimize the cost of the supply chain on a process and product basis in response to changes in demand and customer requirements. That is, you could manage the profitability of the supply chain and the flow of materials on demand.

Finance Bias Examples

In our last example, we highlight economic value added (EVA) as an important measurement tool with a financial bias. EVA is used for optimizing capital investment decisions within a broader corporate context, and it is extremely effective. Wouldn't it be nice, however, if EVA could provide insight into the effectiveness of a capital investment decision at the process and resources levels? A manager might want to know if a particular investment in a new machine or facility, for example, would be able to achieve the process goals and financial objectives specified by an EVA approach. In theory these objectives might go hand in hand, but EVA alone can't tell you about how the two interact with each other in practice.

We do not take issue with any of the above-mentioned approaches and their biases. Each of these approaches serves a specific business need. What is important is that you don't automatically jump to a biased approach; you need to be aware of the potentially missing perspectives with any approach. Furthermore, if a particular operational philosophy or improvement method lacks a dimension that you need, you can seek to enhance the approach by adding the missing perspective(s)—which we show you how to do in this book.

NAVIGATING THROUGH YOUR CONSTRAINTS
AND OPPORTUNITIES

Despite so much effort and cost, the various innovation cycles that contributed to the management roller coaster failed to create a sustainable competitive advantage. These failures and the causes behind them have been the subject of intense study. Several arguments with varying degrees of validation have been proposed. Our intent here is not to dwell upon the causes of failure and assign blame, but to overcome the deficiencies while building upon the successes.

Some operational philosophies have proven quite useful over time, but nonetheless encounter speed bumps and blind spots in their day-to-day application. We believe such challenges result when strategy, with its multidimensional nature, is executed through an operational philosophy of executing along one dimension at a time without correlating that dimension with the other concurrent efforts. For these cases, we offer a complementary approach to help managers get the most out of their initiatives by gaining critical insight that is not otherwise available into the execution drivers.

Historically, new concepts have emerged when people observed situations in which the previous philosophies had failed. The new anecdotal evidence gave rise to new correlative reasoning, and the cycle continued over and over. We, however, do not offer yet another rung on this evolutionary ladder, nor do we wish to propose a new ladder based on yet another round of anecdotal evidence. Our approach is not built on correlative reasoning and anecdotal arguments, but stands upon the fundamental principles of all of the involved operational disciplines. It therefore complements and enhances an organization's particular operational philosophies; it doesn't try to change them.

The lack of success with prior approaches is typically attributed to four broad causes: an irrational decision-making process, a static view of the value chain, an incoherent communication and execution of the business strategy, and a lack of enthusiasm and purpose on the part of employees. Our favorite is the last one. When one cannot find a cogent reason for failure, subordinates are often blamed—and, of course, subordinates tend to blame their inept managers. The blame game has provided great fodder for the *Dilbert* cartoon strip over the years.

In our collective experience of over four decades, we cannot recall many people in senior or middle management who do not put forth their best efforts within the constraints under which they operate. We believe that, instead, they lack timely and pertinent information, which is compounded by their lack of the tools and the methodologies needed to assimilate and analyze information to ensure success. Above all, they lack synchronization between their actions and the corporate objectives as they seek guidance from the corporate vision.

How can a manager make an informed decision about improving a process if he or she does not know, for example, the correct cost of every product or service that is affected by the process before and after implementing the decision? This problem is compounded by rapidly changing market conditions and product or service mix requirements. The number of dimensions requiring management's attention is so overwhelming and the entire situation is changing so dynamically that no individual can assess the impact without using comprehensive analytical methodologies and tools. The slogans don't help, and neither do tools that require a long lead time and plenty of expertise to use.

The absence of a comprehensive analytical framework leads to an irrational decision-making process. That is to say, the decision-making process becomes marred by one-dimensional correlative reasoning without any acknowledgment of the interrelationships among the various rules of thumb. Without a factual and forward-looking analysis that includes the validation of assumptions, the decision-making process succumbs to jockeying for power and remains captive to corporate culture. Objectivity is lost. Business analysts typically resign themselves to the fait accompli. Indeed, some degree of irrationality is bound to be present in decision making, but it ought not to be an identifiable and significant factor. It should be an exception and not the rule.

No corporation operates in isolation, either within or across organizational boundaries. Often the factors that enable a business to compete successfully today will not be those that will enable it to be successful tomorrow. Competitive factors such as market conditions, customer demands, internal capabilities, and partner arrangements are by definition dynamic—some change more quickly than others, but change is virtually guaranteed. Although everyone recognizes that these and a myriad of other factors are not static, most managers do not have the tools to include this variability in the planning process. With increased globalization and the advent of rapid communication, the dynamic nature of the value chain has become even more pronounced. Hence, if an organization has a rigid, inflexible business strategy, then that organization is unlikely to remain vibrant over the long haul. The agility to adapt to the changing business environment at all levels of an organization is critical to staying ahead of the competition.

Organizations do not think, make decisions, or execute strategies; people do. If every activity is not synchronized with corporate objectives, then the execution will falter, leading to wasted resources, confusion, and loss of competitiveness. The organization's internal processes should empower people at all levels of the organization to ensure alignment of their actions with the corporate strategy. A lack of synchrony is particularly acute in large organizations, where distinct groups of individuals are responsible for setting directions at strategic, tactical, and operational levels. This is generally the case because different sets of tools and methods are used for goal setting at different levels. Execution thus occurs in a waterfall effect, with goals crashing down from higher to lower levels without regard to any explicitly demonstrable capability for a sustainable execution. Such an approach is prone to creating *pie-in-the-sky* goals without a clear roadmap for attaining them, since the creation of the roadmap is not a part of the exercise, leaving the organization vulnerable to the implausibility of a successful execution.

IT'S NOT AN AD HOC GAME

We firmly believe that the pathway to creating and sustaining a profitable present and future is to be found in elevating and organizing the various concepts of execution into a discipline, which we refer to as the *discipline of business execution*. A discipline identifies an area of expertise, study, and/or practice and is specifically demarcated by our focus on business operations. Why approach execution as a discipline? Management needs a disciplined approach to execution because it is typically harder and takes longer to execute strategy than to make it. As Hrebiniak[7] points out, "The problem with poor performance typically is not with planning, but with doing. That is, strategies often aren't implemented successfully. Making strategy work is more difficult than strategy making. Sound plans flounder or die because of a lack of execution know-how." The disciplined approach that we describe in this book is offered as a means for overcoming any gaps between strategy and execution, particularly when one or more operational philosophies are an important part of the picture. This is how you get off the management roller coaster.

In their enlightening book *Execution: The Discipline of Getting Things Done*, Larry Bossidy and Ram Charan[8] state, "Strategies most often fail because they aren't executed well." They go on to define three core processes of execution: the people process, the strategy process, and operations processes. All three have to work in sync to deliver success. They cite the example of flaws in budgeting for operations processes at most companies. The crux of the flaw lies in the fact that the process is built around management's desire for achievement, but is not grounded in the reality of what can be achieved. When there is a basic disconnect between the business processes (whether they are at strategic or operational levels) and the execution capabilities of the organization, failure is virtually guaranteed.

The discipline of business execution is designed to assess and build the paths to success at all levels of the organization before setting the process in motion. As shown in Figure 2-1, the business execution discipline is most helpful for bridging the gaps between operational processes, strategy, and operating plans, and also the gaps with other interdependent operational processes. These are the reality gaps that we described in Chapter 1. Business strategy and operating plans must be grounded in the realities of an organization's actual operational capabilities and limitations. The arrows represent the synchronization that must occur to prevent reality gaps.

The mantra for the market leader has changed; it's now *be the lowest-cost producer with the highest product quality and customer service with a wide variety of customizable products, delivered when and where customers want them*. That's a mouthful, but customers expect you to deliver this, for they have more choices in an increasingly competitive and global business environment.

Figure 2-1. Business Execution Discipline

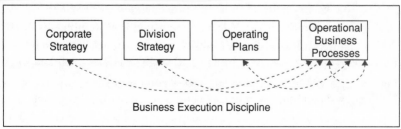

Can a cell phone manufacturer offer new phones with large feature lists but with high price tags and marginal quality? Can an automaker rest on its laurels and not introduce updated products quickly? Is it good enough for a company's customer support center to meet its desired service levels, if it still has very dissatisfied customers? We argue that in today's global market, operational excellence and product leadership are no longer separable, and you cannot win a customer with strong hand-holding only. You win customers today by providing excellent customer service (sales or marketing) along with product leadership (actual product or service) at a reasonable price (operational effectiveness).

In the commodity market for computer hardware, why does Dell continue to gain market share while others do not? Market leaders such as Dell are gaining because they are relentlessly cost-competitive and maintain product leadership by continually diversifying their product offerings. They do so without sacrificing quality and customer service. Market leaders today create an excellence proposition with an uncompromising focus on all three disciplines. They extend their core competencies to all facets of their business.

Leading companies like Dell, GE, and Wal-Mart are successful because they operate within a discipline rather than take a haphazard approach to execution. We present the ProFIT-MAP methodology in this book as a means for realizing the promise of the discipline of business execution. ProFIT-MAP helps managers reach decisions on what operational actions to take, elevates the level of factual knowledge and reduces the amount of irrationality in decision making, accounts for the increasing variability in demand, and helps managers and employees synchronize their actions with one another and with corporate objectives. The ultimate promise of ProFIT-MAP, however, is the ability to quantify in advance what has largely been thought of as unknowable: the specific course to the destination, the company's desired operational state.

When viewed within the context of a discipline, the ProFIT-MAP methodology provides a certain rigor in its application to operational business challenges. Ideally, it is not something that organizations step into and out of, but rather a mindset and a systematic approach for improving operational performance. ProFIT-MAP is useful both in maintaining operational health and in dealing quickly with more acute challenges. The choice is yours. Do you want to see the "now" and into the future as an integrated and interdependent whole, or do you wish to continue to approach operations in a piecemeal and disconnected manner, relying on outmoded rules of thumb and perceptions of fact rather than on reality?

Globalization of the markets with competition coming from low-cost producers, integration of value chains, and increased concentration of end-delivery providers (consolidated retailers) have permanently changed the competitive dynamics. In today's fast-moving environment, even a small gap between the promise and the results of strategy and actions becomes overwhelming and can have remarkable consequences. You can no longer create and maintain your competitiveness by creating an elaborate strategy that takes months or years to implement. Companies must develop core competencies in all disciplines and create a culture in which every decision, no matter how large or how small, must take the company a step closer to meeting its objectives while ensuring its success in execution. Agility in producing products and services is as important as agility in realigning strategy. Synchronization, however, should not have to mean re-creating the strategy in response to every shift in market conditions; the organization should only need to adjust the roadmap and its execution to get to its desired future state.

We believe that cycles of business innovation will continue to yield new or improved management tools, some of which may be followed with exaggerated zeal for only a short time period, while others will gain permanent traction with management. Companies have their own unique operating philosophies and dominant principles. They have their own strategies, process improvement frameworks, and measurement approaches. Particular strategies, frameworks, and approaches may move in and out of favor over time, but the fundamental need to execute never loses importance or goes away. Binding the entire organization together into its own unique expression toward a common goal requires a disciplined culture of business execution.

REFERENCES

1   Gary Hamel and C. K. Prahalad, *Competing for the Future* (Boston: Harvard Business School Press, 1994).

2   James P. Womack and Daniel T. Jones, *Lean Thinking: Banish Waste and Create Wealth in Your Corporation* (New York: Simon & Schuster, 1996).

3   Michael Treacy and Fred Wiersema, *The Discipline of Market Leaders* (Reading, MA: Addison-Wesley, 1995).

4   Robert S. Kaplan and David P. Norton, *The Balanced Scorecard: Translating Strategy into Action* (Boston: Harvard Business School Press, 1996); Robert S. Kaplan and David P. Norton, *The Strategy Focused Organization: How Balanced Scorecard Companies Thrive in a New Business Environment* (Boston: Harvard Business School Press, 2001).

5   Jim Womack, e-mail received October 17, 2005.

6   Womack, e-mail.

7   Lawrence G. Hrebiniak, *Making Strategy Work: Leading Effective Execution and Change* (Upper Saddle River, NJ: Wharton School Publishing, 2005), p. xvii.

8   Larry Bossidy and Ram Charan, *Execution: The Discipline of Getting Things Done* (New York: Crown Publishing Group, 2002), p. 15.

PART 2

Business and Theoretical Underpinnings

Business Execution Challenges

To make knowledge productive, we will have to learn to see both forest and tree.

—Peter Drucker, *Post-Capitalist Society*

COMPANIES ARE UNDERTAKING a veritable alphabet soup of initiatives ranging from business process reengineering, to corporate realignment, to lean manufacturing or operations, to outsourcing, to Six Sigma, to supply-chain rationalization, to advanced technology implementation, to major IT systems, among others, to execute their business strategy. What's clear is that every corporation values the ability to execute, yet few excel at it. A myriad of business execution challenges stands in your way, threatening your position in the marketplace. Dealing with these challenges without a proper framework and methodology is risky. You cannot address them in a piecemeal manner; your approach must be holistic and strategically focused, or you are doomed to mediocrity.

THE VALUE CHAIN

The Increasingly Cost-Competitive and Dynamic Environment

Competitors big and small are squeezing your markets, stakeholders are pressuring for growth and profitability, and your customers are increasingly vocal about their price, quality, and service expectations. Sound familiar? With the rise of the global and interconnected economy, cost structures are under relentless challenge. Historically, driven by the brutal pressures to find lower-cost production alternatives to enable them to remain competitive, manufacturers were the first to outsource and offshore. More recently, business services have been following suit. The options can seem limited and overwhelming when a competitor moves production to a lower-cost environment through "rural" sourcing to NAFTA partners or by completely offshoring. Not all companies have jumped on the outsourcing bandwagon, and many have been less than successful with their offshoring endeavors, but the fact remains that the outsourcing question will be at the forefront for years to come. Outsourcing is merely one response to the pressures for cost competitiveness.

The increasing investments and a growing abundance of highly educated workers in the developing world, coupled with the ease of communications and collaboration facilitated by the Internet and global communication networks, have put tremendous pressure on the cost of goods and services in North America. Taken together, manufacturing and service economies might be described as being in a struggle for the future of their respective competitive spaces. Many companies are engaged in a professional game of competitive catch-up. Thinking about emerging opportunities typically gets relegated to a lower priority in this paradigm. One might argue that manufacturing and service companies are actually locked into a global winner-take-all profits battle for operational, product, and customer leadership.[1]

Clearly such competitive factors are pressuring value chains—the collection of activities that create and sustain competitive advantage and customer value. Broadly, the value chain is composed of inbound logistics, operations, outbound logistics, marketing and sales, and service.[2] Operations, whether manufacturing- or services-oriented, represent a significant chunk of these value-chain activities and are the specific source of competitive advantage that we focus on in this book. Value chains are even more complex given that they depend on suppliers and partners to deliver customer value and that customer demands are moving targets.

Not only are companies struggling to increase their cost competitiveness, but they are also operating in an increasingly unstable business environment in which customer expectations, product and technological leaps, and nimble competitors are contributing to an overall increase in the speed of change. The value chain is not a static phenomenon, and its variability has substantially increased in recent times (as illustrated by the amplitude and oscillation in Figure 3-1). This pattern is compressed as the distance between the peaks and troughs in the lower chart shrinks when compared to the historical graph.

The actual amplitude and frequency of the wave depend on the nature of your business, but the pattern remains the same. To survive, organizations need greater flexibility so that they are able to respond rapidly to customer and market changes. Otherwise, the energy contained in these waves can be so great that they can overwhelm you.

Looking back perhaps 20 years ago, it may have been reasonable for companies to wait a quarter or two before receiving feedback and making adjustments. In today's dynamic environment, however, product mix changes frequently, and products are not necessarily made for a long period of time. The product life cycle is simultaneously shrinking and becoming more complex, and no one wants to be saddled with a large inventory that might either have to be liquidated or become obsolete. Operational thinking around the underlying activity profiles is changing from long durations to short ones, in many cases from months to weeks or days, or even hours. You can no longer wait for a quarter to end; you need answers now.

Figure 3-1. The Value Chain Is Becoming More Dynamic

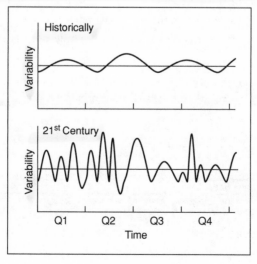

Measuring and Managing Dynamic Processes Are Becoming More Difficult

Understanding operational processes and their interconnections in the value chain is central to any decision making. However, unless you are a small business that performs only a handful of activities, you cannot directly "see" the entirety of your dynamic operational processes because of the inherent complexities of their activities, geographies, costs, and so on. As a matter of fact, it is very difficult for even most small businesses to grapple with this. Operational processes and all of their variability have to be observed through measurement instruments that estimate, for better or worse, what's going on in this complex environment. Figure 3-2 highlights the difficulty of measuring real dynamic processes against a backdrop of global competition and continuous change in product demand and operational response.

Because one cannot easily see and quantify operational processes in their entirety, management relies on estimates of these processes. Measurement instruments may include demand profiles, efficiency reports, financial statements, and other similar tools. The quality of identification (also known as estimation or reconstruction) depends on the definition of the processes, the nature of the data collected, the measurement instruments, and the algorithm for reconstruction.

Management looks at reports to provide insight into performance. These reports are subject to the particulars of the reporting system's reconstruction of the underlying process. Some management systems, such as financial accounting, quantify past performance. Others, such as supply-chain systems, may look ahead to enable performance to keep

Figure 3-2. Measuring and Managing Dynamic Processes

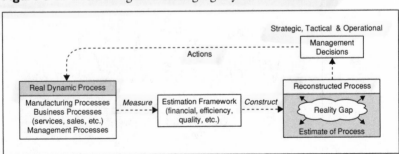

pace with known or projected demand. A critical challenge with all reporting approaches is to ensure the accuracy and reliability of the way in which they estimate processes. While some degree of error can be expected, the greater the difference between the real dynamic process (i.e., the actual entity) and the reconstructed process, the greater the potential for a disconnect between perception and reality, resulting in a reality gap.

Unfortunately, reality gaps are all too common. Moreover, they are exacerbated by the constantly changing nature of customer demand, organizational capabilities, and the mix of products and services. Despite the presence of reality gaps, managers must move ahead in managing their manufacturing capabilities and services; hence process improvement initiatives abound. These are necessary and good things, but what is good can be made better, and what is not good should be improved, shut down, or divested—that's our bias. Yet, in striving to achieve desired improvement gains, many companies are unaware of or are blindsided by the reality gap. They end up settling for something that is less than ideal or less than they are capable of achieving—a form of institutional learned helplessness.

Collectively, these business execution challenges will probably not diminish in the near term. Companies operate in an increasingly cost-competitive world, the need for operational agility is a given in an environment marked by continuous change, and it is becoming increasingly difficult to understand both the forest and the trees of your operational processes. Successful business execution also requires a firm grasp of your company's fundamental value proposition, which, in turn, drives operational priorities and execution objectives. It is therefore important that managers understand the nature and implications of their company's particular quest for excellence.

MANAGEMENT PERSPECTIVES

The way you look at a problem is critical in shaping how you go about solving it. Although everyone brings a different perspective to the table, there are some important commonalities that influence how and what you manage as you execute the corporate strategy. Managers must understand the commonalities that are broadly shared across the organization as well as the unique elements that tend to cluster around different management groups. Operational decisions and actions do not occur in a vacuum; they often have significant ramifications throughout the company.

The terms *context* and *perspective* are often used interchangeably. A system may be so complex that you don't necessarily see what you have. Perspectives are simply a view of what you observe from your vantage point. The context comes from inferring and reconstructing the entity from a perspective, which is why measurement frameworks become so critical. That is, the context of business execution is complex and dynamic, and it can be "reconstructed" from a number of different perspectives. The excellence proposition, as discussed later, lends a perspective from which the context of the business execution can be assessed.

What Is Your Excellence Proposition?

Leading companies actively pursue an excellence proposition, and others may stumble upon it through a long-drawn-out process of trial and error. Regardless of how it evolved or its specific composition, all companies provide value by way of their unique excellence proposition. Treacy and Wiersema[3] describe three general value disciplines: operational excellence, product leadership, and customer intimacy. In their insightful book *The Discipline of Market Leaders*, they argue that companies must choose to excel at one of these disciplines.

In today's competitive environment, however, it is no longer sufficient to excel at just one of these disciplines. Companies must master all three, and in ways that each organization uniquely defines for itself. Our purpose here is not to sketch out how to accomplish this juggling act, for this is the domain of the strategists and operational managers that make it happen. Rather, we argue that companies must translate their excellence proposition, either implicitly or explicitly, into terms that are then rigorously executed to achieve their strategic goals. This book shows you how to master the operational processes required to achieve your excellence proposition—whether they are for manufacturing processes, business services, or some mixture of the two.

Corporate vision and strategy drive initiatives and projects that seek to capitalize on the opportunities presented by market conditions and customer demands. As shown in Figure 3-3, these are combined with management expectations about organizational capabilities and performance.

Figure 3-3. Excellence Proposition

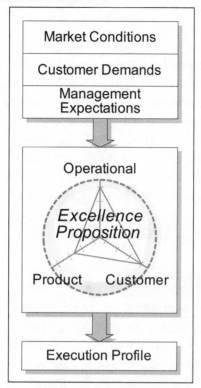

The collective strategic expression of these factors yields an excellence proposition, as shown with the radar graph. Each dimension of the excellence proposition represents the specific processes and costs of the particular domain, reflecting the way in which the business really works. We believe that successful companies make a conscious decision about how to organize their particular excellence proposition by identifying their ideal mix of operational, product, and customer excellence.

The business implications of an execution profile are daunting. Organizations must learn to master all three excellence disciplines. The profile itself is a moving target as organizations constantly sense and respond to changing market conditions, customer demands, and management expectations. Moreover, the disciplines are affected by general industry trends, such as technology improvements and changing cost structures. For example, knowing that the cost of LCD or plasma screens tends to fall systematically over time has implications for the

material costs of PC and TV manufacturers. When combined with consumer expectations of more for less and increased competition, manufacturers must constantly adjust their execution profile to respond accordingly.

The question is, do you want to execute your execution profile
through educated guesses and correlative reasoning about actions and
outcomes, or would you rather make better proactive choices based on
knowledge of your actual processes and cost capabilities—not just those
that exist today, but those that you will face in the future? Strategic
thinkers want the ability to proactively articulate what the ideal excellence profile should look like, based on an understanding of what the
organization is actually capable of delivering, including any additional
resources that may be required. Operational managers need tools to
help them rigorously execute the corporate strategy as expressed in the
execution profile. ProFIT-MAP is designed for this specific purpose.

What a Manager Wants to Know

Companies that understand and proactively shape their excellence profile are empowered with a crystal-clear focus on their business execution targets. This clarity of purpose enables them to move aggressively
to dominate the existing situation or to stake out an innovative future in
which they can reign supreme. Dell Computer and Wal-Mart offer
enlightening examples of how to carve out a commanding position in
their respective industries. Dell wasn't the first, but it soon came to
dominate the direct-to-consumer build-to-order PC industry, changing
the rules of the game and driving industry consolidation along the way.
Wal-Mart has done the same thing in retail industry by using its sheer
size and a relentless focus on continuous improvement to drive down
costs. In fact, its domination, to a large extent, can be attributed to its
cost-oriented approach to the market.

Wal-Mart's unyielding quest to dominate has created tremendous
problems for its competitors. Wal-Mart CEO Lee Scott says, "What
makes us different is our logistics, our information systems, our culture."[4]
It is a culture of ruthless pursuit of reshaping cost structures. Both Dell, a
product company, and Wal-Mart, a retailer, are innovators in their own
industries, but not in a traditional sense of product or service innovation.
They both emphasize operational efficiency by being "cost innovators"
and thereby create product and market leadership through the value they

offer in their products and services. Good customer service adds to the mix. As one Dell executive emphasized, "Contrary to what most companies say, it's not necessary to be price competitive. It's most necessary to be cost-competitive."[5]

Regardless of your company's particular industry or strategic focus, there are three fundamental ways to go about improving operational business processes. You can (1) improve existing processes, (2) replace them with new and superior processes, or (3) outsource them to someone else who will presumably do a better job, or at least a comparable job at lesser cost. Actually, there is a fourth option as well, which is to discontinue the process altogether, such as exiting a particular line of business.

These are all complex decision pathways, and they are all becoming more difficult to navigate, given the increased variability of the value chain and relentless cost pressures. Management methods and tools have not kept pace with managers' needs to quantify their options for shaping current and future operations quickly and dynamically based on an organization's actual capabilities, constraints, and costs. We believe that there is a core set of questions that managers want answered prior to making important operational decisions.

- Is an objective achievable, and will it ever be profitable?
- Will a proposed change have the intended effects?
- What impact will a proposed change have elsewhere in the organization?
- How do I transform operations from point A to point B? That is, what precise steps do I take to get to the desired operational destination?

Operational decisions can have tremendous process, people, technology, and investment implications. Knowing the answers to these questions in advance leads to better decision making, allowing managers to efficiently structure the activities and resources that will be required to achieve operational, customer, and financial success. They help managers avoid making decisions that may have insignificant positive or altogether negative impact, and look for opportunities to make potential high-gain decisions. They also help close the reality gap.

We have observed many corporate initiatives that have tried to empower management with the data, information, and knowledge necessary to answer these questions. Some have resulted in costly "boil-the-ocean" approaches to understanding and improving corporate processes and associated costs. Sometimes, such initiatives fail because of the lack of a proper framework that links to or aligns with corporate strategy. In other instances, they fail because the available tools have been unable to meet the demands of management. ProFIT-MAP fills these voids.

Management Roles and Time Frames

Decision makers typically frame the decision process through a lens selected for their particular role in an organization. Front-line workers can literally reach out and touch operational problems on the shop floor or listen to customer complaints firsthand at a call center and intuitively know how to resolve the source of dissatisfaction. They live and breathe the operational "ground truth" day in and day out. Strategists may see things as a high-level chess game, where moving resources leads to desired outcomes. The point is that we do not all see the organization through the same lens. Some might have a telephoto lens, viewing up close the activities required to achieve an end result. Others see the organization though a wide-angle lens, focusing on the big picture. Yet others may employ a microscope, looking in infinitesimal detail at a single activity in isolation from other organizational processes.

Such differences in operational perception highlight the need to distinguish between three interrelated roles in an organization—strategic, tactical, and operational—and to explore the different issues and challenges faced by each (see Figure 3-4). Corporate strategists typically devise high-level plans that, if successful, will ultimately result in growth and improve profits and/or reduce costs. Business-unit managers are the tacticians who translate corporate or division strategy into actions to achieve the desired end. Operational managers are responsible for the business transactions and activities that give shape to the company's products or services.

The layering and interconnections among strategic, tactical, and operational considerations are an important theme that we return to throughout the book for two reasons. First, it is important to acknowledge the critical and unique collection of skills and capabilities that each role brings to the organization. Second, acknowledging the distinct yet

Figure 3-4. Strategic, Tactical, and Operational Roles

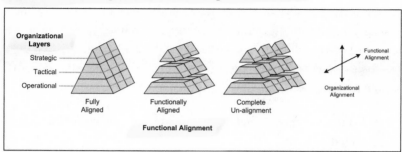

complementary nature of these roles leads to awareness and consideration of organizational alignment—or the lack thereof. Segregation is an
impediment to organizational success. In the extreme example of complete un-alignment, not only do you have silos at the organizational
layers, but you also have silos within the functional groups of the
organization. For example, product design might not talk to or collaborate well with engineering, and both groups might keep finance at
arms length.

As the term implies, organizational alignment or synchronization
refers to bringing people, processes, and the structure of the organization into a common relative position, presumably to achieve an overar-
ching plan and objective. Alignment is both a noun and a verb—a state
of being and a set of actions.[6] The promise of organizational alignment
comes when it is embedded in the corporate culture in the latter form—
as a set of actions. When actions are treated as a series of disconnected
exercises across strategic, tactical, and operational layers, synchronization suffers. On the other hand, managers who view their actions as part
of a larger portfolio of integrated strategic, tactical, and operational
options will see their operational performance rise as a result of the
increased alignment.

The promise of synchronization is that operational decisions will
seamlessly "roll up" and be consistent with overall corporate strategy. On
the other hand, everything must "roll down" so that corporate strategy is
consistent with operating plans and organizational capabilities. As suggested by such an integrated approach, the issues and challenges experienced by each organizational layer are not mutually exclusive. For
example, an operations person might be concerned about throughput

and quality issues on a particular line, a tactical person might be focused on optimizing similar processes across a portfolio of facilities, while a manager responsible for strategy might be considering new products and markets, and how to meet customer demands. The methodology outlined in this book provides an operational discipline and tools that enable managers to

- Translate corporate and division strategy into a series of interconnected projects.
- Influence business strategy with information about current or future organizational capabilities.
- Create an environment in which strategic, tactical, and operational management can work together seamlessly.

Operational time frames also contribute to the challenge of organizational synchronization. Like roles, decisions tend to cluster around three related realms of time (see Figure 3-5). Strategic decisions are at the highest level, representing a long-term plan of action for the organization. At the next level, tactical decisions are smaller-scale actions with a shorter-term end in view. Operational decisions, at the base level, represent the here and now actions.

Managers need to be cognizant of this continuum in operational focus. Organizational synchronization improves only when managers understand and effectively collaborate across their professional boundaries as demarcated by their management roles and primary time orientations. ProFIT-MAP creates a common ground that greatly facilitates communication and collaboration.

Figure 3-5. Strategic, Tactical, and Operational Time Frames

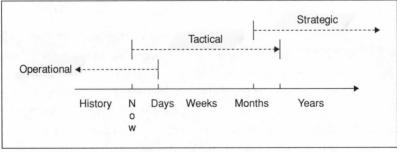

Strategy to Execution: A Time for Retrospection and Alignment

The concept of business strategy and the process of creating strategy mean different things to different people. This is a much studied and written-about subject that is somewhat amorphous. Our intent is not to lay out a new strategic framework or to jump on any particular strategy bandwagon. Rather than perpetuating the modus operandi of execution, our objective is to question if there is a better way.

Suffice it to say that both your approach to developing corporate strategy and the actual strategies that emerge must suit the needs of your particular organization and customers. There is no one-size-fits-all approach for corporate and business-unit strategists. Yet there are some common themes or characteristics that are shared by the multitude of strategic frameworks. At a fundamental level, strategy can be put into operation as a position a company takes—that it is going to do this thing or that thing (e.g., reduce inventory, become lean, innovate with new products). Given a range of strategic options, companies typically adopt a strategic position that comprises the answers to the following three questions: Whom should I target as customers? What products or services should I offer them? How should I do this?[7]

From our perspective, strategy becomes somewhat more tangible when an organization gets tactical and begins thinking about developing projects designed to achieve the strategic endgame. What sorts of projects, for example, might be required to produce the right products at the right costs for the right customers?

There may be certain implicit assumptions about how best to translate strategic intent into actions that lead to the desired outcomes. Moving to lean manufacturing, for instance, is intended to increase efficiency and reduce costs. However, unless companies create a direct synchronization between the tactical objective of becoming lean and the strategic objective of increasing efficiency and profit, the tactical issues can take on a life of their own. As some companies have discovered, in their quest to be lean, they have become too lean, leading to major expenditures on expedited shipping, which destroys the original profitability promise of lean operations. In many instances direct costs have been shifted to indirect or from one department to another thereby offsetting any overall gains or even costing more. Let's be clear: we are advocates for lean operations. Our point is simply that lean operations exist within a larger context—all of which needs to be considered and measured together, i.e., synchronized.

In Figure 1-2, "Translating Strategy into Action," we illustrated a closed-loop process linking strategy to projects, to measuring performance, and then to making adjustments based on analysis of activities-based process and cost data. Projects may be either tactical or operational in nature, and the measurement frameworks can quantify strategic, tactical, and/or operational performance. The process of iterating between projects and their measurements based on an activities composition of the operational process enables organizations to construct their roadmap to the future.

An important consideration, therefore, is how organizations measure and adjust based on actual performance along the pathway to achieving a larger strategic objective. "A strategy is a set of hypotheses about cause and effect. The measurement system should make the relationships (hypotheses) among objectives (and measures) in the various perspectives explicit so that they can be managed and validated."[8]

This is a two-step process—to measure against the strategy, and to use the measured information with additional functional knowledge to adjust the activities to ensure adherence to the strategy.

The Balanced Scorecard is a leading example of a popular and effective tool for measuring and managing business strategy. The Balanced Scorecard is a multidimensional framework that incorporates both lagging indicators, such as financial performance, and drivers of future performance. Forward-looking indicators include investments in customers, internal business processes, and learning and growth.[9] Unfortunately, these are not truly forward-looking indicators. Rather, they are extrapolations of lagging indicators into the future. They do not explicitly incorporate the conditions of the new environment of the future.

We see several additional challenges with current approaches. First, management is not taking advantage of the latest advances in functional sciences. Better techniques are available, such as dynamic modeling and activities-based costing (ABC). There is too much dependence on data mining—a great solution often in search of a problem. Second, managers rely on steady-state analytical approaches that inaccurately assume that the constantly changing business and operational environment is invariant, which in fact is not the case. In the days when business cycles were long this assumption was reasonable, but in today's hyperactive environment this assumption is usually not valid. Third, the standard costing approach does not work well for understanding past performance because it has to be corrected with variance analysis. It is even less up to the task for creating the future. The reality is different from the assumptions.

The tools for managing operational performance have not kept pace with the complexities of manufacturing and services environments. Most existing techniques use the measured information to extrapolate but are unable to create a roadmap to achieve the strategic objectives. Smart decision making requires discipline and a repeatable systematic approach. The missing link is a framework with a structured methodology that explicitly includes the functional knowledge about the business to construct an estimate of its state.

Why a framework for making decisions? To paraphrase a competitive maxim, plans are not as valuable as the ability to plan and adjust once the battle begins. A framework-based methodology is easier to use precisely because its structured nature provides greater flexibility than would otherwise be available to managers. Overwhelmingly, management philosophies are mere guidelines based on correlative reasoning and anecdotal evidence. They lack functional knowledge about the business. Although they advocate doing the "right" things, their lack of a fundamental methodology limits their ability to show the connection between management actions and subsequent process performance, resource requirements, and financial implications prior to taking action.

Without having an easy-to-use systematic framework, current approaches break down under pressure. Systematic decision making, if there was any to begin with, goes by the wayside and is replaced by correlative reasoning and extrapolation from history. Crises lead to stopgap decisions in order to keep operations moving. Such situations arise because the time required for a systematic approach is a luxury that is lost when you are operating in a crisis mode. This is true whether you are attempting to achieve long-term strategic or short-term operational goals. The show must go on; hence, managers make decisions without fully assessing the consequences.

In order to align every step of execution with strategy, a multidimensional activities-based approach is required. It must incorporate functional knowledge about how the business operates to construct and adjust the roadmap to attain the strategic objectives. Furthermore, the methodology must be easy and intuitive to use. It must support a disciplined approach regardless of the time pressures. ProFIT-MAP is the only methodology that meets these objectives.

THE PROFIT-MAP APPROACH

If your operating environment includes new or improved products or processes, changing customer demand, pricing pressures, and increased competition, among other factors, you need a structured methodology to successfully navigate through your business challenges. Let's consider a typical scenario in creating competitive advantage. The executive team has presented the strategic plan in order to target the most promising and profitable opportunities. The CEO has a clear vision of where he or she needs to guide the company, and that vision has been widely communicated throughout the workforce. Several high-profile initiatives have been launched. Employees have embraced the new rallying cry with a sense of purpose and competitive spirit. Further, each business unit has meticulously translated the corporate strategy into divisional strategies.

Now comes the hard part: planning, prioritizing, implementing, and managing the collection of individual projects that, if successfully completed, hold the promise of a better future. Unfortunately, many organizations never achieve their goals and do not realize that they are at a competitive disadvantage because they are operating from a position of financial and process hindsight rather than foresight.

As with cable news, we have grown accustomed to instant analysis. The speed of society is increasing. To win the challenge, we need a framework that can cope with unyielding dynamic demand. IBM calls this "On-Demand" and talks about the operational resources required to fulfill the need. We contend that On-Demand is not just for operational resources, but has to include an operational response that is in sync with the corporate strategy. You must be able to adjust your strategy as well as your execution on demand as market conditions and other external factors change. A company must create a pathway to deliver value that is completely aligned with its overall strategy. Localized actions or a piecemeal approach is not acceptable in a global economy.

A Parametric Approach Allows You to See into Your Future

Any methodology for making operational decisions requires a conceptual structure that is capable of capturing the essence of business execution. ProFIT-MAP relies on a parametric activities-based decision approach that provides the critical integrated process, resource, and financial information that managers require in order to make informed proactive decisions. These are the three central business execution "perspectives" that we return to throughout this book.

Historically, fully enumerating actual operational capabilities, constraints, and costs has not been easy or practical. Many methodologies have attempted to do this, with varying degrees of success; all have run into a wall of inadequate management tools. Some required new ways to do business, whereas others called for new business systems to be installed. None worked with existing setups (e.g., systems, processes) and management thinking. A chorus of corporate strategists, strategy consultants, and leading business book authors has advocated doing the "right" things to guide or lead execution—although the specifics may vary by source. This is a good thing and leads to a more disciplined and repeatable approach to execution. However, none of these advocates can tell you the *specific set of activities* that, if done properly, will actually execute the strategy.

To gain foresight—to be able to proactively shape both the forest and the trees—we use the Parametric Activities-Based Framework (what we call pABF) for decision making to complement but not replace existing financial and operational systems. The pABF approach is the only framework, to our knowledge, that works equally well from the executive suite (making strategy) all the way to the front lines (strategy execution) and back again in an iterative fashion so that operational capability and resources can influence strategy. ProFIT-MAP is built on top of the pABF.

As the name implies, pABF is an extension of the traditional ABC model, which goes beyond a static view and allocated—or aggregated—costs, providing an actionable roadmap of expenses and profitability based on activities performed by an organization. Kaplan and Cooper[10] stated, "An activity-based cost system provides companies with an economic map of their operations by revealing the existing and forecasted cost of activities and business processes, which, in turn, leads to knowledge of the cost and profitability of individual products, services, customers, and operating units." Unfortunately, ABC is an accounting tool that looks at history from a single financial perspective. The pABF, on the other hand, incorporates additional perspectives and is specifically designed to look forward in time.

An activities-based approach allows an organization to determine the actual cost associated with each product and service produced by the organization. The method is independent of the organizational structure and focuses on activities performed by employees and machines throughout the organization. The advantages of ABC over the traditional cost-accounting methods are well documented and widely accepted. Despite agreement on the superiority of ABC for managerial decision making, however, it is not widely accepted or used in corporations. Typical existing financial systems do not support an activities orientation. The cost of capturing the activities data is prohibitively high, and there are significant data inconsistencies. Moreover, ABC accounting methods are historically focused, capturing what has transpired and not what is going to happen in the future; hence, it is not very useful for decision making.

Like ABC, our parametric framework also works at the activities level, reflecting more closely the way the business operates, but with several critical differences. It enhances an ABC approach in three ways. First, pABF is strictly process-oriented, providing an activities-oriented description that carries with it the critical functional knowledge conveyed within operational processes. Second, the functional knowledge is dynamic and made up of several elements. The pABF approach understands the activities composition of a process, including how each station interacts with every other station in a dynamic manner. It accounts for the dynamic nature of resources and how they are used. It quantifies the corresponding financials of the dynamic system. Third, the pABF approach is able to look into the future, using parameters as surrogates for expected activities that have not yet occurred. These parameters, which are derived from the functional knowledge of processes, are based on an organization's actual dynamic performance and cost data (not an aggregated snapshot) and can be tuned to reflect anticipated future operational conditions. We build the pABF from the ground up in the next chapter.

The absence of an activity-based approach to planning and measuring processes, resources, and their costs puts an organization at a severe competitive disadvantage and can lead to management by "perception of the facts" rather than management by facts. For instance, companies may adopt an offshoring strategy, developing manufacturing and service capabilities in lower-cost countries, based on the assumption that having the lowest product costs is vital for survival. In contrast to the rush to outsource and offshore, Dell has chosen not to outsource its manufacturing. It has a factory in China to serve China and Japan, but not the United States. For Dell, the deciding factor is knowing its cost structures, including the logistics costs of its dynamic value chain. More specifically, the cost of transporting the finished goods is greater than the cost of the labor required to build PCs.[11] Dell expands its manufacturing capability to meet demand closest to each primary market, such as the United States or Europe, even when its competitors are pushing to send manufacturing overseas. Winners know precisely why they are better, whereas competitors may simply think that they are better.

Implementing the Parametric Approach with the ProFIT-MAP Methodology

The ProFIT-MAP methodology—which we describe in detail starting in Chapter 6—is the implementation methodology for the pABF. It is the conduit that links the pABF to the realities of the shop floor and weaves it through to the executive suite. The impetus behind ProFIT-MAP is to help organizations execute their operational strategies. ProFIT-MAP is wholly complementary to all strategic initiatives and measurement frameworks. It goes a step further by helping to identify an optimal portfolio of activities and processes for efficiently transforming the organization into what it wants to become.

The concept of a dynamic activity-based approach is central to the methodology. One cannot execute with sufficient precision based on the static view of the value chain offered by the steady-state analyses, the allocated cost structures, and the historical efficiency and resource utilization reports. With existing methodologies, you can set a general direction for the future, but you cannot chart a step-by-step path to the future. You need a comprehensive and dynamic activity-based implementation methodology to do so.

One of ProFIT-MAP's greatest strengths is that it is an iterative and flexible methodology that allows organizations to adjust execution on demand. This is particularly useful for decision makers because it lacks the rigidity inherent in most approaches. It allows managers to answer specific operational questions quickly and to refine and adjust as they continue to learn and build expertise.

Moreover, the ProFIT-MAP methodology does not require organizations to have complete and accurate information. You can begin within the limits of currently available organizational data. You can use the methodology now with whatever you have available and refine it later as needed. ProFIT-MAP provides visibility into the future through a systematic process of successive iterations. If the future is insufficiently clear, the methodology enables organizations to capture additional detail quickly and to continue iterating until the future emerges with sufficient clarity. In our view, it is not necessary to paint the full scenery of one's journey. You could, but this is typically a very time-consuming and costly "boil-the-ocean" exercise. We believe it is more practical to invest the minimal amount of time and energy to illuminate the basic roadmap that gets the organization from point A to point B and to continue to refine the roadmap as you progress.

Let's illustrate how ProFIT-MAP uses existing data to understand the future with an example of a hybrid "lean" and "low-cost" manufacturing strategy. Imagine that you are an automotive OEM or a Tier 1 supplier that is "burdened" with union agreements limiting or flat-out precluding your ability to outsource any or some portion of your manufacturing. This is what we refer to as the reverse of the "China strategy." Whereas China competes on an abundance of cheap labor, in our scenario you are constrained to compete using an abundance of high-cost local labor. This sounds like an impossible position, but it is not. By helping you understand your actual activities-based processes, the labor costs, the logistics cost, and other relevant factors already contained in various enterprise systems, the ProFIT-MAP methodology enables you to work within your existing constraints to identify alternative profitable pathways to your future. For example, knowing that you have more labor than necessary might enable your organization to put off investing in expensive capital equipment and divesting extreme automation that can be replaced by labor, as it would not have sufficient payback over and above the cost of the abundant labor.

ProFIT-MAP is revolutionary, yet it is not a reinvention of the multitude of methods, frameworks, and tools employed in business today. Rather, it is a unified and disciplined approach that enhances what companies are already doing. ProFIT-MAP provides a multidimensional and integrated perspective on operations. We took the best ideas from market and thought leaders and incorporated them into a cohesive framework with a strong foundation in theory, as discussed in Chapter 4. Our goal is that this methodology should be easily deployable by any manufacturer or service provider without significant effort. The discipline imparted by this approach serves multiple audiences at all the levels of the organization—strategic, tactical, and operational—without requiring the organization to rip apart and replace current operational initiatives or enterprise systems and processes. ProFIT-MAP builds upon the work of the giants who preceded us. In the fast-moving global business environment, ProFIT-MAP's integrative approach stands ready to deliver a source of competitive and sustaining advantage by solving current operational problems and offering a methodology for anticipating and proactively responding to future challenges.

REFERENCES

1   Michael Treacy and Fred Wiersema, *The Discipline of Market Leaders* (Reading, MA: Addison-Wesley, 1995).
2   Michael E. Porter, *Competitive Advantage: Creating and Sustaining Superior Performance* (New York: The Free Press, 1985).
3   Treacy and Wiersema, *The Discipline of Market Leaders.*
4   David Faber, "With a Small-Town Culture, Wal-Mart Dominates," MSN Money TV, HYPERLINK http://www.moneycentral.msn.com, November 10, 2004.
5   Gary McWilliams, "Dell Fine-Tunes Its PC Pricing to Gain an Edge in Slow Market," *Wall Street Journal*, June 8, 2001.
6   George Labovitz and Victor Rosansky, *The Power of Alignment: How Great Companies Stay Centered and Accomplish Extraordinary Things* (New York: Wiley, 1997).
7   Constantinos C. Markides, *All the Right Moves: A Guide to Crafting Breakthrough Strategy* (Boston: Harvard Business School Press, 2000).
8   Robert S. Kaplan and David P. Norton, *The Balanced Scorecard: Translating Strategy into Action* (Boston: Harvard Business School Press, 1996), p. 30.
9   Kaplan and Norton, *The Balanced Scorecard*; Robert S. Kaplan and David P. Norton, *The Strategy Focused Organization: How Balanced Scorecard Companies Thrive in a New Business Environment* (Boston: Harvard Business School Press, 2001).
10 Robert S. Kaplan and Robin Cooper, *Cost and Effect: Using Integrated Costs Systems to Drive Profitability and Performance* (Boston: Harvard Business School Press, 1998), p. 80.
11 John G. Spooner, "Dell to Open New PC Plant in United States," *CNET News.com*, October 19, 2004.

Driving the System: A Parametric Framework

In a state which is ordered with a view to the good of the whole we should be most likely to find justice.

—Plato, *The Republic*

In theory there is no difference between theory and practice. In practice there is.

—Yogi Berra

UNDERSTANDING OPERATIONAL processes and how they evolve over time and continually change is indispensable for achieving success. Driving the process, whether it is for manufacturing products or delivering services, to a desired future state requires management to build a roadmap in the form of a multistage action plan. The action plan is dependent on a thorough understanding of the state of the process, including the capabilities and constraints of the organization at every step along the pathway to the operational destination. Incorporating functional knowledge about the process is a critical component of defining the actions required to take the process to the next step. A process can be observed and measured, and its status can be estimated from these observations. The quality of the estimation framework and the ability of the methodology to develop the roadmap are, therefore, intimately tied to each other.

In this chapter we present the theoretical underpinnings of the Parametric Activities-Based Framework (pABF), then link it to practice by highlighting how it applies to solving business execution challenges. The pABF provides a unified and flexible framework for understanding and driving business execution. ProFIT-MAP is the implementation methodology for the pABF, which is why we sometimes use the terms interchangeably in this chapter. If you are already sold on the pABF approach and the ProFIT-MAP methodology, then you can proceed directly to Chapter 6, where the hands-on description of the methodology begins. We, however, recommend reading this and the next chapter to fully comprehend the advantages of using ProFIT-MAP over other existing methodologies.

"HOUSTON, WE HAVE A PROBLEM"

A fundamental management conundrum is the necessity for making important decisions without really knowing what the totality of their impact will be. Will there be any unanticipated effects? You can eliminate all the "waste" from a process to improve efficiency, for example, but do you really know the cost and profitability implications of the leaner process before you make the change? If cost and profitability are important elements of your process and you are planning for the future based on steady-state analysis and allocated cost structures, you are limited because you are using static information to understand an ever-changing dynamic environment.

Allocated Cost Structures Are No Longer Adequate

Allocated costs are aggregated estimates of costs assigned to a particular function or department. They are not actual costs because the estimates are static, are based on an older environment, and often are not up to date with the present realities. The use of standard labor hours for allocated costing was a suitable approach in the days when labor was one of the largest contributors to the product cost. The process was dedicated to delivering the same product or service day after day without any change or modification. Products had a long life cycle, and they were produced to build inventories. The long life cycle protected against product obsolescence. Companies added value by operational excellence, doing the same thing over and over without fail in a methodical manner. Work was segmented among the various disciplines and departments. People were experts in their own line of work and focused primarily on doing the best job they could within their own department. They were not cognizant of the broader perspective, and, frankly, it did not matter. The product mix, product volumes, and most other externally driven variables did not change significantly, so that the allocated cost structure built on standard labor hours was a good representation of the actual situation. Today things are very different.

Currently, product or service leadership has been added to operational excellence as an essential requirement for business. As a result, companies are introducing new and improved products with greater frequency. Product life cycles have decreased and continue to shrink. The market is shifting from mass production to mass customization. Product variations have increased, creating an avalanche of changing product mixes and volumes on a daily basis. No company can expect to build the same product without variation for a long time; the flexibility to produce and deliver many products on a single line has become essential. People have to be trained to do many things and can no longer focus on one task only, as they once did. Automation continues to reduce the role of labor. In summary, the activities composition involved in creating and delivering value has become more dynamic as companies continually sense and respond to new opportunities and challenges.

The variety of activities required to deliver products and services has changed dramatically in accordance with changes in customer expectations. The environment is highly dynamic, with changes in the activities composition or operational processes being driven by external factors. The necessary activities are no longer confined to the operation's four walls. Changes in product mix and volumes, technologies, and other factors, such as the efficiency of the supply chain, play a greater role than labor. The role of labor has also shifted significantly from a direct function of "touching" the product or service to an indirect back-office mode. For example, shorter life cycles require more product designs, which require more engineers and analysts—people who do not physically "make" the product.

Automation has reduced the number of direct laborers working on operations while increasing the need for knowledge workers such as CNC (computer numerical control) programmers, field service engineers, and customer relationship managers. Information inventories and know-how have replaced product inventories. Many of these functions are not directly "in-line" for delivering the goods and services, and hence are being outsourced to cheaper labor markets. The crux of this discussion is that direct labor no longer accurately represents the variety of activities performed today; therefore, a cost model built on direct labor hours is outdated.

Common Workarounds for Allocated Cost Structures

Many companies recognize the problems with allocated cost structures based on labor standards and have adopted variations on these structures. A common adaptation is adjustment of labor hours based on machine use, called equivalent labor hours (ELH). Some companies have switched completely to machine hours, creating machine run rates (MRR) as a mesh of labor and depreciation. Similarly, the service industry introduced the standard task rate (STR), which is akin to the machine run rate. More complicated workarounds separate labor, machine, or ELH standards by individual products—or other related variations.

The commonality among these various techniques is the use of some sort of single time-invariant parameter to represent the magnitude of the effort involved in creating and delivering value. Although a lot of value-adding steps have been moved to the back office, offline, or, as it is often called, to indirect or overhead costs, these techniques continue to use an artificially created parameter. The portion of overhead has increased tremendously in recent years, but the cost structures currently in use are deficient in acknowledging this reality. They continue to modulate the overhead cost based on a single artificial action parameter.

Deficiencies in Common Fixes

Valuing overhead expenses—which today can exceed direct costs—on the basis of a single parameter is a potentially calamitous approach. It amounts to defining a significant portion of cost, in many cases more than half, as a multiple of one artificially created factor. Mathematically, the sensitivity of this single parameter is so overwhelming that it creates volatility in the final results. Small deviations create large swings in cost estimates. Despite the refinement of the parameter definitions, the magnitude of instability is often so overwhelming that the cost numbers are simply not believable. This has created a crisis, as managers do not know the true cost of producing and delivering products and services until it is too late. They do not realize the true cost until the accountants close the books at the end of the quarter or, in many cases, at the end of the year. By then, taking corrective action has little, if any, value.

Realigning the single parameter does not address the dynamic changes occurring daily or weekly. Managers respond to opportunities or challenges on one time scale, but the allocations do not respond accordingly. Although the changes in broad resource policies and improvements in technology happen over a longer duration, the product-mix diversity and volumes vary frequently. Such dynamic system behavior requires a rethinking of the allocation strategy.

There is a more intuitive approach for proactively understanding the process and financial implications of management decisions. Why depend on workarounds or patches when there is an integrated methodology that accounts for the dynamics of business execution from multiple perspectives, including a cost and profitability focus, and can be used to build a process roadmap? Before describing ProFIT-MAP's integrated framework, we discuss its theoretical underpinnings, setting the stage for why it radically improves the management decision-making process.

PROFIT-MAP'S THEORETICAL FOUNDATION

ProFIT-MAP is built on the foundation of systems theory. Systems theory is an interdisciplinary field that draws on principles from physics, biology, and engineering to study dynamic, complex, and interdependent systems as a whole.[1] Talk to any manager responsible for executing the business about his or her operational challenges and you are likely to get an earful of real-world stories about the daunting nature of the management problems. Any manager who tells you that synchronizing business execution with the strategy is easy is probably dealing with some form of a reality gap—unless, of course, the manager is dealing with a static system! The discipline of business execution is a perfect fit for a systems theory approach.

The applicability of systems theory to the challenges of business execution is contingent upon satisfying several conditions. These characteristics or postulates help frame ProFIT-MAP's formulation of an integrated systems model and are delineated here:

1. *Existence.* Operational processes exist in every organization, even if they are not fully documented or completely understood. The rest of the postulates emanate from this one.
2. *Dynamic structure.* Operational processes vary over time. The change is a combination of factors internal and external to the corporation.
3. *Realization/identification.* Operational processes are measurable. Even if they are not well defined, they can always be observed through measurements.
4. *Reachability/controllability.* The ProFIT-MAP methodology preaches the ability to create a roadmap to a desired future operational state. Systems theory requires (a) that the endpoint must be attainable or reachable, and (b) that the process to reach the future state must be controllable. That is, managerial actions must be able to assert controllability not only at the starting points and endpoints, but also throughout the path on the drive to reach the desired future state.
5. *Reconstructability/observability.* Operational processes can be re-created through measurement. It is possible to accurately reconstruct the underlying phenomenon from the various measurements of it taken at every step along the path. Poor reconstructability— the inability to accurately reconstruct the relevant portions of the process along the path—is a root cause of the reality gap. It is difficult to make good decisions based on poorly reconstructed performance information.
6. *Stability/sensitivity.* Operational processes must demonstrate structural stability so that small disturbances do not cause them to diverge or become stagnant. The process must demonstrate parametric sensitivity so that management actions can alter the system. That is, management must have the ability to change the process through specific actions. The stability means that it behaves within the bounds that you want it to. If the system deviates outside the bounds, then it is not stable. The stability concept can be illustrated with health-care or pension costs. If

the costs are at a level at which the corporation can still operate (not necessarily profitably), then the company is "stable." But if the costs become so large that the company cannot operate, the system becomes unstable, as you have created a divergence in the system.

Operational business processes satisfy all of these postulates. Although a process is a conceptual object, it can be observed through various measurements. Even if an organization does not explicitly define all of its processes, they do exist. The application of systems theory to the discipline of business execution demonstrates a way that you can control the business through parametric actions. But this controllability doesn't mean that you can drive the business anywhere you want. The areas where you can drive it are restricted and depend upon the system and its surroundings. For instance, luxury automobiles are designed to run on paved roads. SUVs have the capability of driving off-road in rough terrain. You could enter a luxury car in the Baja 1000 off-road race, but the results are not likely to be competitive.

The reconstructability concept is critical because if you do not recognize the facts surrounding the type of system you have, then you cannot drive it very effectively. You might be driving the wrong system in the wrong place, but you would not know this without reconstructability—or until much further down the line, when the disappointing final results become apparent. This is the biggest cause of the reality gap. *If you don't recognize what your system is really capable of doing, you will not be able to drive it properly.*

A product is a figurative term for any output of the process, whether it is tangible in nature or not. For example, a manufacturing process produces "widgets," whereas a service process, such as accounts receivable, collects payments. Just as each widget is a complete product, each receivable when it has been collected is one complete unit of the product. In either case, the process is not a static system, but a time-varying dynamic entity that reacts and responds to internal and external forces. Corporate policies, human know-how, and resources, among other factors, define the constraints that shape the process and regulate its capabilities.

Macro-level factors are constantly bombarding the corporation and affecting the dynamics of the operational response. These external factors include both controlled and unforeseen events, such as fluctuations in product mix and product demand, process improvements, market opportunities, technological developments, and so on. A process is also susceptible to internal or micro factors, such as equipment failure or fluctuations in time to carry out a process step, among others. Both macro and micro factors are dynamic, but they operate at different time scales, and each factor can have its own dynamic behavior. Hence the dynamism of the overall process is complex, with a great deal of interaction among the various factors.

"Control" actions, such as management decisions, also perturb the process and change its response. Whether the results are measurable or not is secondary to the fact that the management action (or inaction) is always part of the system. The sensitivity of the process to the management action or other event determines the relative importance of the action or event to the process.

CURRENT APPROACHES ARE LESS EFFECTIVE FOR MANAGING COMPLEX DYNAMIC SYSTEMS

Managing a Complex Dynamic System

One could argue that the role of management is to shape processes to achieve the desired outcome. Reshaping occurs through redefining the capabilities and constraints to change the way the process responds to its internal inertia and external events. This can be done by changing either the dynamics of the process or the infrastructure surrounding it to affect the constraints. Systems have a life of their own. Their inertia causes them to continue to evolve even in the absence of management action. That is to say, taking no action does not make the system static.

Figure 4-1 shows a generic management action framework. Here we have explicitly separated reconstruction as a function distinct from management. This highlights an interim step between measurement and management. The difference between the actual dynamic process and the reconstructed process is the source of the reality gap. In this model, the reality gap is not a function of poor management. Rather, it says that management is making critical decisions based on faulty or inadequate information about the process.

In the management literature, reconstruction is not typically recognized as a separate step. It is usually integrated directly into the management logic. Bossidy and Charan[2] cite the budgeting process as an

Figure 4-1. Managing Dynamic Processes

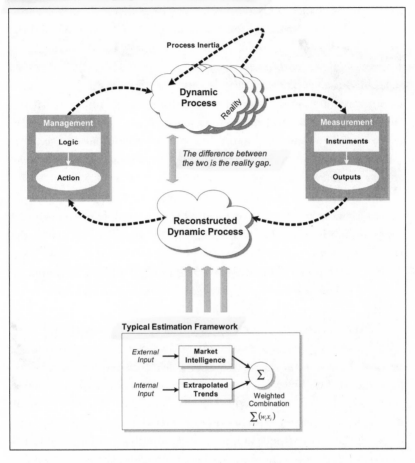

example of a process that is marred by this deficiency. The budgeting process is built around management's desire for achievement, but it is grounded neither in the reality of what can be achieved nor in how to achieve it. Detailed analysis to ensure that the path to the future state is feasible is usually not done, as the definition of the future state is based on management desires and not on what is achievable.

In the typical estimation framework shown at the bottom of Figure 4-1, the state of the system is being estimated in good faith, but with an inadequate, partially dynamic approach. In this mixed model, market intelligence (which is often time-based) is combined with extrapolated and static internal trends about historical process capabilities to form some sort of weighted combination that is projected into the future to predict performance. This approach force-feeds dynamic variables from static capabilities. The extrapolated trends are based on aggregated historical indicators. They can tell you a lot about the past, but they do not translate well to the future, particularly as conditions are no longer the same as those under which the trends were developed. For example, resource requirements, demand, product mix, and so on are constantly changing. The common practice today is to take real-time data from transactional systems and then force-fit them into a static view of the future. However, in the immortal words of Yogi Berra, "The future ain't what it used to be."

If your measurement framework is not delivering the value that you expect, chances are that the reconstruction is incomplete. Management is not at fault because it cannot see the reality gap. The problem is that the reconstruction algorithm does not give management the visibility to understand the gap. There will always be a reality gap, as you cannot get rid of it unless you have perfect measurements. You can nevertheless reduce it to a negligible issue.

Reconstruction can occur by way of a mental model as well. You don't necessarily need a formal model. Malcolm Gladwell[3] talks about this as "'Thin-slicing' . . . the ability of our unconscious to find patterns in situations and behavior based on very narrow slices of experience." Experienced managers can quickly size up a situation based on the details of a very thin slice or brief period of observation—perhaps only a few minutes. In either case, the reconstruction approach should be intuitive and should scale sufficiently to meet the exponential complexities and interactions of the entire operational system. We believe that a healthy balance of human expertise, including domain knowledge and experience, combined with the "systematic" thinking facilitated by ProFIT-MAP, leads to a winning combination for making better management decisions.

The Need for a Better Reconstruction Framework

"Nature, the Practical Joker, armed the systems analyst with a set of linear tools and then insisted upon creating a nonlinear world to tantalize and frustrate him."[4]

Success in reaching the desired future state is possible only when each stage on the way is attainable and can be estimated to be in the same place that was desired. It is like connecting the dots between the various waypoints on a roadmap to ensure the connectedness of the path from its start to its destination. It requires knowledge of where you are beginning and where your actions in each successive stage will lead you. Disconnections in the pathway can occur at three possible places—at the beginning, at the end, and along the path. These are sources of the reality gap. Management decisions can move the system off course at any time, but they also have the ability to enable it to recover from deviations. If deviations from the expected path are not recognized through reconstruction along the way, and the process is allowed to evolve, then the process cannot reach the desired final state. It will ultimately end up at an unexpected final state.

Reconstruction is an essential part of building the pathway, whether we do so explicitly, as with ProFIT-MAP, or implicitly, as practiced currently. Current technologies for reconstructing or estimating the process are based on two inputs: the extrapolated historical trends and the market intelligence, as shown in Figure 4-1. This is the domain of data warehousing, data mining, and reporting, or, as it is more commonly known these days, business intelligence. We use the term *market intelligence* in a broad sense to represent the knowledge or best estimate of the external environment, including market conditions and customer demands. Current approaches cannot ensure that the path to the future state is feasible, nor can they identify and connect the waypoints along the route to the destination.

Figure 4-2 illustrates the reconstruction challenges for business execution. We cannot really know the pathway's true "shape," so the figure shows a hypothetical curved plane representing a time slice of business execution. The surface is continuous. There is no beginning or end, but it does have a direction. Within this time period, the origin represents the current state, and the dots represent potential measures and their reconstruction waypoints on the journey to the future state. The system is directional in that it moves forward, and there are a multitude of possible system states at each time sample, as it can move in any forward direction.

Measurement may point out that there is or is not a problem, but without proper reconstruction, you cannot know what the true problem is or why it is occurring. If your measurement "scorecard" is properly constructed, then it gives you the reconstruction capability—the proper

Figure 4-2. Reconstructing the Business Execution Waypoints

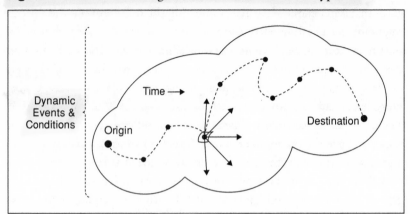

view of the system in its current state. Reconstruction tells us where we are and helps articulate the problem for the particular time slice. This may sound a little complicated, and it is. That's our point, but with proper tools and training, it is far more manageable and intuitive than you might think.

Reconstruction can occur through the use of a disciplined approach like a methodology. Let's look at a challenge from outside of the business world to illustrate the value of systematic reconstruction. Gladwell[5] describes a fascinating series of studies of relationships and marriages in which the psychologist John Gottman has shown that by analyzing only one hour of a husband and wife talking to each other, he can predict with 95 percent accuracy whether the couple will still be married 15 years later. His success rate falls only to 90 percent if the observation period drops to 15 minutes. How does he do this? Through many years of study, he has developed a coding system containing 20 different dimensions spanning every conceivable emotion expressed by couples in conversations. The videotapes are sampled every second, and scores are assigned, leading to thousands of data points for the hour, and these data are combined with measures from electrodes placed on the skin and other measures. Feeding these data into a complex algorithm leads to the remarkable prediction success rate.

Gottman's work shows what can be done with conscious and deliberate measurement and reconstruction. Through years of practical experience, he determined that the marriage "system" can be accurately predicted by sampling a little over 20 dimensions (adding in the physiological dimensions). Likewise, the pABF was developed and refined over two decades, yielding three key management perspectives, each with many dimensions—which in this instance vary in number and type depending on the particular business execution problem.

Reconstruction can also occur through mental models—that is, experienced managers do it effortlessly in their minds. Gladwell[6] describes the adaptive unconscious as the part of the brain that rapidly processes a lot of data (called "thin-slicing") to identify a problem, make important decisions, or even make predictions. It's when you sense that there is something wrong with the way your car is handling and pull over to the side of the road to investigate. In that brief moment of time, your brain said "danger," and you took action even before you could articulate the problem. A quick walk around the car shows that you have a flat tire. There were warning signs—a loud pop, deceleration, a sensation of pulling toward the side of the road—but you might not have pieced the clues together unless you had had a similar previous experience. "The adaptive unconscious does an excellent job of sizing up the world, warning people of danger, setting goals, and initiating action in a sophisticated and efficient manner."[7]

Gottman has become such an expert at "thin-slicing" couples that he can literally overhear a couple talking in a restaurant and quickly know whether their marriage is ultimately doomed. In a business context, expert managers quickly thin-slice the environment and instantaneously know whether or not there is a problem. They are adept at rapidly assimilating measurements (i.e., management reports) and their own observations and formulating a general sense of what's going on. There is a gap, however, between the intuitive knowledge that there is a problem and being able to reconstruct its root cause. That's why the reconstruction step is so important. It's where the manager combines his or her intuition with a reconstruction model that can clearly identify the actual source of the problem and its cause, enabling the manager's actions to be connected to the problem. *The true value of proper reconstruction is that it can provide previously unavailable insight into what actions will be effective for driving the system to the desired destination.*

Reconstruction does not have to be exact or even complete as long as it is suitable to use for the specific task. You don't need to pay attention to everything, just to what is important and relevant. Knowing precisely what to pay attention to is half the battle. After years of practical application and refinement, ProFIT-MAP captures the essence of business execution through three primary perspectives: process, resources, and finance. Each of these perspectives, in turn, contains multiple dimensions. We are not saying that these are the only perspectives, just that their systematic reconstruction is sufficient to give you what you need if you are to make effective, forward-looking decisions that are capable of achieving your business objectives. The ProFIT-MAP methodology's emphasis on "validating the results with reality" acknowledges the value of combining systematic thinking with mental models that factor in managers' functional knowledge and experiences.

Functional Knowledge Trumps Extrapolation

In current estimation approaches, there is no formal incorporation of the functional knowledge about the business itself—about how the business really works, including important contextual information. These approaches typically involve gathering data from various sources and compiling them in a particular limited context. The focus undoubtedly is historical in nature, with little regard to the future. The lack of functional knowledge in the improvement process is the single largest source of the reality gap.

Applications of functional knowledge in broad managerial decision making have been few and far between. Although the desire to use functional knowledge for operational, tactical, and strategic decision making exists, the lack of proper frameworks and analytical tools has prevented its use. To work around the dearth of such tools, managers often find themselves oversimplifying operational problems and doing the best they can under the circumstances by applying correlative reasoning.

Important functional knowledge includes the capabilities to produce the products and services, including resource requirements, policy constraints, and corresponding financials. It defines the boundaries of the constraints. It provides an estimate of the shape and the size of the system so that we do not violate the capabilities and the restrictions of the process in making decisions. Such information is necessary to fill the gap between the reality and the promise that Bossidy and Charan[8] wrote about: "The gap between promises and result is widespread and clear. The gap nobody knows is the gap between what a company's leaders want to achieve and the ability of the organization to achieve it."

The primary driver for the traditional approach is the need to report performance that has already occurred. This approach is historical in nature, predominantly based on measurement data and not on the integration of data with functional knowledge. This is the basis of the data mining, statistical analysis, and reporting commonly found in a business intelligence toolset. The only futuristic knowledge that can be inferred from this is based either on statistical extrapolation or using older rates in the future and requires that the conditions remain invariant—that the future operating environment is identical to the present. The extrapolated data lend insight into the future based only on the past; they cannot identify opportunities or problems that may occur as a result of dynamic changes. In the absence of functional knowledge, one has to believe that the measured outputs and the extrapolated trends contain sufficient and accurate enough information to take the place of an estimate of the process as it evolves into the future. Clearly, this is a dangerous assumption.

Can we accept the extrapolated trends as representing the process of the future? Decisions made now cannot affect the past, only the future. If no external or internal factors change, and if the process continues to evolve over time driven primarily by its internal inertia, then in most cases the extrapolation will be suitable. That is, in some instances extrapolation is acceptable. Functional information about the process is the only way to analyze how the process would evolve thereafter.

With a functional knowledge model, the current state and its constraints, which restrict the functional capabilities of an organization, are the only relevant information from history. How the process reached the present state is not relevant. History is an imperfect teacher, but one needs only to know where one is and understand one's capabilities at present to proceed to the next step. Similarly, understanding the capabilities at the next step is important for moving to the subsequent step, thereby building a multistage path to the final desired state.

It's Not a Journey into the Past

A system that depends on the present value and not on the historical journey is called *autonomous* or *Markovian*. The concept of a Markovian process is related to the principle of optimality put forth by the famous mathematician Richard Bellman.[9] It states: "An optimal policy has the property that whatever the initial state and the initial decisions are, the remaining decisions must constitute an optimal policy with regard to the state resulting from the first decision."

Rutherford Aris stated the same principle in more colloquial language: "If you don't do the best with what you have happened to have got, you will never do the best with what you should have had."

Bellman often spoke about the principle of optimality and its application as the embodiment of a common phrase: *don't cry over spilled milk.* He suggested picking up from wherever you are and making the best decision to move forward, keeping in mind the limitations and the constraints that you have to operate within. Similarly, accountants speak of "sunk costs," or money that has already been spent and cannot be recovered; hence, they advise making investments for the future based on the current capabilities.

Let's illustrate this with a simple example of two identical cars starting from a common location. Their destination is the same. Car A takes one path, whereas car B takes another. After a while, the driver of car B realizes that he is heading in the wrong direction and adjusts his route. He made the decision to change his route based on the destination and current location, and not on how he arrived there. The history of his journey (the path and the decisions along the way) brought him to his current location. The relevant factors to move forward from here are his location and destination. In addition, his capabilities and constraints determine his ability to reach the destination.

After some time, both cars reach a common crossroads, arriving from two different directions. Their destination is the same, so they both take the same road going forward. Car A had taken the shorter route and did not consume as much gas, so it reached the destination without requiring a fuel stop. Car B, on the other hand, which had taken the longer route, had to stop on the way to get more gas. The decision to stop and get gas was essential if car B was to reach the final destination. The history of the cars prior to their arriving at the common junction is irrelevant except for one fact: they had different amounts of gas remaining. The amount of gas is the constraint that controlled their future decisions and their ability to reach the destination. This represents their capability for forward movement. Extrapolating the route would not affect either of the two decisions—to adjust course and to get gas—made by the driver of car B or the decision not to get additional gas made by the driver of car A. Their decisions were independent of the path they took and depended only on their capabilities. The history is irrelevant to proceeding further. This simple example highlights two critical issues in managerial decision making: what should be measured, and how to use that information.

Measurements—A View into Internals

Simply stated, measurements provide an instantaneous view or a snapshot inside the process—nothing more than that. They represent a static image or time slice of a small part of the object under observation at a given time. Without putting the measurement output into its context, this information has very little value. You cannot measure the whole system, so your measurements must be carefully and judiciously picked so that they give you an accurate view of the system. The "perspective" of the measurements must be in concert with your reconstruction algorithm.

More formally, a measurement output is a time-sensitive projection of the process onto a small set of variables, as shown in Figure 4-3. Typically, the measured set has a smaller dimension than the original object. That raises the question of what information it contains and what to do with that information. Rephrasing this question in a business context, the question becomes: is there sufficient information to reconstruct the process for decision making? In other words, can we gain meaningful insight into the process by combining the measured output with the functional knowledge?

The type and quality of measurement depends on the measuring instruments and the perspective under which they are used. The instruments are independent of the definition of the process or the object they are observing. Further analysis and interpretation of the measurement—whether to extrapolate trends or to use them with functional knowledge—are built on top of the measured set, not the actual object. Hence, the biases inherent in the measurement instruments and

Figure 4-3. Measurements—A Poor Reflection of Reality

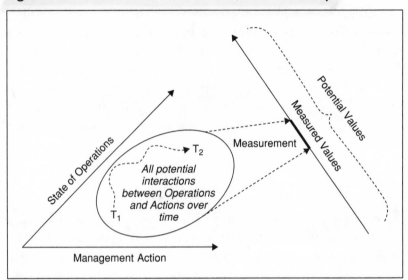

the perspective are present in the observed values, and therefore in the analysis as well. For example, as shown in Figure 4-4, a simple object looks different depending on the location of the observer. A square base pyramid may look like a simple square or even a triangle depending on the position from which the observer is viewing it. Consequently, an inadequate or restrictive perspective can lead to incorrect and partial conclusions—with potentially catastrophic business outcomes.

Analytical Framework

The need to have a correct perspective is not restricted to measurements only; it is critical to the whole analysis. The analytical framework has to be appropriate to the reality of the process and the objectives. An improper analytical perspective also leads to a reality gap. A common example is when a dynamic and time-variant process is analyzed using static and time-invariant measurements or analytical principles.

This practice is common in capacity or throughput analysis in the manufacturing industry. For example, it is common to find product and service costing algorithms in use that are based on static product or service mix, demand, technological capabilities, and so on, despite the fact

Figure 4-4. Reality to Observation Depends on One's Perspective

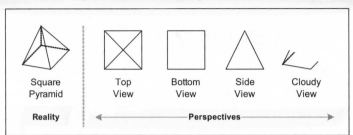

Square Pyramid

Top View

Bottom View

Side View

Cloudy View

Reality ◄——————————Perspectives——————————►

that changes in these variables occur frequently. This is the de facto standard costing algorithm used by the overwhelming majority of manufacturers today. To correct the deficiency in the analytical framework, accountants use variance analysis. It is possible to do this when the analytical view is historical and the actual costs have already occurred. Without a variance analysis—which can be done only for the past and not for the future—projections are based on a deficient analytical framework. This creates a large reality gap by default. Such an approach leads to correlative thinking and rules of thumb. One can only hope that these rules of thumb represent the behavior of the actual system under future conditions.

As Figure 4-5 shows, a mismatched analytical framework spanning from measurement to decision analysis will fail to capture significant business changes, such as a lost contract, a new contract, or product changes. These examples require the business to change so that it can address the new conditions of the system. A static allocated costing approach misses the new reality. A trend analysis is invalidated, since the underlying assumptions have changed and the new dynamics of the system are different.

An activities orientation is needed to understand the new conditions—to facilitate management decisions that lead to appropriate actions for the current reality. An activities orientation, where resources and costs are distributed across the activities, provides increased visibility into the process and eliminates the reality gap. That is, without an activities focus, one cannot adequately plan and manage the operational changes required to drive the business.

In order for the measurement data to be useful, they must contain sufficient information about the object to reconstruct its original form for the required purposes. They should also conform to the analysis frame-

Figure 4-5. Forecasting Challenges

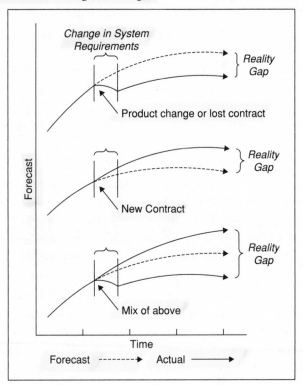

work for the objectives at hand. At the very least, the data and the analytical framework should give the user the confidence that the object can be reconstructed satisfactorily along the path on which she is attempting to drive the system.

Activities-Based Analysis Is the Right Idea

Activities-based costing (ABC) allows an organization to determine the actual cost associated with each product and service produced by the organization. The methodology is independent of the organizational structure and focuses on activities performed by employees and machines. The merits of ABC over the traditional costing methods, which are based on accounting principles for the purposes of managerial decision making, are well documented and widely accepted.[10]

Despite agreement on the superiority of ABC, it is still not commonly used in corporations for managerial decision making. It is underused primarily because existing financial and other enterprise systems do not support the activities framework. They are designed to support the organizational structure and hierarchy. Implementation of a new concept and the support infrastructure to maintain it is expensive and requires a change in the management thought process. Another complicating factor is that ABC in its strict form is not a suitable alternative to everyday and operational accounting, so it is not easy for an organization to embrace it.

Several flavors of ABC have emerged over the last few years under various names, such as lean accounting and throughput accounting, among others. Activities-oriented approaches will give you better costing results than allocated costing approaches. Keep in mind that these approaches all have different objectives and use different algorithms for "reconstructing" what they measure.

An Activities Orientation—Not to Be Confused with ABC

Like everything, an activities basis presents both opportunities and challenges. The effort involved in implementing an activities-based accounting system is monumental and often does not lead to any improvement. Unfortunately, it can lead to distrust among people and lends a flavor of Orwellian "Big Brother" because of the way the activities and costs are identified for every conceivable activity. To avoid this Orwellian feeling, some people advocate using management expertise to estimate the activities composition.[11]

We would argue that the focus of all such ABC approaches is historical in nature. Most importantly, we are *not* questioning the value of either traditional accounting or activities-based accounting for the purposes of maintaining corporate books and reporting. We simply want to highlight the difference between the historical view for accounting and the managerial view for the future. We believe that understanding the activities that will take place in the future in response to the external and internal parameters is the only way to create the future.

An activities basis is the most suitable form of analysis for managerial decision making. As a manager searches for a new reality that is better than the current situation, the only magic at his or her disposal is reshaping the activities composition. Activities analysis is a comparative form of reasoning, not an absolute view. Its success depends on the ability to redesign the activities composition in a way that improves productivity, eliminates waste, reduces costs, and so on—that is, to achieve the objectives of the strategy.

Accounting for every activity is an extremely resource-intensive task, and it creates an environment of distrust. It is also a backward- and not a forward-looking exercise that captures and reports on what has transpired, not what can happen. Clearly, accounting for each activity is not a suitable framework for decision making, which is a forward-thinking challenge. On the surface, it may seem that we have argued against our own position in support of activities analysis, so we need to clarify some issues.

A direct causal effect exists between activities and financials. An activities-based framework captures this relationship without the intermediation of traditional accounting, which is designed to support organizational structure. Based on the premise that altering the activities composition is the only leverage a manager has in response to a problem or an opportunity, we must design the activities-based framework with a future-looking perspective.

We recommend a disassociation between managerial decision making and the daily accounting function. Accounting is the result of the actions taken within the confines of constraints—constraints that are either controlled or uncontrolled. It is the task of capturing what happened and determining how to understand it. Information extrapolated from accounting reports is valid only when the constraints and the activities composition *do not change*, as we discussed earlier.

The role of managerial decision making is to create an environment that can navigate around the uncontrolled constraints. You may not be able to control high labor rates or health-care costs in the short term, but you can nevertheless do things to improve the performance of the system. Examples include building flexibility, implementing standardization, and creating procedures that yield zero defects. Whether you are dealing with a manufacturing process or a business service process, the concept is identical. In a future-looking perspective, where the activities have not yet occurred, we propose constructing surrogates that represent the potential activities.

THE PARAMETRIC ACTIVITIES-BASED FRAMEWORK

The pABF captures the integrated structure and dynamic characteristics of business processes. It is the only framework that ensures that a problem is being solved within your constraints.

Functional Knowledge Captures the Essence of Business Execution

Figure 4-6 shows the pABF and highlights some of the factors that influence it. The boxes to the left of the triangle represent the parameters used to describe the current state of the system and drive performance. Market factors include demand and product requirements. The strategy defines the organization and establishes boundaries for its products and services. Businesses are always executing the processes that produce and deliver their products and services. These three factors are then translated into the pABF context.

The pABF integrates three interrelated business execution perspectives: process, resources, and finance. These perspectives capture the functional knowledge possessed by people and that resides in enterprise systems. Collectively, this is the domain knowledge of how the business actually works. Most importantly, it is a functional view of the business, replete with important contextual information about operations. The pABF triangle represents a single snapshot in time, and it can be extended into the future by changing the inputs, and thereby the outputs, to create an operational roadmap.

Figure 4-6. The Parametric Activities-Based Framework

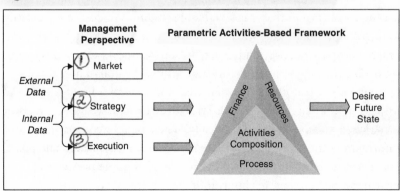

The pABF focuses on functional knowledge because it provides the most fundamental understanding of the way the business works, it is not dependent on the data, and it provides a dynamic parametric framework. The parametric emphasis means that you can change the parameters at will—and the parameters are the link to management control. Stated differently, functional knowledge drives the business execution parameters.

The three boxes to the left of the triangle in Figure 4-6 highlight the sources of the data (both from people and from enterprise systems) that are converted into the pABF context. Market (customer), Strategic (product), and Execution (operational) are simply different management perspectives on business execution. For example, the market may be getting soft or may be improving, so the demand data must be updated accordingly. Product requirements may also change. The strategy is the company's definition of value and where it lays claim to certain core competencies to deliver upon the value proposition. Strategically, a company may alter its objectives, which are translated into the framework. In executing the business, key data may include, for instance, changes in the task flow, such as machine or workstation routings, a new cycle time, or a new inventory policy.

The factors just mentioned are all dynamic factors and can interact with one another in complex ways. If the functional knowledge elements seem obvious, that's because they are intuitive, but their application is difficult. That is why we see so many workarounds in practice today.

Dimensions Are Not Predefined

From a systems theory perspective, we are simply stating that business execution exists and that it is a definable system. We do not necessarily know what it looks like—we do not know its dimensionality—but from practical experience we can identify its key perspectives. This is where we bridge the gap between theory and reality. We don't know if the system actually looks like a pyramid (see, for example, Figure 4-4). We arrived at the three-perspective structure through years of practical experience and refinement. Typically, when people convert data into information, they assume that there is only one perspective. The pABF converts the data into information by way of multiple perspectives and provides a rich context for interpreting the information.

Each perspective, in turn, can have multiple dimensions. The number of dimensions to the business opportunity or challenge depends on the problem. The pABF is not a cookie-cutter approach. The dimensionality depends on what you define as a parameter. You can actually look at the same challenge from multiple perspectives and dimensions. With manufacturing resource planning (MRP) and enterprise resource planning (ERP) systems, in contrast, the dimensions are predefined. With the pABF, you define the system by selecting what is and what is not a parameter. This, in turn, creates a catalog of the functional knowledge.

It is impractical to attempt to learn in advance every possible way in which you might use functional knowledge in your decision making. However, you can learn the fundamentals as reflected in the ProFIT-MAP methodology, which can then be applied to any problem that is posed to you. Capturing the functional knowledge, for example, determines how you choose to look at throughput, but not necessarily the financials. Of course, pABF enables you to connect the financials to the throughput if the financial implications of the decisions are also important to the organization.

The systematic approach of the pABF allows you to express the model in software. Furthermore, you can take the complex operational environment and capture that in software to the extent that analytical models can be automatically created. This eliminates the problem of requiring expertise to create individual mathematical models. You do not need to predefine the dimensions, and the models can be self-constructing—both of which are dramatic improvements over the way things are currently done. That is, the pABF approach facilitates a self-adapting analytical system. In Chapter 8, we show you the requirements for such software.

Activities at the Core

In order to achieve major business goals such as profit growth, process improvement, process standardization, overall productivity enhancement, and the like, management needs to understand the cost, time, and quality of the activities performed by employees and machines throughout the organization. Productivity is a measure of the performance of activities. It can be improved only when managers have the correct information about the financial impact (fixed assets and variable resources) of creating and delivering value to customers. Waste can be eliminated only if wasteful activities can be identified using the correct perspective and either eliminated or replaced by better alternatives. Understanding the role of each activity and the analysis of those activities is at the core of management's functional knowledge.

Successful execution is the result of performing the value-adding activities in synchrony with the objectives. Synchronizing each activity with the top-level objectives is the crux of improving productivity and finances. Activities are the dynamic events that bind a process together. In other words, realigning the activities composition—quality, quantity, and sequence—is the only control that management has over any process. This is the only control that managers have over the destiny of their business. Every decision that managers make somehow affects, either directly or indirectly, the activities performed by the organization—people and machines equally—irrespective of their focus toward any particular discipline, such as customer relations, operational issues, or product concerns. Any decision-making framework, therefore, has to be built on an activities basis.

The pABF approach defines the core of an object as being made up of activities. We may not know how many dimensions are required to define the object, as the number of dimensions will vary depending on the business problem. You can think of the process, resource, and finance perspectives as the coordinate systems that give us different views of the core.

The activities composition of the process is critical because it contains all of the different states of the operations (stations). Operations describe the physical context in which the process activities occur. They are composed of stations (people and/or machines) that perform their work sequentially. Product changes, for instance, have implications for line operations, including the mix of resources (people and machines) required to create the product. Changing one product may also have implications across the operations portfolio, as it may affect other upstream or downstream activities, or it might affect other products that are currently produced in the same facility. Inventory policy changes, for example, can have dramatic throughput and financial ramifications for line behavior. Let's say you have gone to a just-in-time (JIT) inventory strategy to increase efficiency and decrease waste by receiving goods only as they are needed in the production process. The promise of JIT is that it will reduce inventory costs. However, delays in receiving goods can lead to "starvation" problems at manufacturing stations if goods are not received within their critical input window. The station(s) has to stop while it waits for the goods, incurring significant productivity and cost penalties. On the other end of the spectrum, excessive inventory can lead to station "blockage," where a station shuts down because it runs out of physical room to store its completed output. It cannot resume processing until either the next station catches up on its processing or alternative inventory space is secured.

From a business perspective, any decision that affects the states of the operations is in effect changing the business. If the measurement and reconstruction system has sufficient sensitivity, it will see the impact of such decisions—and this sensitivity is perspective bound. Otherwise, you will not have sufficient visibility of the impact of management decisions on operations.

The activities composition is created as a result of the parameter inputs into the functional knowledge about the system. Because knowledge is an amorphous concept, we have to break it down into a context in order to analyze it. The activities are the building blocks of the system. From the activities, we can derive an understanding of the functioning of the business.

Parameters and Metadata

Parameters are different from other operational variables. Parameters are the control variables that can be manipulated by management action. If a variable can't be manipulated, then it is a state variable that describes the condition of the system. State variables can change as a result of management actions taken. State variables can also change as a result of system inertia, where the process changes in the absence of any management action. For example, machines can wear over time, resulting in a greater frequency and duration of breakdowns.

Managers cannot control the business directly. In practice, they try to control the business by changing its parameters. The new parameters change the activities composition of the business, thereby driving business performance. That is why the activities composition is so important. The activities performed by the organization are affected by the parameters that control the business. How you perceive and control temperature in a room illustrates this point.

Your sensitivity to room temperature is influenced by many factors, including the temperature, the humidity, your attire, reflected heat (e.g., through a window), and possibly the wall color and ambient light. The temperature and humidity are state variables and have inertia of their own. For example, the air might be mixing with warmer or cooler sources from the ventilation system or from heat reflection through the windows. The temperature is not uniform and stable throughout the room. The control variables are the settings for the thermostat, possibly a humidifier or dehumidifier, and the window blinds. These control variables affect the amount of air added to and removed from the room, the humidity, and the outside heat sources. As a manager, you can't directly control the temperature of the room, but you can control the parameters that change the factors that drive the perceived temperature. You can create a mental model of the actions that will control the temperature in the room, and take the "management" actions of turning on and off the hot or cold air, and so on, as necessary. Such mental models don't scale very well, however, if you need to control the temperature in an entire building. Managing a multidimensional, interactive, and dynamic system solely by way of mental models is not easy (nor desirable). This challenge is further exacerbated by the fact that the decisions have significant cost implications.

Parametric costing has been around for a long time. It dates back to planning for aircraft manufacturing in World War II. The war dramatically increased aircraft demand, and planners needed a better technique for predicting costs. The pABF is an extension of this costing approach to include integrated activities-based process knowledge and resource information.

The pABF builds on the principles of activities-based costing by incorporating "metadata," or attributes of the process, products, resources, and policies. These are the state variables. Management decisions are made based on their values. For instance, metadata can include the processing time for a particular machine. A scheduling engine might use the "shortest processing time" to determine product throughput. The scheduler can compare the capabilities of several possible machines to determine what machine(s) to use. A manager can use the pABF to quantify several possible decision options: use the current slower machines, supplement the machines with extra labor to increase output, or invest in a new piece of capital equipment. Each decision option has significant throughput, quality, and cost implications that cannot be assessed by looking at the decision from only one perspective. A new machine, for instance, might cost so much that the capital outlay cannot be recovered over the expected life cycle of the machine. The cost per piece might still be significantly lower even when constrained, for instance, with high labor rates.

As this example illustrates, the pABF moves away from a cost allocation to a distribution-based approach. The costs are distributed over the metadata across the activities composition. The metadata provide a rich collection of properties and attributes to describe the activities, and the level of detail is controlled by the depth of the required analysis (i.e., the nature of the business problem).

The parametric framework extends activities-based costing, which is an accounting tool for reporting on what has already occurred, into an integrated, future-looking efficiency, resources, and financial instrument. It is a unifying formulation that spans operational, tactical, and strategic decision making. Both the specific management decision level and the type of business problem define how to apply the framework, the required information, the level of detail, and the "what-if?" strategy.

The crux of the parametric framework lies in its ability to generate the activities composition from the process of producing the product or the service. The dynamic process analysis, when subjected to the demand and the processing constraints, generates the activities composition. The activities composition is the parametric basis for evaluating the resource requirements and the financials (see Figure 4-6).

One of the advantages of a parametric approach is that you do not need an ERP or MRP team to deploy the pABF. For most organizations, the data already reside in enterprise systems. It is simply a matter of identifying the requisite data for analysis. In fact, the parametric approach does not predefine the data or their level of detail. However, it does provide critical insight into needed refinements. For example, pABF enables the rapid deployment of a cost model based on readily available data. A sensitivity analysis of this initial model will yield a prioritized list of needed refinements. Over time, the refinements can be implemented, if necessary, by creating the infrastructure to gather the identified metadata. Often, the additional detail already exists, and it is simply a matter of gathering more refined data from the enterprise systems.

From Information Overload to Insight

With the proliferation of enterprise systems, companies are drowning in data and information. Often, the extra information is confusing and complicates decision making. Managers need more context; they need to see the trees in the context of the forest. They need to strike a balance between "systematic" thinking and their expertise and intuition. The pABF gets at the essence of the business execution problem. It takes a complex challenge and reduces it to its simplest elements (perspectives) for decision making. We may be accustomed to reacting to information from only one perspective, yet other dimensions may also contain important information. The pABF presents the information in an integrated context, with sufficient sensitivity that the effects of management actions can be observed holistically within and across perspectives. It provides critical insight into the behavior of the system so that you can link specific management actions to specific outcomes prior to implementation.

Management insight is derived by viewing the inner workings of the process. It gives you enough visibility to identify the right problem and use your expertise to solve it. In a management twist, let's say that you are managing someone else's operational process. This is more common than you might think. If your company has outsourced any portion of its business to an external vendor, then you are managing the portion of that vendor's operational processes that serve your company. Keep the core and outsource the rest—that seems to be the operational mantra of late, and it touches upon everything from taking over the corporate information technology (IT) function to human resources or customer service, or even manufacturing.

Managing an IT service-level agreement (SLA) is a prime example of this phenomenon. An IT vendor meets all the conditions painstakingly negotiated in its SLA. Yet employee satisfaction ratings for the vendor are falling through the floor. Employees are very dissatisfied with the vendor's service. What is the source of the disconnection between the vendor and the perception of its services? Closer inspection of a representative operational process, managing computer servers in a central server farm, reveals that service requests are being successfully processed within three days, as required by the SLA. However, the vendor has staffed the central facility with junior employees who are lacking in expertise. Thus, service requests are requiring extensive hand-holding on the part of the customer's employees, sometimes taking 10 to 15 separate calls and e-mails to complete the transaction. This wastes the employees' time, raises the costs of resolution for both parties, and lowers customer satisfaction.

This is not unlike the temperature and humidity example described earlier. The vendor meets the "temperature" requirements, but the humidity factor (or in this case the customer involvement factor) was never included in the SLA. It may be 100 degrees outside, but if you live in Arizona, it is a dry heat and therefore more tolerable. The same temperature may be a lot less comfortable if you visit Florida, where the humidity is much higher. The point is that the SLA is missing at least one important dimension for synchronizing vendor performance with employee satisfaction.

The larger message is that we tend to measure complex phenomena in a few dimensions that are not able to adequately reconstruct the entire system. A more practical approach is needed to measure the right variables in order to reconstruct the whole system, and pABF does this by using the three perspectives and the dimensions that underlie each. From a management standpoint, you need to be cognizant of what perspective or perspectives you are applying to the problem, and to ask yourself if they are giving you enough information to determine what you are indeed looking at. The pABF does this, and it overcomes the limitations of current approaches by eliminating the need for patches or workarounds. The pABF is a better framework because it

- Is designed based on systems theory specifically for dynamic, interconnected systems.
- Is based on a representation of the activities required to deliver products and services instead of some concocted allocation scheme that is outdated as soon as it is implemented.
- Does not require a new infrastructure, such as an ABC system.
- Is driven by functional knowledge—the knowledge and experience of the people who execute the business.
- Has three integrated perspectives that lead to better reconstruction and provide a unified and common framework for strategic, tactical, and operational decision making.
- Distributes costs across the activities composition of the process.
- Is capable of sensitivity analysis that can be used to prioritize data requirements and data quality issues.

- Is nonintrusive. Operations are not affected by the modeling until management actions (if any) are undertaken to implement the desired changes.

In the end, pABF is an estimation and reconstruction framework. A framework without a methodology or a process for applying it leaves a big gap in implementation. ProFIT-MAP is the methodology for applying pABF to business execution, and it is our focus for the rest of the book. ProFIT-MAP is the management decision-making tool that capitalizes on the power and agility of the pABF infrastructure.

REFERENCES

1   See, for example, John L. Casti, *Nonlinear System Theory* (New York: Academic Press, 1985).
2   Larry Bossidy and Ram Charan, *Execution: The Discipline of Getting Things Done* (New York: Crown Publishing Group, 2002), pp. 226–33.
3   Malcolm Gladwell, *Blink: The Power of Thinking without Thinking* (New York: Little, Brown, 2005), p. 23.
4   Casti, *Nonlinear System Theory*, p. 1.
5   Gladwell, *Blink*, pp. 20–33.
6   Ibid., pp. 11–13.
7   Timothy D. Wilson, quoted in Ibid., p. 12.
8   Bossidy and Charan, *Execution*, p. 19.
9   Richard Bellman and Rutherford Aris quotes are from Omer S. Benli, "Dynamic Programming," *Industrial Engineering Applications and Practice: Users Encyclopedia*, International Journal of Industrial Engineering, 1999, http://benli.bcc.bilkent.edu.tr/~omer/research/dynprog.html. See also Rutherford Aris, *Discrete Dynamic Programming: An Introduction to the Optimization of Staged Processes* (New York: Blaisdell, 1964); Richard Bellman, *Eye of the Hurricane: An Autobiography* (Singapore: World Scientific, 1984).
10   See, for example, Gary Cokins, *Activity-based Cost Management: An Executive's Guide* (New York: Wiley, 2001).
11   Robert S. Kaplan and Steven R. Anderson, "Time-Driven Activity-Based Costing," *Harvard Business Review*, 82(11), 2004, pp. 131–38.

Win Before Taking Action with a Structured Methodology

A victorious army first wins and then seeks battle; a defeated army first battles and then seeks victory.

—Sun Tzu, *The Art of War*

MOST APPROACHES to operational improvement are guidelines that are based on sound principles, but do not have specific structured methodologies for implementation. As a consequence, well-intended managers stumble with execution. "Managers . . . routinely face a bewildering set of decisions about a host of strategic and operating problems, including those dealing with execution. They need guidelines, a 'roadmap' to steer them logically to execution success."[1] Many frameworks can help identify cost and profit sources to some degree or other. They typically tell you where you are today and describe operational targets. In order to explain various approaches to management, consultants often present these guidelines in the form of generic rules of thumb. Unfortunately, rules of thumb lack structured approaches for implementation and often end up competing with one another, undercutting their potential benefits. Moreover, rules of thumb do not scale well in a complex operational environment.

In the absence of a structured methodology, the performance derived from using guidelines is often below expectations. Since rules of thumb are simplistic and easy to misapply, there is a great need for a structured methodology and specific tools. You win before taking action by having a well-designed and forward-looking methodology that is properly connected to the way your business operates. The methodology must create a direct link between parameters that managers can control and the business results. The underlying parametric framework discussed in the previous chapter enables the ProFIT-MAP methodology to connect the parameters to the business objectives, thereby complementing and enhancing your preferred approach for crafting and implementing strategy.

YOU CAN'T WIN WITH RULES OF THUMB

All operational philosophies and improvement methods (lean, Six Sigma, continuous improvement, and so on) have their merits. That's the good news. The bad news for practitioners is that these methods don't provide a uniform and complete methodology for their implementation. The approach depends a great deal on the user and how he or she chooses to apply the method to the situation at hand. As a consequence, organizations struggle with misguidance and isolated implementations. The guidelines are often boiled down to rules of thumb to suggest what you might do if you were faced with a given situation. These rules of thumb emanate from experience and intuition about causes and effects in isolated, or idealized, situations. Stated differently, even though we may ask the "right" questions as managers, we frequently attempt to answer them with an inappropriate tool for the task.

Rules of thumb are the quintessence of correlative reasoning. They are effective so long as they are applied within the confines of previous experience, or in situations that do not deviate from that experience in any substantial manner. But they often have little or no effect in cases where they are applicable, or have unintended effects as they begin to compete with one another and break down in complex and different situations. Table 5-1 lists some common manufacturing rules of thumb and their possible desired effects. Although the terminology may differ somewhat for business services, the concepts are similar.

Rules of thumb carry a certain level of comfort, for they are easy to understand. Unfortunately, this comfort comes with a huge risk. If your

Table 5-1. Sample Rules of Thumb and Possible Outcomes

Rule of Thumb	Possible Desired Effect
Reduce lead times	Improve customer service
Lower batch sizes	Improve customer service; make products more frequently; reduce inventory
Move bottlenecks to front (balanced flow)	Reduce inventory and defects
Theory of constraints	Improve efficiency
Reduce work-in-process inventory	Improve efficiency of the flow and reduce defects; reduce cost of manufacturing
Reduce inventory	Improve balance sheet
Increase flexibility (agility)	Be able to use the same equipment to make multiple products; efficiency; reduce capital investment
Reduce changeover time and cost	Efficiency

goal is to make better operational decisions, then you need to understand the potential limitations of this approach and decide on the best course of action. Figure 5-1 shows two hypothetical rules of thumb and their relationship over time. At the start of the process, Rule 1 is very effective, while Rule 2 is not of much value, as illustrated at Time 1. In the ad hoc approach to applying rules of thumb, we say to ourselves that "we are reaping the benefits of Rule 1, so let's crank up Rule 2 so that we can start to benefit from it as well, resulting in even greater benefits." This is linear thinking—that doing one thing at a time in a sequential manner will bring about continuous improvement. Not recognizing the interrelationships between the two rules, since they were created in isolation from each other, we start to implement Rule 2, with the result that we experience a decline in benefits instead of the expected rise. The dominance of Rule 1 is being challenged by the competing Rule 2. As we move further in time, the rule dominance becomes equal and then reverses as it passes the crossover point. Eventually, Rule 1 drops out of favor and Rule 2 becomes the dominant one. Later in this chapter, we provide a real-world example of this phenomenon in the context of lean operations.

Figure 5-1. Rules of Thumb Compete with Each Other

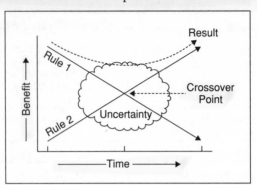

Rules of Thumb Are Risky

A rules-of-thumb culture typically flourishes in functionally segregated organizations. While a functional view of an organization is helpful for understanding an organization chart, it does not offer much insight into the way in which processes are carried out. Processes have a workflow reflecting the activities of the work performed, who performs them, their relative order, and so on. They are the pathways through which organizational work is done. The gap in process and workflow information represented in a "functional" view of a company has been described as the "white space" seen on an organization chart. Bridging the white space is the impetus behind much of the performance improvement and reengineering literature.[2]

The origin of many rules of thumb is an attempt by one functional group to bridge the white space by describing the role of another group in simplistic terms without an understanding of that group's functioning. For example, supply-chain planners typically view product lead times as a fixed quantity, irrespective of the product mix and demand. Such simplifications are perpetuated because managers either don't understand the complexities of scheduling production or don't have the tools to incorporate such complex information into their analyses.

Is there a rule of thumb to predict how rules of thumb will interact with one another? That is, can you optimize the simultaneous use of multiple rules? Theoretically, the answer is yes. The practical problem, however, is that one would need to know all the rules that exist and how they scale together in order to define an optimal relationship. Unfortunately, in a complex and dynamic operational environment, you are not likely to be able to identify all the rules and their scalability characteristics. The only way to overcome such a situation is by adopting a multifaceted framework, such as the Parametric Activities-Based Framework (pABF), in which each action can be connected to the business objectives and implemented with a systematic methodology.

Why Improvement Philosophies Fail

All improvement approaches carry with them certain biases and presuppose the possible source of problems. When the North American auto industry faced competition from Japan, it rushed to adopt the waste-reducing practices of Toyota Motors, known as the Toyota Production System (TPS). The lean manufacturing movement arose as many of the TPS concepts were adapted to North America. These same practices were extended to lean operations (i.e., service processes).

While lean initiatives have brought about many high-profile successes, the North American auto industry is still not competitive. Was going lean the most pressing issue facing the industry? Probably not. Our intent is not to state that implementing lean is a bad thing, but simply to question whether businesses are solving the correct problem, and whether they are solving the right problem correctly. For many companies, becoming lean instead of being cost competitive has become the mission. The industry assumed, as the Irish proverb states, that "What's good for the goose is good for the gander." That is, the industry created a rule of thumb that lean principles were the solution to its problems, and therefore lean was implemented with abandon. Moreover, lean was typically implemented as a big collection of well-intended rules of thumb, which, as we illustrate later, can get you into a lot of trouble.

Let's translate this hypothetical discussion into concrete terms. One of the first steps in making a process lean is to create a flow of content (material and/or information) such that little or no content is stored between operations or tasks. In manufacturing settings, the content between operations is called work in process (WIP), and in services it is often referred to as backlog. "Reducing in-between content" and "creating continuous flow lines" are two rules of thumb, among many, that are essential elements of lean principles. The "in-between" content is called "waste" and thus is a target for reduction or total elimination. The logic goes that reducing WIP reduces inventories and postpones the value being added by an operation until it is absolutely necessary, hence freeing up cash flow. Improved cash flow reduces the need for working capital (favorable for the balance sheet), requiring less borrowing, and thereby reducing the cost of borrowed capital (favorable for the income statement).

These are good rules to live by, but they are among the most misapplied. How can you really know if reducing WIP (and by how much) will produce the desired efficiency and cost results? For example, in their zeal to convert a batch operations line, with lots of costly WIP, into a flow line with no or minimal WIP, manufacturers often end up with a financial disaster. In some instances, the positive aspects of reducing WIP are negated by increased costs for expedited shipping and losses to the process dynamics. In other instances, becoming too lean can harm the collective throughput of the process, reducing the ability to meet customer demand. The fault is not with the individual guidelines, but with the lack of a structured methodology with appropriate tools to analyze the applicability of the guidelines for a particular company and how they behave collectively in the specific situation at hand.

Unintended process and/or financial consequences of these rules have two primary causes: (1) proper consideration is not given to work-stoppage and breakdown dynamics of the workstations involved, and (2) labor and asset requirements are considered variable costs in the analysis. You will see the impact of such dynamics in the case studies presented in Chapter 10. One case study shows how a financially viable manufacturing line becomes unprofitable when the two guidelines are not properly applied. A second case study shows how an award-winning lean manufacturing line could not satisfy customer demand because maintaining lean inertia became the end game, causing management to lose sight of the bigger picture. In our opinion, relying solely on rules of thumb and simple guidelines is dangerous and misguided.

CONNECTING PARAMETERS TO OBJECTIVES WITH PROFIT-MAP

The business world is dynamic, and things constantly change; thus, the framework used for analysis must reveal the effects of each change on the business objectives. The framework has to be comprehensive enough to relate individual actions to the overall objectives. Lacking such direct connection and working with a surrogate intermediary such as rules of thumb results in a rules-of-thumb quagmire. The emphasis moves away from solving the real problem to solving a fictional one.

As discussed in the previous chapter, the pABF recognizes that every operational process is dynamic. At the crux of a business, according to pABF, lies the activities composition, which is an organized collection of activities performed by people and machines. The activities composition is another way to look at the operations of any business. Any change in parameters, whether for internal or external reasons, causes a response in the business operations *via* the activities composition. In order to understand the state of the business, you must understand its constantly changing activities composition and the ramifications of the activities composition for the business objectives.

The activities composition changes as a dynamic response to changes in the parameters on an ongoing basis. To understand the state of the business and its evolution, one must therefore have insight into the activities composition at meaningful instances over time. The pABF provides a causal relationship between the activities composition shaped by the process parameters and the things that drive business execution. Figure 5-2 shows this relationship, which is the underlying structure of the ProFIT-MAP methodology. The execution drivers are connected to the execution objectives by way of a business execution profile. The execution objectives come from strategy and are the business goals that the organization wants to achieve. Execution drivers are the process, resources, and finance perspectives of the business that must be shaped to meet the needs of the execution objectives. Managers use the profile to connect the strategy to their environment and actions. This is how ProFIT-MAP fosters the alignment of strategy and execution.

When one or more parameters undergo change as a result of either internal or external considerations, their impact is first observed at the execution drivers. Parameters are the precise actions or controls that cause the change. The drivers are the views into the activities composition through particular perspectives, thereby defining the state of the business. Processes consume resources and have financial implications at the execution drivers' level. The secret to business execution, therefore, is to successfully construct the precise activities composition that produces the desired results for the execution objectives.

Figure 5-2. Connecting Parameters to Objectives with ProFIT-MAP

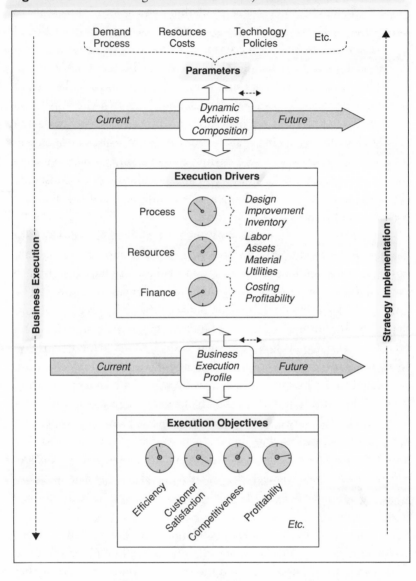

3 KEY
DRIVERS*   The significance of each driver depends on the execution objective.
Any number of drivers is possible, but we believe that the three we
present—process, resources, and financials—are the most critical ones.
The ProFIT-MAP methodology is flexible enough to incorporate
whatever additional drivers you choose to include. This flexibility is of

particular importance in an "experience economy," where the customer doesn't purchase the collection of activities that go into a product or service, but rather buys the total experience surrounding that product or service.[3]

While financial profitability is the ultimate measure of corporate performance, other execution objectives can also be used as critical measures (e.g., customer satisfaction, efficiency). For instance, call centers are cost centers and must strike a balance between customer satisfaction and effectiveness in order to provide the right mix of service at the best cost. This concept may seem contrary to other popular process improvement philosophies. For example, total quality management programs and lean initiatives focus on eliminating waste, which can take the form of any number of inefficiencies (non-value-adding activities or content). However, sometimes a little "waste" can go a long way toward building customer satisfaction. Few people like to be put on hold, for instance, when calling customer support. If you find yourself on hold with Southwest Airlines, however, you just might find yourself chuckling as you listen to the company's humorous prerecorded messages. One could argue that taking the time to create these messages is a "waste" of time, yet for Southwest they contribute positively to the total customer experience that is Southwest Airlines. In a value-driven environment, one size does not fit all, and leading companies understand that it is the value that the customer wants, not just the price.

As shown at the top of Figure 5-2, the activities composition of a process is influenced by a number of interrelated parameters, including demand, process, resources, costs, technology, policies, and so on. The manager can set the dynamic activities composition "slider" anywhere along a continuum from "now," referring to real time, to as far out into the future as the manager wishes to analyze the process and cost dynamics of interest. Each change in one or more parameters creates a new activities composition, thereby resulting in a new view of the drivers. The drivers then are collected and combined through the business execution profile to construct the response in relation to the execution objectives. The result shows whether the proposed change in the parameters has any significant effect. If yes, then by how much and in which direction? It is entirely possible to obtain an unfavorable response from what seemed a good thing to do because of the complex interactions among the various factors in the drivers. ProFIT-MAP is not a cookie-cutter approach and does not have a presumptive bias—other than that the process exists, as described in the previous chapter. The business problem, in ProFIT-MAP, defines the precise linkage and synchronization between parameters, drivers, and objectives.

The ProFIT-MAP methodology is versatile enough to be used both from the bottom up and from the top down in organizations. It can help you understand the impact of parametric changes on the business objectives as you formulate and execute strategy. In the reverse direction, going from bottom to top, you can find out which parameter(s) require how much of a change to achieve the desired execution objectives. If it is not possible to attain the execution objectives, then the business drivers help you to understand the reasons for this and adjust your strategy or tactics accordingly. ProFIT-MAP allows you to explore potential solutions by altering parameters at will to do "what-if?" assessments. This bidirectional versatility makes ProFIT-MAP a common tool that is applicable for shop-floor through top-floor use. It provides a holistic view of the business independent of the organizational structure.

PROFIT-MAP IS AN INTEGRATIVE TOOL

ProFIT-MAP provides the structure for understanding business execution from multiple perspectives. It is a fundamental tool to assist in decision making. In this section, we set the stage for ProFIT-MAP by describing the conditions that it must meet in order to overcome the above-mentioned management challenges.

An implementation methodology must

- Be capable of managing *thought* projects (i.e., strategic analyses) as well as design or improvement projects that are *implemented* on the shop floor (i.e., business execution).
- Provide a common language for communication among strategic, tactical, and operational management, as well as across the functional silos in an organization.
- Facilitate the understanding of business execution challenges from interrelated perspectives: process, resources, finance, and any other, if present.
- Be conducive to creating a forward-looking operational roadmap.

- Not burden the organization with a new data collection initiative. It should leverage the vast amount of data that already resides in enterprise systems.
- Not affect operations until an implementation decision (if any) is made, enabling the impact of decisions to be quantified prior to carrying out those decisions.

Any approach must be able to create a roadmap for executing the strategy, which in turn must synchronize with tactical and operational approaches using the same methodology. The objectives at each management layer must translate into concrete, measurable actions, which are manifested in the form of a business execution project. In its simplest form, a project starts with an intention to modify or improve an existing process or to create a new one, with an eye toward making the process as effective and profitable as possible. Managers make the judgment calls about which processes to improve and how to measure success. A business execution project can point out which of the processes may have the greatest payoff if redesigned or replaced.

Once defined, the methodology must enable business execution projects to be conducted prior to their actual implementation. Doing so enables managers to see the effects of their actions prior to taking any action, which is an important factor in avoiding costly experimentation with changes that may or may not have the desired effect. The basic premise is to let managers see the future before making critical operational decisions.

Synchronizing Thought and Implementation Projects

Business execution *thought* and *implementation* projects span the continuum of strategic, tactical, and operational decision making. *Thought* projects represent strategic analysis and planning. For example, should you invest or divest to reach specific manufacturing objectives? What is the impact of price changes in your value chain on profitability? What is the impact of changing your product mix on manufacturing costs? These are all questions that *thought* projects can tackle. As improvement initiatives move toward the tactical and operational issues, managers can employ *implementation* projects to plan and optimize plant-, line-, and/or station-level improvements. These represent tangible changes on the operations floor.

To address the challenge of vertical synchronization, a methodology must support both types of projects. That is, the approach must apply the same common methods from the executive suite to the front lines, reflecting the interdependence between strategy making and execution. Execution is not something that organizations should "worry about later"; it should be incorporated into the strategy-making process as early as appropriate.

Figure 5-3 highlights both the conceptual distinction and the overlap between *thought* and *implementation* projects. Your particular role in an organization frames the types of issues and challenges you are likely to face as a manager. It also frames the types of projects you are likely to conduct.

An operations manager, for example, might wish to optimize a process line for quality and throughput, while a strategic manager might need to make decisions about moving or consolidating manufacturing capabilities within a specific plant or across a portfolio of plants. The operations manager may possibly be responding to an actual problem somewhere on a line (implementation project), whereas a corporate or business-unit manager might be interested in rationalizing production capabilities among several plants (thought project). In this instance, using activities data from the actual facilities, the corporate manager can explore multiple scenarios, all of which are built upon the data from existing plant processes. Decisions are then made about the optimal locations and plant-specific configurations for the new production logic. Such decisions may then lead to implementation projects such as optimizing throughput and minimizing waste in the new lines.

Figure 5-3. Business Execution Projects

Iteration and Alignment

The organizational journey of business execution is iterative by nature, both within the strategic, tactical, and operational levels and in the handoffs between the levels. Figure 5-4 illustrates the typical life cycle of thought and implementation projects. As with other strategic initiatives and process improvement methods, understanding the current situation is a crucial first step. A business execution project pays particular attention to the process, resources, and financial characteristics of the process under the microscope. Next, an implementation methodology must enable the manager to iterate through a range of possible future endpoints to identify the best decision options along the pathway to the desired future state. The new or improved process changes are then implemented, measured, and managed. If continuous improvement is a corporate priority, managers must be able to cycle back to the start in the form of a feedback loop and navigate through the process challenge anew.

We distinguish between the need for two types of iteration. First, managers iterate from "here" to "there" to explore the decision alternatives and their ramifications before taking action. Second, once the decisions have been implemented, managers can iterate through decision options to continue to validate and adjust performance as the organization senses and responds to opportunities and challenges.

Figure 5-5 highlights both forms of iteration and shows how they also present organizational alignment opportunities if performed using the same methodology. This enables apples-to-apples comparison and planning. Thought projects cascade down the organization to drive implementation projects. That is, strategy drives execution. Implementation projects can spawn or affect other implementation projects, and also cascade strategic issues back up to the executive suite. In the latter case, for example, an R&D breakthrough might present new business opportunities for senior management to ponder and quantify.

Managers typically conduct projects one at a time, and organizations can have many concurrent projects under way at once. The connections or handoffs among all such projects provide a rich ground for fostering organizational alignment. These handoffs occur because most operational processes are cross-functional and interdependent with upstream and/or downstream processes. Organizations are living, dynamic systems with numerous interconnections. Every change must be synchronized

Figure 5-4. Iterating to the Future

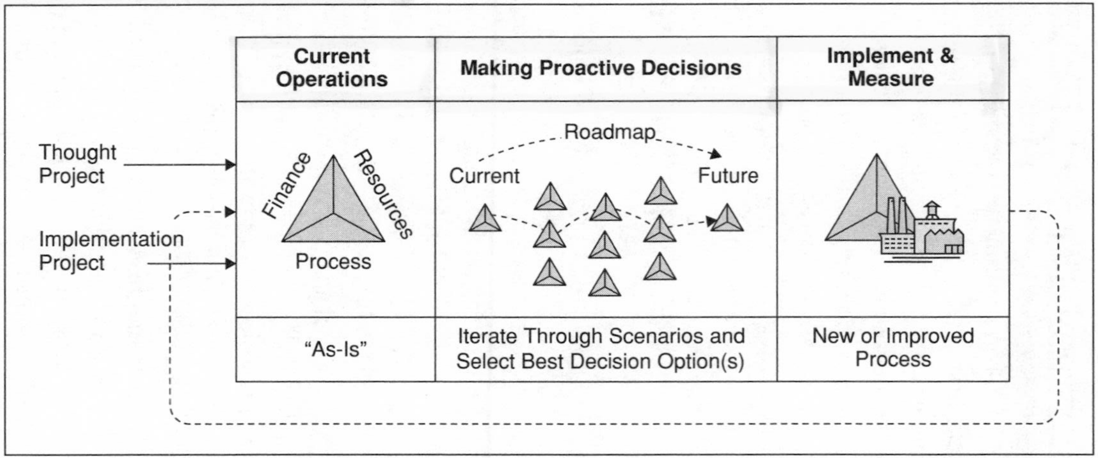

Figure 5-5. Alignment Opportunities

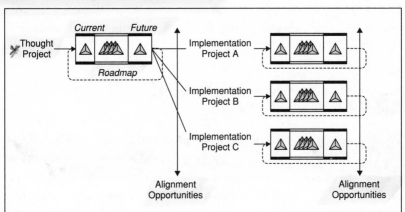

with other linked processes and the corporate strategy—and must be facilitated by the implementation methodology.

Thought and implementation projects are interconnected. Managers must ensure that implementation projects are aligned with the strategy. As any particular strategy can spawn a multitude of implementation projects, each of these projects should be synchronized with all the others, so that the right hand knows what the left hand is doing, and they are both coordinated in action. A corporate initiative such as moving to flexible manufacturing may begin, for example, with a thought project (as shown in the left column in Figure 5-5) exploring the redesign of an existing facility, including equipment modernization. If implemented, the project may trigger one or more implementation projects (in the right column), ranging from real-time job scheduling, to labor planning, to buffer planning, and so on. Each physical project can be a predecessor or successor to another one. The final implementation would most likely be a combination of several of the implementation projects. It is, therefore, imperative to ensure that the final implementation results in overall benefits, and that the individual projects do not negate one another.

Thought projects are typically conducted to consider a range of strategic options, or even to use as input in helping to shape corporate strategy. From an alignment perspective, thought projects can help set or refine the anchor point from which implementation projects seek their relative position. In working on implementation projects, tactical and operational managers are thus presented with an opportunity to ensure that the desired future process state is prealigned with corporate strategy—assuming that the implementation methodology is capable of this.

The ProFIT-MAP Methodology in Action: A Manufacturing Example

We describe an example in depth to illustrate the broad applicability of ProFIT-MAP. The specific example is from the manufacturing industry, but the concepts are identical in the business services arena. Products delivered by manufacturing organizations are widgets, whereas those delivered by business services organizations are completed tasks. Both use similar processes and resources, although with different skill sets, and are identical in their orientation within a process.

Figure 5-6 presents a generic functional view of a manufacturing organization. It is not necessary for each manufacturer to have all the different groups we have identified as separate departments, but more or less these functions exist. Mid- and larger-size manufacturing companies

Figure 5-6. Sample Manufacturing Company Functional Organization

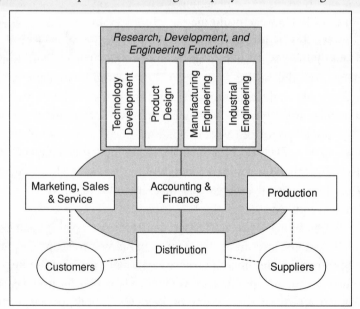

tend to view themselves as "engineering"-driven and sell "products" to their customers through a distribution channel. Our example represents this cultural bias; hence, we have chosen to skew this representation toward the research, development, and engineering functions by breaking them out into four distinct functions. Our motives will become clear as we proceed into the example.

Technology Development is a "pure" research function, where new materials, manufacturing techniques, and so on are investigated and developed. The Product Design group is what the name implies. Manufacturing Engineering focuses on converting the design to the manufacturing processes that create the product. Industrial Engineering concentrates on refining the manufacturing processes, with a concentration on continuous improvement. Depending on the particular company, some of these functions may be performed by the same groups, particularly as you move down the spectrum from large to smaller companies.

Framing Thought and Implementation Projects

Having described a functional view of the organization, let's get more specific about the business execution challenges. In this section, we explore the framing of a strategic improvement project and its tactical offshoot for illustrative purposes.

The process begins by "framing," or defining the objectives of the particular initiative. To *frame* a project is to establish its performance objectives and understand its place in the organizational context. Your CEO has just mandated that your division's profitability is to be improved by consolidating manufacturing that is currently performed by several plants. The operational context for this strategic project is that each plant is capable of producing the same products. The company may have accumulated multiple locations over time for a variety of reasons. Distribution from one site rather than another may historically have been optimal. There may have been better cost factors at a particular location (e.g., availability of raw materials or labor). Merger and acquisition activities may also have added a facility or two to the portfolio. At present, the distribution advantages are no longer there: your distribution strategy may have changed, there may be unfavorable material costs at one or more locations, and your cost structure is burdened with redundant capacity. This is a common scenario for a mature company in North America.

Let's say that the plant consolidation strategy work has been completed, and it resulted in a decision to move all manufacturing to plant B, freeing up plants A and C for retasking, mothballing, or divestment. Management in plant B then undertakes an initiative to consolidate the production in its plant. Can the existing lines make the products that were produced in the other facilities? What kinds of capital and labor investments might be needed? If the products being moved in are similar, Product Engineering may not need to be involved, but Accounting and Finance, Production, and Industrial Engineering will surely be integrally involved.

In order to expand the level of detail on this plant consolidation initiative, we first look at how the tactical plant-level decisions are framed. By this we mean the level of analysis and data that management explores in order to generate relevant information for making operational decisions. Manufacturing Engineering examines whether and how the products can be built, including designing the processes to build them. For example, what types of holes need to be drilled in a particular part? Is a lathe or milling machine needed, and so on? Marketing has already defined the expected demand, so Manufacturing Engineering can determine how many machines are necessary, given the cycle time to drill the hole, clear the waste, and finish the part. The potentially useful information ranges from routings, to labor and capital requirements, to basic costs spanning the entire bill of materials, and more, and these are the contributing parameters in each of the implementation projects in ProFIT-MAP.

Next, Industrial Engineering determines that it needs extra machines to do the drilling, cleaning, and finishing. Are such machines already available at this location, or can they be brought from other locations? Do we have to purchase new machines, and with what specifications? Each one of these questions is an implementation project in ProFIT-MAP, as seen in Figure 5-5. Working with Finance, Industrial Engineering determines the cost and continues to tackle implementation challenges such as successor and predecessor steps, which may include, for example, conveyers or lift trucks, as well as space requirements. Is an existing line adequate? Is a new facility required? Can it be built on an existing location, or is a Greenfield advised? These are additional contributing parameters to the implementation projects in ProFIT-MAP. After selection of the appropriate decision scenario that best meets the corporate strategy of consolidation and improvement in financials, the implementation is ready for actual deployment. Industrial Engineering delineates the process details and policies, and then works with Production to erect the line.

Merging the functional and workflow components into a coherent framework more accurately reflects actual operational processes. Every step of the way bridges one or more boundaries between the functional organizations. By threading these silos together within the integrated framework of ProFIT-MAP, an organization can build a management framework that works within its existing organizational structure.

Let's return to the original strategic plant consolidation challenge that resulted in the decision to settle upon Plant B. In practice, a strategic project is not a "real" project per se. However, this is where it gets real: to conduct a strategic project, one must first divide it up into multiple tactical initiatives. With ProFIT-MAP, instead of creating artificial aggregated data from the real data, you use your real data and manufacturing processes as inputs for the tactical decisions. Next, you analyze each component individually, correlate the components, and cascade them to develop an implementation roadmap. The tactical decisions may also lead to operational decisions, where operational managers run with the strategy, looking for additional ways to improve operations on a specific line(s) within the facility. In order to build a realistic view of the organization that treats the functions as contiguous extensions of one another, one needs the dynamic and activities-based parametric framework for analyzing and planning processes, resources, and finance that is implemented with the ProFIT-MAP methodology.

YOU DON'T HAVE TO REINVENT
YOUR OPERATIONAL PROCESSES

The example just given shows that you do not have to change the way you do business in order to improve your operational processes and performance. The general idea is to lace your functional areas and workflows together into a collaborative operational process and management framework, thereby bridging intra- and interorganizational spaces and closing the reality gap.

In our experience, operational processes are typically larger than any single functional area. Each functional group may work on its particular processes, but it must realize that those processes are likely to be subprocesses of other core operational processes. An operational process is not something new. Good managers intuitively know what operational processes are and how they work.

The ProFIT-MAP methodology bridges the functional and organizational gaps with an activities-oriented approach to planning and optimizing operational capabilities and costs. Our approach to building a roadmap not only lays out the steps to the destination, but also points out the organizational requirements, limitations, costs, and potential payoff prior to implementation. This is how you win before taking any action!

This chapter concludes the first part of our journey though this book, having explored today's business environment, business execution challenges, and the theoretical underpinnings of ProFIT-MAP. From this point forward, we adopt a much more hands-on focus, presenting the methodology and demonstrating its practical application through examples and case studies.

REFERENCES

1   Lawrence G. Hrebiniak, *Making Strategy Work: Leading Effective Execution and Change* (Upper Saddle River, NJ: Wharton School Publishing, 2005), p. 27.

2   See, for example, James Champy, *Reengineering Management* (New York: HarperBusiness, 1995); Thomas H. Davenport, *Process Innovation: Reengineering Work through Information Technology* (Boston: Harvard Business School Press, 1993); Michael Hammer, *Beyond Reengineering* (New York: HarperBusiness, 1996); Michael Hammer and James Champy, *Reengineering the Corporation* (New York: HarperCollins, 1993); V. Daniel Hunt, *Process Mapping: How to Reengineer Your Business Processes* (New York: Wiley, 1996); Raymond L. Manganelli and Mark M. Klein, *The Reengineering Handbook: A Step-by-Step Guide to Business Transformation* (New York: American Management Association, 1994); Geary A. Rummler and Alan P. Brache, *Improving Performance: How to Manage the White Space on the Organization Chart* (San Francisco: Jossey-Bass, 1995); Alec Sharp and Patrick McDermott, *Workflow Modeling: Tools for Process Improvement and Application Modeling* (Boston: Artech House, 2001).

3   B. Joseph Pine and James H. Gilmore, *The Experience Economy: Work Is Theatre and Every Business Is a Stage* (Boston: Harvard Business School Press, 1999).

PART 3

Practical
Application and
Case Studies

Getting Started with ProFIT-MAP

Unless organized, information is still data. To be meaningful it has to be organized. It is, however, not clear at all in what form certain kinds of information are meaningful, and especially in what form of organization they are meaningful for one's own job. And the same information may have to be organized in different ways for different purposes.

—Peter F. Drucker, *Management Challenges for the 21st Century*

THE PROFIT-MAP methodology, the GPS navigation system for business execution, transcends the functional boundaries and management layers in an organization to deliver an integrated solution to business execution challenges. It helps evaluate the impact of changing parameters on the business drivers and objectives. By now, we expect that we have convinced you of the potential value of ProFIT-MAP for your organization. Moving forward from this point, we adopt a hands-on approach for using ProFIT-MAP to solve business problems. We delve into the step-by-step details of how and what to do, and we demonstrate the value of the methodology with two case studies.

ProFIT-MAP is a practical and easy-to-use methodology. It was developed based on extensive interviews with 40 senior managers at medium- to large-size companies in a range of industries, and it has been validated and refined over many years. The methodology prescribes a six-phase gated process starting with framing the problem; then incorporating process, resources and finance data; conducting "what-if?"

Figure 6-1. ProFIT-MAP's Six Phases

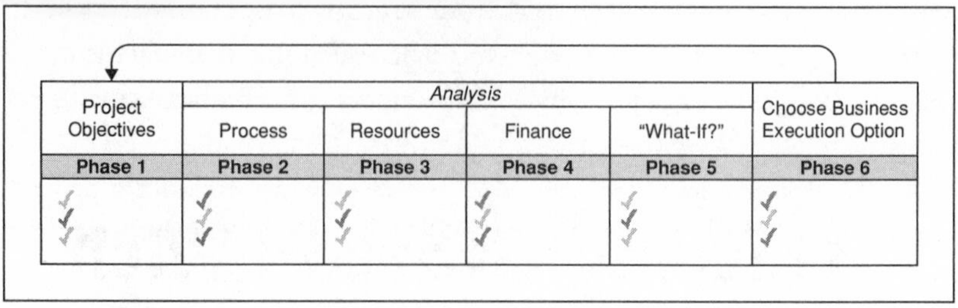

Project Objectives	Analysis				Choose Business Execution Option
	Process	Resources	Finance	"What-If?"	
Phase 1	Phase 2	Phase 3	Phase 4	Phase 5	Phase 6

analyses; and finally selecting the best decision option for implementation (see Figure 6-1).

The methodology begins with quickly identifying and communicating the particular operational "pain." It does this by creating a business execution profile that helps articulate the nature of the business challenge. The role of the business execution profile is to create the context within the organizational framework. Early in Phase 1, where the profile is constructed, practitioners can make a quick first pass at developing a preliminary business execution profile in order to organize the necessary information to gain support and funding for the business opportunity. This is our focus in this chapter, as this is a critical enabler for achieving success in any project. Once the project has been approved and funded, you can update the profile as you formally begin the journey in Phase 1 (see Chapter 7).

CREATING THE CONTEXT AND GETTING YOUR PROJECT FUNDED

One of the realities of business is that managers are competing against one another for limited organizational resources in order to realize their vision of what the organization could be, or to deal with existing problems. In this section, we offer a quick and accurate way for managers to translate their strategic challenges or "pain" into a format that can be easily communicated to others to help them gain organizational buy-in and funding to proceed with a viable project. We refer to such initiatives, efforts, or activities as business execution projects.

Business execution *projects* are the pathways for achieving operational objectives—for closing the gap between the goals of strategic initiatives and tactics, and the ensuing operational results. This is where the rubber meets the road. Business execution projects provide a common language, enabling all levels of management, from strategic to operational, to find a common ground for communicating and executing manufacturing or service changes or improvements. This chapter contains but a small sampling of possible business execution projects. We have identified over 30 different types of such projects. But, before you can conduct a project, you need to create the profile that will help you get the authority and funding to proceed.

A business execution *profile* is used to articulate the particular strategic initiative or process design/improvement strategy and value proposition for an organization. Not only do managers need to identify the "right" challenges and problems to address, but they also need to communicate the business and operational context implicit in their project in order to get the green light from the organization. Once the go-ahead has been received, the manager can quickly convert the initial business execution profile into a set of clear business execution project objectives. This is the second step in Phase 1 of the ProFIT-MAP methodology and is described in the next chapter.

A business execution profile consists of three elements: a problem statement, seven dimensions that characterize the nature of the problem, and any additional profile notes. We describe these elements here and present two sample profiles to illustrate their utility for framing business execution challenges. It is important to keep in mind that the profile is intended to help you get started in defining a business execution problem. You should not get bogged down and spend too much time creating a profile. Limit yourself to an hour or two the first time around. The profile is a living document, and you can always come back and refine it as necessary.

Problem Statement

Crafting a problem statement is the first step in defining a business execution opportunity or challenge. If your business demand is growing, if you have acquired another company, or if you are expanding into new markets, for instance, then this is a statement that crystallizes your product or service opportunity. If you are responding to a current execution problem such as a production or service delivery issue, then this statement might describe your "pain" and how you hope to quickly relieve it.

(2) The Seven Dimensions of a Business Execution Profile

The purpose of creating a business execution profile is to identify the specific parameters and sources of enterprise data that ProFIT-MAP will use to create a business execution roadmap. There are seven dimensions to a business execution profile: roles and stakeholders, strategy, decision level, assessment focus, ProFIT-MAP components, enterprise tools and data, and parameters. While the use of seven dimensions may seem a bit complex at first glance, these dimensions are designed to help a practitioner develop an initial profile within a matter of minutes. A "quick" profile can be invaluable for facilitating discussion and debate and garnering organizational support.

The waterfall diagram in Figure 6-2 illustrates the cascading relationship among the seven dimensions of a profile. You can think of this figure as representing a visual outline of the steps for building a profile that we describe later in more detail. The outline shows the conceptual connections between the seven dimensions, starting with roles and stakeholders and concluding by delineating the parameters and data sources required for a ProFIT-MAP analysis. As you move down the waterfall, the rows become the columns as the relationships between dimensions are articulated. This will become more apparent as you read the specifics of each dimension.

Keep in mind that the waterfall is a conceptual tool, and that there may be some overlap among the seven dimensions. More importantly, the same business execution opportunity or challenge can make use of multiple profiles, each serving the needs of a different management audience, and it is not uncommon for companies to have more than one business execution project underway at any given time. The disciplined nature of the ProFIT-MAP approach enables you to develop a flexible pathway through the waterfall. You can start at any level you want and work your way up or down the waterfall as you go about building your business execution profile.

Dimension 1: Roles and Stakeholders

A central challenge for any business execution project is that different stakeholders may define success in different ways. It is not that one perspective is more "right" than another; rather, your role and your professional discipline tend to filter what captures your interest and attention—as well as determine how you are evaluated and compensated.

Figure 6-2. Business Execution Profile Waterfall

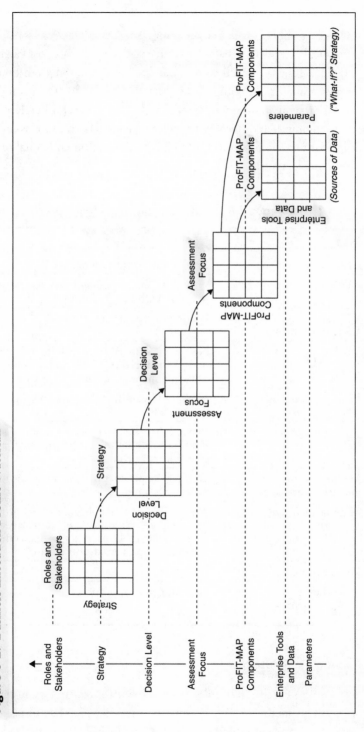

Table 6-1 highlights several key organizational roles and the corresponding financial perspective that is typically used as a guidepost for each role.

Table 6-1 also shows the commonalities and differences in financial priorities among a sampling of key management roles. What might be important to you might not be immediately central for another. Explicitly acknowledging such differences enables managers both to focus on what is important to them and to facilitate communication and collaboration with their colleagues.

Table 6-1.   Organizational Roles and Financial Guideposts

Role	Financial Guidepost
CEO	Profitability, return on net assets
CFO	Cash flow (ensure enough cash to operate; optimize cash flow to improve profitability)
VP operations VP manufacturing	Profitability, return on assets
VP development	No direct financial responsibility other than budget; financial role is to support operations and manufacturing
Plant/general manager	Measured by profitability; operates business by cash flow
Engineering manager	Profitability (but no tools or authority to monitor profitability; uses "efficiency" as a surrogate for profitability)
Manufacturing/ operations manager	Getting the product out the door; cost not necessarily a high priority
Materials manager	No specific financial obligations; may provide input to purchasing and/or plant management; a supply-chain role; uses supply-chain efficiency as the primary measurement
Financial controller	Cash flow
Any other interested party	Determined as appropriate

Dimension 2: Strategy

For a business execution profile, strategy refers to the strategic initiatives, improvement methods, and measurement frameworks that an organization currently uses or intends to deploy. The ProFIT-MAP methodology complements all such efforts and does not require an organization to change the way it does business—although this is always a management consideration. Table 6-2 lists sample strategic initiatives, process improvement methods, and measurement frameworks.

This list is not exhaustive, nor is it meant to be prescriptive. Organizations typically pursue one or more of these items in their quest for success, as the methods are not mutually exclusive and many are complementary. In defining this dimension of a business execution profile, the practitioner simply indicates the relevant strategies, methods, and measures.

Table 6-2.   Sample Strategic Initiatives, Process Improvement Methods, and Measurement Frameworks

Strategy/Philosophy	Process Improvement Method	Measurement Framework
Lean manufacturing	Value-stream mapping	Balanced Scorecard
Lean business operations	Six Sigma*	Economic value added
Flexible manufacturing	Continuous improvement	Value analysis
Design for manufacturability	Theory of constraints	Activity-based costing
Toyota Production System	Value-chain mapping	Lean accounting
Toyota Production System—II	Discrete event simulation	Economic investment analysis
Concurrent engineering	Parametric modeling	Business process management
Design for initial quality	Stochastic modeling	Benchmarking
	Financial modeling	Risk analysis
	Reengineering	

* Or other quality initiatives.

Dimension 3: Decision Level

The previous two dimensions contain some implicit assumptions about who is interested in what, and when. When taken together, the organizational *roles and stakeholders* and *strategic* dimensions suggest a particular management layer or level of analysis. Figure 6-3 shows the three primary layers—strategic, tactical, and operational—and the time frame that is of greatest interest to each layer.

These layers help articulate a management and decision context as well as a corresponding time horizon for any given manager. Corporate management, for example, might seek out a merger or acquisition opportunity, the ultimate success or failure of which may play out over several years. Tactical management might tackle plant and/or product rationalization challenges. Operational management might focus its energy on optimizing one or two lines at a single site. The boundaries between the layers are not cut-and-dried; they can overlap, and multiple layers are often relevant in any given business execution opportunity or problem.

Figure 6-3. Organizational Layers and Time Frame

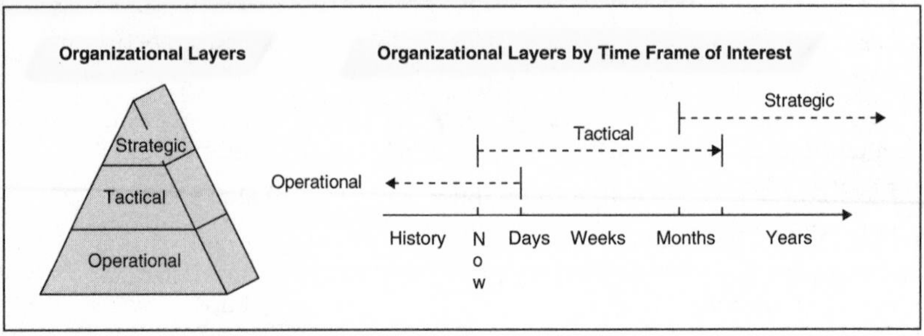

Dimension 4: Assessment Focus

The assessment focus helps frame the nature of the business execution challenge or opportunity. Table 6-3 describes six interrelated characteristics of a ProFIT-MAP assessment. These characteristics are not mutually exclusive. Their relevance or importance to a business execution project depends on what kinds of operational questions are being asked by management. While the full complement of characteristics is always available, managers typically emphasize the subset of characteristics that best meet their needs.

The *reality gap* assessment incorporates functional knowledge to proactively determine whether or not a given objective is possible. And if the result comes back negative, it allows the practitioner to identify what additional capabilities and resources are needed to bridge the gap.

Table 6-3. Assessment Focus

Assessment Focus	Description
Reality gap	The *business reality gap* quantifies the difference between a strategic objective and an organization's ability to realize that objective.
	The *technology reality gap* quantifies the difference between a technology objective (e.g., a new technology required to produce a product) and an organization's ability to successfully deploy the technology.
Multidimensional impact	This describes the integrated relationship between process, resources, and financial performance.
Dynamic impact	This characterizes changes or fluctuations over time in process dynamics, materials and supplies, labor and utilities usage, and their costs.
Interaction impact	This explores the impact of a decision across the company's process and product mix.
Financial impact	This assesses the profitability implications of all the process design or improvement decision options.
Pathway identification	This outlines the series of steps that will move an organization from its current operational state to its desired future state.

In practice, there are both *business* and *technology* reality gaps. They assess the difference between their respective management objectives and the ability of an organization to actually achieve the particular objective.

Let's take a closer look at a sample technology gap. A consumer electronics (CE) company has expertise in manufacturing micron-size (i.e., narrow-bore) tubing. Executive management is approached by a medical device company that needs a manufacturing partner with narrow-bore tubing capabilities because it is having problems with its current supplier. Management views this opportunity narrowly as a technology leap challenge. However, there might also be other related but unknown technological challenges. For instance, the CE company may not in fact have a technological advantage if the tubing materials used are different. Moreover, processes at the medical device company's current supplier may differ substantially from the CE company's related processes. There are also different regulatory requirements. The CE company's current practices meet environmental regulations but may require a substantial upgrade to meet FDA medical device regulations. A technology gap assessment could quantify the process and financial impact of all of these issues, aiding senior management in making the "right" strategic decision.

The *multidimensional impact* is quantified by the integrated process, resource, and finance information that forms the nexus of the ProFIT-MAP approach. This contrasts with the multitude of existing tools that analyze at most two, but not all three aspects simultaneously at an activities composition level.

Compared to a traditional static analysis, where snapshot data are collected and extrapolated to predict the future, ProFIT-MAP automatically accounts for *dynamic* fluctuations in process and resource costs and usage. This is relevant when it is important to understand the expected changes in processes over time as a result of changing process conditions, followed by corresponding changes in the use of resources and costs. For example, improving a current operation might increase the efficiency of a process, enabling a plant to produce more output or to produce the same amount of output with less labor.

The *interaction impact* assessment helps managers understand how a particular decision can have ripple effects across an organization's process and product mix. It explores how changes in one process affect other upstream or downstream processes and products. For example, introducing a new product or service to an existing line has throughput and cost implications for other products already produced on that line as well as on other dependent lines.

Managers want to know the *financial impact* of their process and product-mix decisions in the context of the overall portfolio of projects before the decisions are implemented. As an example, the cash flow improvement argument is at the crux of implementing supply-chain management (SCM) tools. Initially, SCM tools bring about a dramatic improvement in profitability but have difficulty delivering improvements on a continuous basis thereafter. A tighter supply chain amplifies process dynamics. Further improvements are difficult because the benefits of reducing inventory are eaten up by increased system volatility.

The *pathway identification* is the business execution roadmap, indicating how to improve the delivery of a product or service. It delineates the requisite steps that enable an organization to move from its current to its desired future process state (see Figure 6-4).

Figure 6-4. Business Execution Roadmap

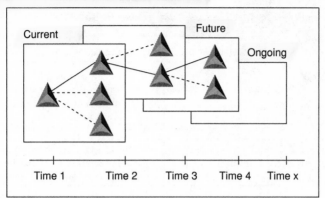

Each box in the figure represents one complete iteration through the ProFIT-MAP methodology. The left triangle in the first box shows the current state, with three lines connecting to the three decision options. The solid line shows the selected decision. The complete roadmap is generated by iterating through the methodology and selecting the best decision option as many times as necessary to reach the desired future state.

All business execution projects generate a process roadmap containing a minimum of one step, with the potential for many steps along the route to achieving the business execution objectives. For example, a manager may simply want to know which station, A or B, is more efficient to set up and operate. This type of decision is binary; it requires only one step to conclude, to select A or B. Alternatively, management might wish to consolidate products among several plants. The roadmap in this case, for instance, can include decisions as to what products to move among what plants, and also include guidance on how to further improve efficiency and profitability once the initial consolidation plans have been implemented. This is an example of a more complex multiple-stage roadmap.

Dimension 5: ProFIT-MAP Components

The ProFIT-MAP methodology contains five categories of interdependent components, which are described in Table 6-4: process, capital, resources, inventories (including work in process [WIP]), and finances. To create this portion of the business execution profile, the practitioner simply

Table 6-4. ProFIT-MAP Components

Element		Description
1. Process		A simple thumbnail description of the process to be improved.
2. Capital		What kind of capital is currently deployed, such as operations or buildings? What do they cost? Are any new sources of capital available?
3. Resources	Materials and supplies	What kinds of materials and supplies are available? What kinds of constraints exist?
	Labor	Describe the available labor pool. Are there any labor constraints?
	Utilities	Are utilities data (e.g., from a utilities audit) specific to the process available? Should utilities even be considered?
4. Inventories and WIP		Describe the current inventory and WIP policies. What kinds of changes to the policies is management willing to consider? Include supply chain expectations and limitations here.
5. Finances	Manufacturing or service cost	What are your fixed costs, above and beyond current capital requirements, resources, and inventory and WIP policies? What is the cost of capital? These are any additional costs that are required to produce, but not to sell or distribute, the product.
	Income statement	Are sales and marketing data available by product? Similarly, are logistics and distribution costs available by product?

describes the current situation as it pertains to each element, including any relevant organizational constraints. It is rare, for instance, for an organization to have an unlimited capital budget, so any investment limitations need to be stated. In another common situation, a company may have a labor agreement that dictates certain fixed costs that cannot be changed—at least until the agreement comes up for renewal down the road.

The *process* is composed of a sequence of value-adding activities, as well as some that may not add value, that create the product or service. Management can refine or reshape the process by way of its constituent activities in order to gain a desired advantage, such as profit growth or regulatory compliance. Detailed process or value-stream maps are not required here, but can be included in the Notes section, which is described later.

Capital refers to an organization's fixed capital structure and whether or not it can be changed. It is a financial "lever" that can be pulled to help solve a problem, provided that the organization is willing and able to provide it.

Resources can be thought of as constraint boundaries, affecting the effectiveness, quality, and cost of processes. Organizations rarely have unlimited resources. There may also be opportunities to use current resources more effectively. For instance, an organization may have a labor agreement that dictates the number and cost of workers. Identifying this as a resource constraint enables the investigation of viable competitive options, such as delaying a planned capital equipment upgrade because there is an abundance of (expensive) labor to meet demand without need for the new equipment.

Policies drive *inventories and work-in-process (WIP)* practices. For instance, should finished goods inventory be held for one week, two days, or four hours? WIP is unfinished or "working" inventory in the case of manufacturing. In a services context, WIP is the backlog of customers at each step in the process. For example, a medical transcription service has multiple customers, with multiple steps required to acquire the work, transcribe it, and return it to the customer. Both types of policies have cost implications. For example, if operations are designed with infinite-size buffers, then it is theoretically possible to have infinite WIP, which requires more working capital to pay for the cost of the materials and warehousing space.

Manufacturing or service cost is a catchall category that gathers leftover fixed costs and variable costs that were not accounted for in the previous categories. These costs range from things such as the salaries of white-collar employees, equipment leases, computers and IT infrastructure, and corporate allocation, among others. Sales and marketing and distribution costs are not included here because they are not associated with producing the product.

An informative *income statement* requires that sales, marketing, logistics and distribution, and other relevant cost data be available for analysis on a product-by-product basis. With the ProFIT-MAP methodology, cost data are estimated using a parametric activities approach—the pABF. Such a product focus inherent in the ProFIT-MAP approach is one of its strengths. Most enterprise tools such as MRP II are process-focused, and discrete event simulation tools explore line efficiency, but neither have a product focus.

Dimension 6: Enterprise Tools and Data

The *tools* dimension is really a marker for relevant sources of enterprise *data*. For example, important financial data may reside in the financial module of an enterprise resource planning (ERP) system. Likewise, valuable production information may reside in a manufacturing resource planning (MRP II) system. Rather than manually collecting available data, the goal is to identify appropriate sources of operational data that can be gathered for subsequent analysis. Figure 6-5 shows some of the more common sources of enterprise data. One of the strengths of the ProFIT-MAP approach is that it enables you to start with the data you already have and then expand the level of detail later if necessary.

Figure 6-5 distinguishes between tools used for operational management, business management, engineering, and other purposes. This is only a sampling of pertinent enterprise tools, and in practice these tools often overlap, both within and across the major categories. Their particular structure and deployment will always be unique for each organization.

This category may in fact be merely the tip of the iceberg in terms of all of the personal files used by managers to do their work. This kind of information is unavailable to the organization unless there is an enterprise content management system in place that facilitates the sharing of documents. For some organizations, printed documents such as shop floor routing sheets may not be automated, but gleaning such information from paper documents for future analysis can be extremely helpful.

Operational tools emphasize operations, "supporting" processes, general operating practices, and accounting. Business management tools emphasize profitability and other aspects of performance measurement and management. We have also included business execution manage-

Figure 6-5. Enterprise Tools and Data Sources

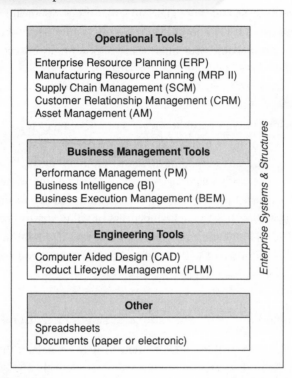

ment tools, which are used for planning and managing strategy execution, in this category. Such tools have limited value in providing useful data for a parametric framework. They are typically oriented around extrapolation of historical data. These tools are for data mining and do not convey functional knowledge about your business, as ProFIT-MAP does.

Dimension 7: Parameters

Parameters are variables that you can change. These are the variables that managers can control to drive the business. For example, the thermostat setting that regulates the temperature in a room is under someone's control. However, even if the variable is under control, you may not be guaranteed the desired results. You might set the thermostat at home, but perhaps you do not do so at work. However, you may have the ability to call someone else, who does control the thermostat. This, of course, doesn't guarantee that the thermostat setting will be changed on your behalf. It also does not guarantee that the temperature will reach your desired level. It is important to recognize and identify the parameters that are controllable over those that are potentially controllable.

Profile Notes

We find that the seven core dimensions of a business execution profile meet the needs of most managers. There may be times, however, when additional information should be added to supplement the basic profile. Notes is an open-ended category designed to catch important relevant detail, and it is often used to highlight issues that require further clarification. This is the place to capture process or value-stream maps, other prior studies, and any additional information that can help the project. However, be very careful with the details, as they have the potential to overwhelm and distract the team.

Some Concluding Comments about Business Execution Profiles

Business execution profiles are intended to help managers think about and begin defining strategic initiatives and process changes. They are intended as a "rapid definition" tool, helping an organization to move from having some sort of operational problem to an initial definition that can be used to gather critical organizational sanction and support. The ProFIT-MAP methodology provides a "shared" language that facilitates communication and collaboration among a wide range of strategic, tactical, and operational management roles.

Business execution profiles are not static definitions. In fact, they can vary quite extensively over time as managers continually learn and adapt as a part of their daily experiences. Management decisions can also refocus projects at any given time, so profiles must be updated accordingly. For instance, a company may consider outsourcing a product or service. The initial profile may focus on a fundamental outsourcing question: Should we outsource or not? If management decides to follow the outsourcing route, then the profile needs to be updated to reflect that decision. Alternatively, if the decision calls for backsourcing or continued insourcing, then the profile can be updated to reflect the pursuit of internal process improvement opportunities.

We also find that business execution profiles become much more specific over time. Managers commonly approach their first business execution project with some initial high-level ideas. As they embark upon business execution projects, they typically generate further or more refined questions. For example, if a company decides to go the outsourcing route, it may next wish to determine the "best" of several candidate outsourcing companies to partner with. Managers who approach business execution projects as an iterative undertaking will find that the ProFIT-MAP methodology is well suited for addressing the natural progression of their management decision needs. Each new scenario spawns additional business execution options.

At this point, you should have enough material or ammunition to justify the project. You can package it in whatever form works best for your company (e.g., proposal or presentation) and go forth and seek funding and approval for your initiative. In the next section, we explore two sample business execution profiles for a manufacturing company and a services company. These profiles enable managers to move from an amorphous collection of thoughts and ideas to a concrete conceptualization.

SAMPLE BUSINESS EXECUTION PROFILES

The following examples show the business clarity that execution profiles bring to describing an operational challenge or opportunity. Creating a profile is relatively straightforward. We present two examples, one from manufacturing and another from the business services sector. Both examples are strategic in nature but simple enough to fit within the space limitations of the chapter. The creation of division strategy, which is too long to present here, is simply a logical extension of the following examples. We present detailed tactical examples as case studies in Chapter 10. The samples here address not only two distinct industries, but also two different types of opportunities: integrating operations after acquisition and outsourcing. We selected such diverse examples to demonstrate the versatility of ProFIT-MAP.

Let's begin with the strategic manufacturing example. The process of creating a profile is greatly facilitated by the fact that it is created for an organization with which you are intimately familiar—yours!

Business Execution Profile: Manufacturing Company

CBA Manufacturing (CBA) has 22 U.S. plants that produce various parts and modular systems for light and heavy commercial trucks and military vehicles. CBA has growing customer demand and has acquired several smaller competitors.[1]

Problem Statement

CBA's manufacturing leadership is dealing with a number of postacquisition challenges. First and foremost, management wants to know how best to integrate the newly acquired manufacturing site and capabilities into the company's existing operations. Manufacturing has inherited a new site that makes the same basic products as two other CBA plants, but uses different processes. The objective is to integrate the three operations.

Seven Dimensions of a Business Execution Profile

The CEO has already done her job. She bought the new company, and now the integration is the responsibility of her management team. Table 6-5 presents the seven dimensions of CBA's business execution profile for the strategic integration.

Profile Notes

This profile reflects a plethora of important management questions to be answered with ProFIT-MAP and illustrates a natural ordering of the way managers pursue the answers. The primary question of how best to integrate the new site and its capabilities into the organization raises a series of follow-up management questions: Does it make any sense to close a plant? Should equipment be moved between plants? Should the product mix be redistributed among plants? Each of these questions will spawn a series of follow-on projects for analysis. This is a zero-sum game because the total amount of product produced is constant unless demand changes. That is, the process and financial optimization need to be connected to product demand.

Management is interested is evaluating information about each of these scenarios. Comparisons need to be made at the process and product level to ensure that demand can be met. Managers want to understand the

Table 6-5. CBA's Business Execution Dimensions

Dimension	Profile
1. Roles and stakeholders	The VP of operations and the CFO need to integrate the three operations. The VP of product development also has a secondary interest because the integration decisions have implications for future product designs and enhancements.
2. Strategy	This is a strategic initiative with a process and product rationalization focus. Once the processes have been consolidated, subsequent efforts might explore how to improve the specific process, which may include one or more plants—we don't know yet because the consolidation decisions still have to be made. The subsequent improvements will spawn secondary projects and will not be a part of this project.
	Key measures include financial indicators (RONA— return on net assets, and EBITDA— earnings before interest, taxes, depreciation, and amortization) and manufacturing indicators (WIP inventory levels, efficiency, and on-time delivery).
3. Decision level	This is a strategic decision with both tactical and operation implications. Options include closing plants, moving equipment between plants, and/or redistributing the product mix among plants.
4. Assessment characteristics	*Reality gap:* The new plant uses different process technology from the other plants. Is its process technology better? Is the market big enough to support what can be produced by the combined operations? Is product demand distributed geographically, enabling production to be redistributed and aligned with geographic demand?
	Multidimensional impact: What is the interplay among the integrated process, resource, and financial implications of product mix, location, and technology options?
	Dynamic impact: The product mix is constantly changing, and process technology improvements are expected as plants upgrade their equipment and capabilities. What are the process, resource, and financial implications of the expected future process and product mix?
	Interaction impact: How do the different scenarios affect other CBA sites, processes, or product mix? A dependency can exist, for example, if other CBA sites feed parts into or receive product from the current sites.

Table 6-5. CBA's Business Execution Dimensions (*Continued*)

Dimension	Profile
	Financial impact: Every scenario has a different financial profile, and the potential impact on the organization needs to be understood.
	Pathway: If the decision is made to move equipment between sites, then which equipment should be moved first? If product is moved between sites, then which should be moved first, as it cannot all be moved at once? What is the optimal inventory buildup while planning product transfer so as not to fall behind in meeting customer demand during the transition?
5. ProFIT-MAP components	*Process:* Which technology should be deployed in the new scenario? What are the production capacity and capabilities of all of the involved plants under all of the scenarios that we define (i.e., under the various product and equipment mix and process options)?
	Capital: How will capital requirements change if we move equipment, add new equipment, or sell equipment?
	Resources: How will the bill of materials (BOM) and supply needs vary under the different scenarios? Likewise, what are the labor and utilities implications of the decision options?
	Inventory and WIP: The two companies have different inventory and WIP policies. Should we standardize on one or the other set of policies, merge them into a new "best practices" set of policies, or start over with a blank slate?
	Finances: How do potential changes in production and corresponding capital requirements affect financial performance?
6. Enterprise tools and data	Relevant data include MRP II (manufacturing resource planning) operational data, financial data from three financial systems, and marketing data. The marketing data include product mix and market conditions and can come from a CRM (customer relationship management) system, other marketing systems, and files. Lastly, product design data exist in CAD and PLM (product life-cycle management) systems.
7. Parameters	(1) The product demand and mix. (2) Equipment mix (process technology). (3) Redesign of the process flows. (4) Bill of materials. (5) Inventory policies. (6) The cost of closing a facility.

effectiveness and the efficiency of the processes at the various locations. For example, to what degree are operations experiencing starvation (i.e., not receiving enough input material) or blockage (i.e., having insufficient room to store output)? What is the impact on WIP? All of these factors are relevant to the ability to meet future growth requirements.

Management wants to know if the additional suggested or required equipment investment can be justified financially. More specifically, what is the impact of any new capital investment (and ensuing processing improvements) on profit? Management also wants to know if resource requirements can be met. WIP was described earlier as a process issue, but management also wants to know the cost implications of the WIP. Moreover, both unfinished and finished inventory must not violate the policies set by the company. Management is also interested in making basic comparisons between the financial statements for each scenario.

Concluding Comments

We intentionally selected a strategic manufacturing challenge to illustrate how a strategic or *thought* project (described in Chapter 5) typically leads to follow-on tactical and operational projects. The business of operational execution is not a static phenomenon. Strategic decisions have downstream implications. Once the high-level strategic decision has been made, such as to redistribute the product mix among plants, then management will want to create a follow-up project to determine the best way to go about doing this. Plant managers will also create operational projects to further optimize performance within their sites— assuming that their operations were not consolidated into another site.

 ### Business Execution Profile: Services Company

In the next profile, we explore customer service and cost issues in the customer relations department of a large consumer electronics company. More specifically, this profile investigates whether to continue in-house telephone support or to outsource the service to an external vendor. Call centers are of strategic importance, as they represent customer touch points. Not only do call centers provide on-demand assistance, but they also provide an opportunity to up-sell and cross-sell as well as doing the things that maintain customer loyalty.

Outsourcing is and will continue to be a political hot potato for the foreseeable future. Politics aside, the ProFIT-MAP approach stresses that the decision-making process needs to attend to the *activities composition* of the particular process. To improve a process, management can change the activities composition of the process and/or change its constraints and/or capabilities.

Call centers are an interesting case study in their own right. Call centers are cost centers. Leading companies seek to improve cycle time and reduce costs while improving customer satisfaction—all of which help the company's bottom line. There is no one-size-fits-all approach for balancing and optimizing these factors. Some companies seek to minimize cycle time, while others will stay with a customer as long as it takes to resolve a problem to the customer's satisfaction.

Often, organizations work from the outside in planning their call-center operations. They ask first, "Where is the best geographic location for a call center?" An implicit assumption here is that other in-country or offshore locations may have lower labor costs. Following the location decision, the organization next figures out how to build the optimum call-center operation. With its focus on the activities composition of a process, the ProFIT-MAP approach enables managers to ask, "What is the ideal 'best practices' operation for my company and my customers?" Next, given this operational target, "What is the ideal geographic location for the operation—one that meets our throughput, quality, and cost requirements?" The ProFIT-MAP methodology doesn't make any judgments as to the best approach; it supports both.

Problem Statement

Management wants to know how to improve the quality and throughput of the call centers while reducing the total cost per call and the number of callbacks required to resolve each issue. This problem statement is normally sufficient for this section, and the practitioner would move on to complete the seven dimensions of a business execution profile section. However, to facilitate a more in-depth understanding of this profile, we are including a description of the process and management's decision tree here.

Figure 6-6 shows the company's general call-center process. This process evolved over several years and iterations. Call-center manage-

Figure 6-6. Call-Center Process

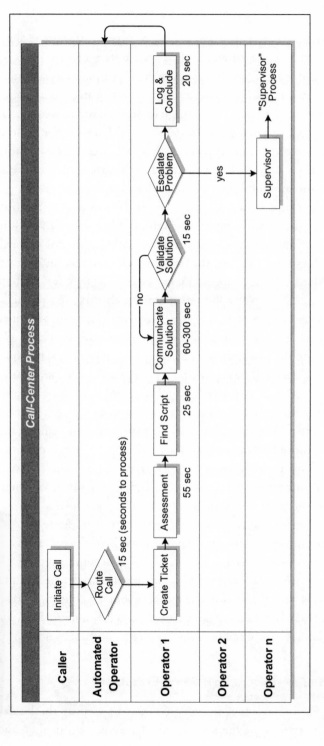

ment is pleased with it and uses it in its two call centers, although each call center uses a different CRM system. Key cycle-time information is shown on the figure underneath the corresponding activity. Incoming calls are routed by an automated system using state-of-the-art voice recognition and natural language understanding processing capabilities. Operators accept calls and conduct a quick assessment. The call-center system automatically creates a ticket and directs the operator to one of several possible scripts designed for the particular service issue. The operator communicates the solution and then concludes by asking if the problem meets the customer's needs. If it does not, the operator can explain the solution again or search for other possible solutions. Assuming that the problem is successfully resolved, the call is concluded and the record updated, and the operator is free to take another call.

Management considers Figure 6-6 a "best practice" and expects that the process will be replicated at any site that handles the organization's customer service. The original problem statement, that management wants to know how to improve response quality and throughput while reducing the total cost per call, suggests a series of related questions, all of which need to be explored. For example: To outsource or not to outsource? If yes, to which of several vendors?

If management decides to continue in-house operations, then how can service at the current sites be improved? This question is actually made up of several subquestions. Which of the two current sites, San Diego or Toronto, has the best balance of service, quality, and cost? Should a new site be opened in Alabama? Regardless of whether or not a new site is opened, should operations be consolidated among the sites? These questions are shown as a decision tree in Figure 6-7.

In considering the outsourcing route, Bangalore is an offshore option with lower-cost labor where English is a second language. Dublin is a higher-cost option where English is the primary language and the population is already fairly knowledgeable about the company's basic products or services (i.e., more expertise exists, and less training is required). New England is a third option, representing an onshore vendor.

Seven Dimensions of a Business Execution Profile

The problem statement given earlier—to identify the best call-center site or sites from the standpoint of throughput, quality, and cost for

Figure 6-7. Call-Center Decision Tree

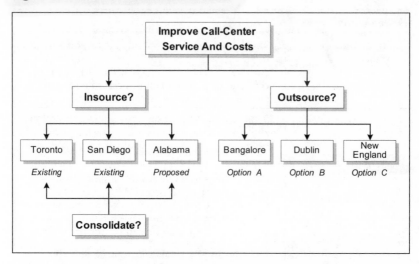

implementation of the ideal process—brings with it a series of implicit follow-on questions that we summarized in Figure 6-7. To simplify this section, we present a single high-level aggregate overview of the dimensions and highlight issues pertaining to the follow-up questions as they arise (see Table 6-6). In practice, a separate business execution profile should be completed for each management question.

Profile Notes

Management's bias in improving call-center operations is that the "best practices" should drive the question of location. That is, the ideal process, service, and cost mix (i.e., the activities and cost composition of the process) should be implemented at the selected location(s). Management does not want to first pick a location and then figure out a process. Location options include two existing internal call centers (Toronto and San Diego), a proposed internal call center (Alabama), and three outsourcing options (Bangalore, Dublin, and New England).

Management's preference is to continue to insource call-center services, provided that the current quality of service is cost-competitive with external vendors and can scale under the same cost structure to meet predicted increases in demand. Labor is the predominant cost factor. If this is deemed too expensive, management will evaluate a capital

Table 6-6. Call-Center Business Execution Dimensions

Dimension	Profile
1. Roles and stakeholders	The VP of customer relations is responsible for the project. The general managers of her two current call centers are assisting with the project. The CFO is also an interested and vital party because of the cost implications.
2. Strategy	This project explores the capabilities, constraints, and costs of the current call centers, a proposed call center, and potential outsourcing vendors.
3. Decision level	This is a tactical project with overlapping strategic concerns to make several important high-level call-center decisions. After the initial decisions are made, ensuing operational projects may be defined to improve efficiency and service within a specific call center or centers.
4. Assessment focus	*Reality gap:* The *business reality gap* is that management is having difficulty understanding the relationship between specific operational constraints and capabilities, on the one hand, and low reported customer satisfaction because of poor process execution.
	The *technology reality gap* is that process execution may be encountering difficulties as a result of technology impediments. Further, each call center has different standard operating policies and procedures, which are reflected in the underlying CRM technologies that each uses. It is unclear whether or how these practices deviate from the "best practice" approach so strongly preached by executive management.
	Multidimensional impact: How do the capabilities, constraints, and costs interact with one another in each actual or proposed call center at the different locations? For example, costs may be lower in certain locations, and language proficiency or technical expertise may vary by geography.
	Dynamic impact: How do these interactions change as demand fluctuates or increases? Is there enough resilience in the process to handle increased demand?
	Interaction impact: How does changing the service requirements, capabilities, and constraints at one site change the dynamics at other sites (e.g., reduce demand, change the nature of callers serviced at one location versus another, such as "easy" versus "difficult" problems)?

Table 6-6. Call-Center Business Execution Dimensions (*Continued*)

Dimension	Profile
	Financial impact: Every scenario has a different financial profile, and the potential impact on the organization needs to be understood.
	Pathway: If the VP of operations decides to revisit the "best practices" issue as a part of this initiative, for example, she might assign her team to redefine the template for the optimal call center. The pathway question then becomes how to migrate from the current to the new best practices call center.
5. ProFIT-MAP components	*Process:* What are the service capacity and capabilities of all of the sites involved under all of the suggested scenarios? Understanding the sensitivity to the demand changes and the variety of calls is critical.
	Capital: How will the capital requirements change between the insourcing and outsourcing options? For example, management might want to expand the natural language understanding (NLU) system to offload some of the call burden. That is, upgrading the NLU system will enable the organization to completely service a significant portion of callers without their having to speak with a human representative. Management might also wish to explore capital requirements to open a new site and/or move operations among sites. There are no capital requirements in an outsourcing mode, unless the company enters into a joint venture with the outsourcing company.
	Resources: Labor is the primary issue. There are no materials and supplies, and utilities are not significant enough to be of concern.
	Inventory and WIP: In a services environment, WIP is the number of customers on hold at each step of the process. Management wants to know how WIP varies under the different scenarios.
	Finances: What are the financial implications of potential changes in processes, location, and so on for each scenario? How do these affect the capital requirements necessary to achieve the desired future performance? The income statement is not important here, as this is a cost center. (If, however, you are a vendor looking at taking on this business and getting paid by the call, then the income statement is very important.)

Table 6-6. Call-Center Business Execution Dimensions (*Continued*)

Dimension	Profile
6. Enterprise tools and data	Management needs performance data from the CRM and/or business intelligence (BI) systems from the two current sites. Data might also come from potential outsourcing vendors. However, many vendors are small and do not have the interest or resources to implement sophisticated performance management systems. In such cases, their data probably reside in spreadsheets. Survey data will also be required to assess customer satisfaction. The consideration of external vendors also suggests another type of *reality gap* centered on vendors' claims for quality and cost performance versus what they can actually deliver. In evaluating performance claims, the contracting company might want to conduct some sort of performance audit before committing to the vendor.
7. Parameters	(1) Task service times. (2) Number of operators and their skill sets. (3) Redesign of the workflow. (4) Capital requirement for redesign. (5) Service delivery time.

investment to upgrade the natural language understanding system, enabling the call center to service more calls without operator intervention. Management wants to know if the capital investment in technology enables onshore call centers to remain cost-competitive. Another option is to add a third onshore call center in Alabama, a state with lower-cost labor, to handle increased demand. A downstream question also includes whether it makes any economic sense to migrate a portion or all of the operations from the two higher-labor-cost operations to the new call center.

Management isn't caught up in the offshoring phenomenon. It cares most about the quality of the service, followed closely by the cost. The question of location is therefore of secondary interest. For the sake of discussion, let's say that a thorough analysis and some serious "soul searching" leads the organization down the offshoring path. The critical question then becomes, which of several potential international vendors is the ideal partner? This is a complex question to answer because labor costs, English proficiency, expertise with relevant products and services, vendor viability, and the like vary by country and vendor. Each of these factors affects cycle time. For example, operators in one country may be more familiar with the product or service, enabling them to turn around calls more quickly, as well as having fewer callbacks because the problem is resolved on the first call without escalation. Management is adamant that the vendor follow its internally developed process and wants assurance that it is able and willing to do this.

In actuality, management is clearly pleased with the current call-center operations. As smart managers, they nevertheless "know" that with a little effort, additional process efficiency gains and cost savings over current operations are achievable without sacrificing quality and customer satisfaction ratings. Factors that the managers would like to explore prior to implementing any changes include (1) a range of technology options to assist or reduce the need for human operators (e.g., upgrades to the natural language understanding or CRM systems), (2) process improvements, and (3) additional specialized training for operators. The cycle-time information shown in Figure 6-6 is integral for determining the effects of these scenarios on total throughput, which when combined with customer satisfaction ratings and costs gives a complete picture of each decision option. For example, management suspects that additional training, combined with a more refined routing of calls to appropriately skilled operators, will cut the average time to "Communicate Solution" in half. Given the wide range required to complete this step (60 to 300 seconds), the hope is to nearly double throughput and also provide more precise cycle-time predictability.

Concluding Comments

These sample profiles illustrate the interconnected and multidisciplinary nature and natural evolution of the decision-making process. A problem might start with a strategic focus, such as to outsource or not, to acquire a competitor, or to enter a new market. It can then evolve into a series of tactical decisions, such as whether or how to consolidate or expand operations. Tactical implementation then leads to operational decisions, such as how to improve a given process at a particular site.

Likewise, operational breakthroughs can spawn tactical or strategic projects to exploit a new product or service capability. In the ensuing chapters we present the ProFIT-MAP methodology in detail and show how to systematically iterate through it to quickly answer the management questions articulated in a business execution profile.

REFERENCES

1   Company name changed to protect identity and confidential information.

ProFIT-MAP Phase I: Project Objectives

Black holes ain't so black.

—Stephen W. Hawking, *A Brief History of Time*

THE PRECEDING CHAPTER introduced the business execution profile as a way to quickly articulate a business execution opportunity or challenge in order to gain the organizational support and funding necessary to conduct the project. The profile is an integral part of the first phase of the ProFIT-MAP methodology, which we present in this chapter, so you already have a head start in defining your project objectives. The methodology may look intimidating at first glance, but it is not, and we demystify it in the ensuing chapters and present lots of applied examples and advice.

In this chapter we describe the first phase of the methodology: Project Objectives (see Figure 7-1). The next chapter presents the four analysis phases together, illustrating their interconnected and iterative nature, and Chapter 9 shows how to create the business execution roadmap in Phase 6. Chapter 10 then presents detailed case studies illustrating the ProFIT-MAP methodology in action. Each phase of the methodology is presented in flowchart form, complete with management checklists describing the required activities that must be completed before proceeding to the next step and/or phase. A complete listing of the entire methodology along with other useful information can be found in the Appendix.

Figure 7-1. ProFIT-MAP's Six Phases

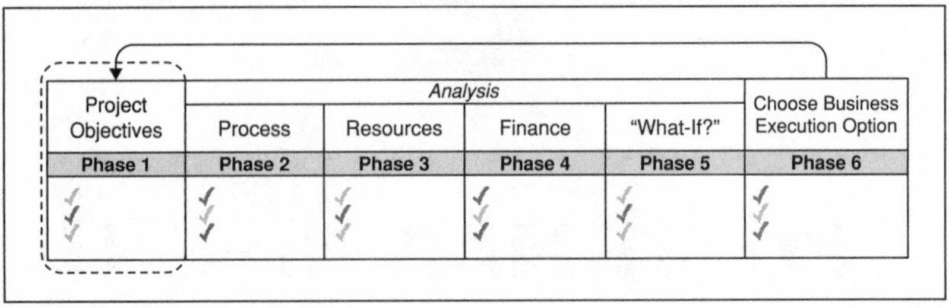

Project Objectives	Analysis				Choose Business Execution Option
	Process	Resources	Finance	"What-If?"	
Phase 1	**Phase 2**	**Phase 3**	**Phase 4**	**Phase 5**	**Phase 6**
✓ ✓	✓ ✓	✓ ✓	✓ ✓	✓ ✓	✓ ✓

The structure and checklists provided for each phase reflect our bias that business execution should be treated as a discipline, yet one that should be accessible and easy for the manager to practice. A significant advantage of this structured, disciplined approach is that these characteristics enable tremendous flexibility in how companies can apply the ProFIT-MAP methodology to resolve their operational challenges and opportunities.

ProFIT-MAP does not prescribe how to manage or impose any structural changes on the organization; rather, it provides a new forward-looking strategy implementation tool in the management arsenal. In fact, ProFIT-MAP's iterative and flexible nature allows organizations to adjust their execution on demand. It is particularly useful because decision makers can adapt ProFIT-MAP to their specific needs and are not rigidly bound, as with some approaches. This methodology allows managers to answer specific operational questions quickly, and to refine and adjust as they continue to learn and build expertise.

The first phase of the ProFIT-MAP methodology involves defining the challenge, including framing the opportunity or problem boundaries, forming a plan for solving the problem, and validating that the plan is structured for success. Figure 7-2 outlines all of the steps in the Project Objectives phase. Unless otherwise indicated, each step must be successfully completed before proceeding to the next step. We recommend using the checkboxes in the figure to track task completion.

BUSINESS EXECUTION PROFILE

The business execution profile articulates the specific challenge or opportunity in sufficient detail to enable the manager to conduct a business

Figure 7-2. Phase 1: Project Objectives

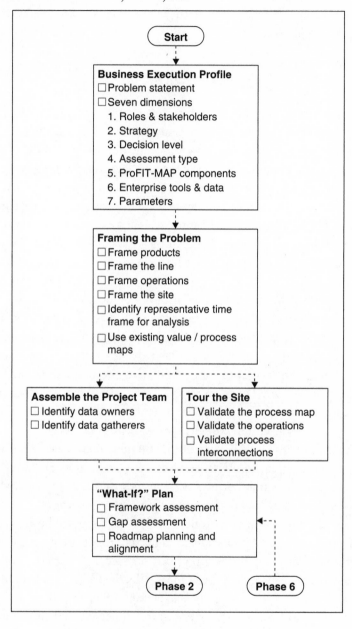

execution project to help the organization realize the operational objectives set forth in the corporate strategy. We discussed the details of the profile in the previous chapter.

FRAMING THE PROBLEM

After delineating the business execution profile, you must define the boundaries of what constitutes the opportunity or the challenge. Just as importantly, you must define what is outside of the scope of the project and will not be examined, enabling the manager to focus on solving the particular problem without unnecessary distractions and costs. We do not advocate a "boil-the-ocean" approach to operational improvement. While theoretically you could choose to analyze absolutely every operational process, we believe it is more time- and cost-efficient to let your specific strategies and tactics drive how you formulate, frame, and conduct the project.

In framing the problem, the practitioner needs to keep in mind three important aspects of business execution. First, *demand* is the most important parameter because ProFIT-MAP is focused on product, and hence on cost and revenue. As product demand and the mix thereof changes, so do the activities composition and, therefore, the costs. This is a customer-oriented focus, as opposed to a purely workflow focus that may look at efficiency from a process standpoint but is unable to foresee dynamic resource and cost changes at the product level.

Second, ProFIT-MAP does not distinguish conceptually between manufacturing and business services. The common denominator between the two is that both types of businesses run by *processes*, which can be described by way of their *dynamic activity compositions*.

Third, if you are approaching ProFIT-MAP from a business services perspective, it is important to understand that the term *service* is just another way to describe a product. A *service* is a *product*. Both are entities that are delivered to customers. Whether what is delivered is a service entity or a physical entity is irrelevant. Typically, when we think of terms such as *product*, *line*, *site*, or *operation*, images of a manufacturing environment come to mind. When you read our definition of these terms, keep in mind that they apply equally as well to describing business services as they do to manufacturing.

Frame Product(s)

How is a product defined? Is it defined at an SKU level, as a grouping in a family, as the whole product family, or at some other level? The level of detail required should flow from the business execution profile. In a service industry, a product might be defined as a decision or some type of transaction. For example, processing an insurance claim can result in a decision to accept or reject the claim. A tax return service might define the actual filing of an income tax return as the end product. In a call center, the product might be defined as the resolution of the call. In an outsourced service environment, where a third party is fulfilling the service, the completion of the service task is the product. The full execution of one business service with an outcome is equivalent to manufacturing one unit of a product. The end product or service is simply an expression of the underlying operational process.

Frame the Line

A process line is an ordered collection of activities that produce a finished product. You can think of a line as a minimum set of activities required to define the process. Like a process, a line must have at least one beginning and only one end where the finished unit or product is counted. Further, it must be a self-contained process with inputs (e.g., resources such as raw materials, supplies, labor, and/or utilities), and the outputs of the line are the product.

The definition of a line and that of a site (defined later in this chapter) are integrally linked to the definition of the product. One way to help clarify the definition of a line is to start with the definition of the product (as discussed earlier) and then look at the line from the viewpoint of how and where the products are created.

From a methodological standpoint, a line cannot "interact" with any other lines. It is important to distinguish here between the physical world, where lines do interact, and an analytical approach where such interactions—if they are relevant for solving the problem statement— are understood by grouping all relevant physical lines into the ProFIT-MAP definition of a line. For example, a line that produces a housing body might require several holes to be drilled in each unit. This primary line may have access to a secondary line of additional drills in a press farm that can supplement the main line if that line cannot keep up with the processing requirements. In this instance, the secondary press line needs to be included in the framework of the primary line. Otherwise, the process dynamics of the secondary line will be excluded from analysis, biasing the results and leading to a reality gap.

Framing the line is also important for defining financial information requirements. Financial information is typically available at a site or location level. Depending on the particular definition of a site, it will be necessary to come up with a strategy to distribute the financial information down to the line level. This can be done, for instance, by creating a set of rules to distribute the financial information to the appropriate unit of analysis. For example, the financial information can be distributed by dividing the number of lines in a site, or by using a percentage distribution based on a parameter such as product demand or some other suitable attribute such as size, weight or other metadata. Keep in mind that ProFIT-MAP is built on a parametric framework. Unlike an accounting allocation, which is based on a single overhead rate, you can choose appropriate and as many parameters as needed for each type of information. We discuss this further in the next chapter.

Frame Operations

Operations describe the physical context in which the line activities occur, and a line is simply a collection of operations that perform their work sequentially. An operation, in turn, is a collection of stations that perform a similar function. For example, an operation might contain three hole-punching machines. The machines can be identical or different, and can operate with different throughput rates and quality levels, but they all perform the same operation. In a call center, an operation might refer to the collection of operators who sit at computer stations servicing incoming calls. Each operator and computer combination represents a unique station, and the sum of all such stations defines the operation. The work within an operation can be done in parallel, whereas operations follow a strict ordering. Figure 7-3 shows the sequential relationship among operations for a line.

Frame the Site

Identify what is meant by a "site." You can define one line as a site, multiple lines as a site, or an entire location (i.e., all the lines at a particular

Figure 7-3. Lines and Operations

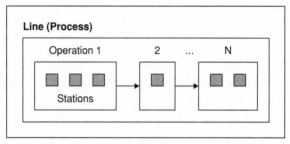

location), a division (i.e., one or more locations), or even a corporation as a site. The idea is to pick the unit of analysis that is most relevant for answering the operational question. This ties back to the management role and how different stakeholders often ask different, albeit related, operational questions.

It is necessary to frame the site only if you intend on doing financial calculations. Certain expenses, such as taxes or the cost of capital, are more likely to be reported at the site level than at the location or corporation level. Other expenses, such as indirect labor not directly associated with the process, can be captured here as well. For example, an engineer or a plant manager might not be linked to a specific line, so that person's costs are assigned at the site level. An appropriate parametric distribution would then charge the line for that person's cost.

There is no requirement that the line, operations, or site has to be located at a single physical location, which is why the framing of these entities is critical for addressing the business execution objectives. An entire division could be described as a site, which would enable site-level expenses to accumulate at a divisional level. In this instance, each plant could be defined as an operation, and each line in a plant could be defined as a station.

Let's say that you want to model a supply chain in ProFIT-MAP. You have three plants; each plant performs a specific task and then passes the partially completed work to the next plant, with a finished product emerging from the third plant. For example, there are many instances where materials are heat-treated or sintered (a process that hardens an alloy), using very expensive equipment. One plant may prepare the product and ship it to the central treatment site (which could be an external vendor) for heat treating, after which it is postprocessed at another plant, so the supply chain spans three sites. From a ProFIT-MAP standpoint, if a supplier is treated as part of the process, then the supplier's structural information and parameters can be included in the definition of a line.

ProFIT-MAP can also model this kind of supply-chain scenario for business services, depending on how the problem and the parameters are framed. In the insurance industry, for example, new policy processing can include an external auditor in the process. In this process model, the policy is sold by a salesperson at a retail outlet. The policy may then go through an internal audit at the corporate office, after which it goes to an auditor at an external agency, and then returns to the company for finalization of the sale. Collectively, this process can be defined as a single line in which each processing step is treated as an operation (or a component of an operation) and modeled as a single interdependent and dynamic product spanning two companies (the insurance company and the external auditing vendor) and three locations (retail, corporate, and external vendor).

Identify Representative Time Frame for Analysis

Each project contains an appropriate time frame for analysis. This time frame is used to demarcate the appropriate enterprise data for the given time period in order to address the objectives articulated in the profile. The time frame defines the smallest amount of time that represents the condition presented in the problem statement.

Analysis periods generally range from one or more days up to about a year, with longer-term options available. A strategic analysis might cover a six-month period, whereas an operational analysis might look at some aspect of weekly production. A manager looking at "seasonality" performance, for example, might look out over multiple weeks, depending on his or her perspective on what constitutes a season.

Use Existing Value/Process Maps

Framing the product, line, operation, site, and time frame of interest articulate critical process characteristics and culminate in the use of process or value-stream maps. If the organization already has process or value-stream maps, they can be used in this step. For some companies, these maps are available but need to be updated, while others will need to create them. Subsequent activities analyses cannot be conducted until the sequence of a process is clearly identified. That is, it is important to identify what comes before and after each step in the activities composition.

ASSEMBLE THE PROJECT TEAM

The project team assembly and site tour can be done in any order, but both have to be done before moving on to the "what-if?" plan. Both steps are important to minimize the potential reality gap from creeping into the ProFIT-MAP analysis.

Identify Data Owners

These depend on what ProFIT-MAP components are to be used. If, for instance, you are interested in process efficiency but not in financial performance, then financial data are not required for analysis, and you do not have to identify any financial data owners. On the other hand, if financial data are needed, then the CFO is an example of a potential data owner.

Identify Data Gatherers

Given the required data sources identified in the prior step, who will actually help the project team gain access to the data? Here, you identify the people who have the authority and means to access the data. The CFO might own the data, for example, but chances are that your project team will work with someone else who reports to the CFO to get the data.

TOUR THE SITE

The objective of this step is to validate that the way you have framed the problem on paper is firmly connected with the realities of the shop floor. You might be surprised by the number of things that are assumed to be true, yet turn out not to be the case when you step out on the shop floor and ask a few key questions. This is the first "ground truth" check.

Validate the Process Map

Compare what you find on the shop floor to how the problem was framed on paper. Identify any problems, such as omissions, misrepresentations, or information that is out of date. For example, you might see an operation on paper that does not exist in real life. It is possible that a process itself has been modified, but the process or value-stream map has not been updated. It is not uncommon to find disconnections between ERP systems and the real workings of the company. The goal is to identify any such problems up front so that they can be dealt with and don't come back to haunt you in the form of a reality gap.

Validate the Operations

A surprising thing can happen when you set foot on the shop floor. Operations can disappear, or you may find extra operations that do not exist on paper. In the former instance, operations don't really disappear; they may have always existed only on paper, or they might have been removed at some point for any of a number of reasons.

You can also observe important aspects of operation performance directly or talk to people on the floor to get valuable information. For example, an operation might be assumed to be working five days a week, but a simple scan around the site may reveal that a maintenance crew comes in once a week at a given time. The operation is not available during scheduled and unscheduled maintenance, both of which can have a profound impact on the performance dynamic of the line.

Validate Process Interconnections

Lines or processes are defined by connecting operations together in the proper order. Validating the process interconnections involves observing the actual flow of materials and information between operations and validating that handoffs are consistent with what is expected. You might discover some interesting things by observing the material and information handoffs between operations. For example, material might not flow directly between two operations, as described in a process or value-stream map. Closer inspection may reveal the presence of an extra activity that no one else previously saw or chose to recognize in the process or value-stream map. For example, an assembly operation might output a subassembly frame that the next bracket-mounting operation takes as its input, drilling several holes and attaching mounting brackets before passing the frame on to the next operation down the line. Walking around the line may reveal, however, that the subassembly is actually placed on a conveyor and rotated after the assembly operation to prepare it for processing at the bracket-mounting operation. The "conveyor and rotation" activities may also need to be included in the line description because they may have significant dynamic implications for the process, as these activities may experience downtime problems that can affect the productivity and costs of the entire line. The inclusion of such operations must relate back to the profile. For example, if you are studying detailed dynamics and their ramifications, then they must be included in the profile.

"WHAT-IF?" PLAN

Because of the iterative nature of the ProFIT-MAP methodology, it is possible to cycle among phases multiple times while constructing individual decision options (i.e., scenarios) as well as during the larger journey to build a complete business execution roadmap. To facilitate building a roadmap, we have added an input to this step directly from Phase 6, Choose Business Execution Option, to allow the practitioner to skip past the project-level detail collected earlier and proceed directly to building the next decision option. If you are returning to this step while building a roadmap, you can simply review the following items, updating them as appropriate.

Framework Assessment

Is the framework that has been identified up to this point capable of meeting the stated objectives? Has the problem been sufficiently defined and the fact that it actually exists validated, and are data available for answering the management questions? Given what the manager wants to accomplish, what data and information are missing? Some relevant data might exist, but might not have been identified. Other critical data might not exist. This assessment is important because it validates that the project is successfully synchronizing the corporate objectives, through the relevant drivers, to the parameters required to solve the particular opportunity or challenge.

Gap Assessment

This step identifies any gaps in the data or problems in framing the project, and describes the plan for overcoming these obstacles or limitations. For example, let's say that utility data are needed for a power-hungry line. However, the company does not have any relevant utilities data at the line level. In this instance, it might be possible to get this information from standard utilization rates provided by the vendor, and then do sensitivity analyses to see if these data have any impact. If they don't have any impact, then the utilities data could be dropped from further analysis.

Roadmap Planning and Alignment

This step involves articulating the management decision options that will be considered, and the order in which this will happen. A manufacturer or service provider, for instance, might wish to evaluate three alternatives: to continue production at a current site, to explore outsourcing to a local or rural vendor, or to consider offshoring production. We refer to each decision option as a *scenario*, and identifying the logical order for evaluating the scenarios helps to build a course of action for tackling the project objectives.

In another example, a manufacturer needs to plan for scaling up its business in order to satisfy anticipated demand. A reasonable first step might be to say that the manufacturer is going to make initial investments in a machining area and use manual labor to meet assembly requirements. Later, the company plans to make some capital investments in the assembly area to reduce labor costs and increase automation. Each of these instances is treated as a decision scenario, with a logical ordering of how they will be explored. Alternatively, the same company is forecasting demand growth at 15 percent per year for the next five years, but it doesn't want to make all of the capital investments today. In this instance, the company can create several scenarios representing different ideas for optimally staging the investments over time.

This step does not yet build the roadmap, but it outlines the planning necessary to ultimately arrive at the desired destination. The actual roadmap is identified in Phase 6. Once this item is completed, it is important to take a step back and recheck that the planning is in order to address the problem statement. This can be done by quickly verifying that the plan sufficiently addresses the seven dimensions of the business execution profile. If it doesn't, you should go back and update accordingly.

Roadmap planning and alignment is the last item in the first phase of the ProFIT-MAP methodology. Each step described in this chapter must be satisfied and checked off on the list prior to jumping into the next phase. At this point, you know what the problem is, but you do not know how it will be solved. You may be asking, for instance, what products are profitable, but you do not know their costs yet. Perhaps you want to reduce product costs by a certain percentage, but you do not know what needs to be done to get there. The decision options or scenarios that you identify lay out the collection of scenarios that will be evaluated to help answer your operational question(s).

As the first phase highlights, the ProFIT-MAP methodology is designed to provide the answers to questions that were previously lost in an operational "black hole," unable to escape the intense gravitational pull of operational complexity to see the light of day. How you apply this methodology is up to you. What's clear, though, is that practicing the discipline of business execution requires leadership and managerial expertise.

ProFIT-MAP
Phases 2 through 5:
Integrated Analysis

Beauty is in the eye of the beholder.

—Proverb

We don't see things as they are.
We see them as we are.

—Anaïs Nin

INTEGRATED ANALYSIS is central to the ProFIT-MAP
methodology (see Figure 8-1). Phases 2 through 4 build up the necessary
information to view the activities composition from three different perspectives—processes, resources, and finance. These are the execution
drivers that connect the business execution parameters to the objectives
of the strategy (see Figure 5-2). The "What-If?" phase then creates the
decision scenarios to be evaluated by management. Collectively, these
analysis phases create all of the information necessary to construct a
business execution roadmap, but they do not yet create the roadmap;
that is the outcome of the final phase, described in the next chapter.

START WITH WHAT YOU HAVE

At first glance, the ProFIT-MAP methodology may appear rather complicated. It can seem intimidating, but in actuality it is quite easy to use.

Figure 8-1. ProFIT-MAP's Analysis Phases

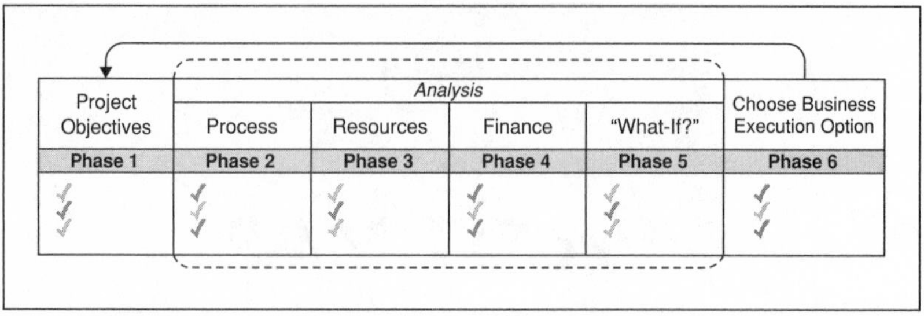

You defined and framed the project consistent with the corporate or business-unit strategy in the Project Objectives phase. Since you have already specified what you want, the next challenge is to select a starting point. One of the benefits of the ProFIT-MAP methodology is that it allows you to start with what you already have. The organization does not need to embark on yet another exhausting initiative to capture new sources of enterprise data.

In fact, you are more likely to have the opposite problem. Chances are that the organization is drowning in enterprise and operational data, but unfortunately does not have a methodology that enables it to fully leverage these data for management purposes—at least in terms of describing current and future capabilities, costs, and constraints. As you begin to explore decision options, ProFIT-MAP's parametric nature will quickly reveal whether you need additional or more refined data. Again, chances are that such data already exist in enterprise databases and simply need to be gathered from the appropriate sources.

The remainder of this chapter describes the four analysis phases. For each phase, we present an integrated flowchart and checklist that indicates the requisite steps and their order. In addition, we summarize the analysis goals, highlight the required parametric information, and discuss any special considerations for application of that phase to business services. Business execution is a complex phenomenon, and the last part of the chapter highlights software tools that can help automate the ProFIT-MAP approach.

PROFIT-MAP PHASE 2: PROCESS

The Process phase builds the foundation for the activities composition of the methodology (see Figure 8-2). Once generated, the activities

Figure 8-2. Phase 2: Process

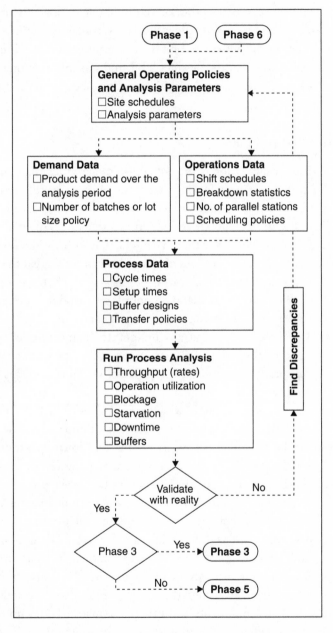

composition contains all the information about the process. The three management perspectives—process, resources, and finance—are the mechanisms for understanding the information contained in the process activities. That is, the activities component captures all of the information about the process at the product level, and this information is then cast into the particular management perspective that is of interest to the practitioner.

Activities Composition

The activities composition is the collection of activities that emanate from the actions of people and machines. The expected activities composition of a process that is to be executed in the future is integrally linked with managerial actions. It is a dynamic collection that undergoes change whenever there is any deviation from the previous operating parameters, regardless of how minor or how great the deviation may appear to management. In other words, when any operating parameter, such as demand, technology, product, design, or policies, undergoes any alteration, a new activities composition emerges. In fact, even without any deliberate changes in any of the operating parameters, the activities composition can change as a result of internal fluctuations in the process. We illustrate this point with an example.

A breakdown of a machine, which is an uncontrolled and natural phenomenon, creates a dynamic wave that has an impact on how other machines on the same line behave. If the broken-down operation is in the middle of the process, then it may starve the operations downstream or block the operations upstream, disrupting the entire process. Likewise, if a person who is critical to a business service or manufacturing process is absent from work, this can also disrupt the process. Such disruptions have resource and financial ramifications. Disruptions can occur for any number of reasons. The breakdown in transportation resulting from the terrorist attack on September 11, 2001, created a shutdown of processes all around the country, leading to enormous consequences. When components and other raw materials did not reach the factories, the activities composition changed dramatically. The cost and profitability of producing the products that were on the shop floor increased dramatically, as a result of production delays, ongoing costs, missed sales, and so on, although the prices did not. Other less traumatic events, such as a dock strike at a major port, can have similar consequences.

In short, the activities composition depends on the time interval of interest. It has four major components:

1. The start time and the duration of the interval
2. Product unit throughput (completed and rejected)
3. Amount of time spent by each workstation in each of various states (e.g., producing or not producing). A workstation can be in one of 11 potential states depending on the level of detail in the analysis
4. The work in process at the beginning and the end of the interval

Depending on the user's perspective—process, resources, or finance—the activities composition contains sufficient information to reconstruct the required view.

At the outset, the activities composition may seem like an innocuous list of information that can be easily generated. Many companies actually collect such information from their real processes in enterprise databases. Complexities arise, however, when you try to construct such information for the future based on the changes in various parameters. It is nearly impossible to incorporate such functional knowledge without the aid of specialized expert system–type software. If it is not properly created for this purpose, the expert system will have to be recreated for each decision scenario, which is an impossible task. An object model for such a system is very complex and requires functional expertise beyond IT skills to construct. Later in this chapter, we will show you how to build a system like this if you have the interest and competencies to build your own.

Process Analysis Workflow

The major work of the Process phase includes gathering information about general operating policies, demand, operations, and the process. Analyses are then conducted to quantify the process performance characteristics and to generate the activities composition. The demand parameter is central to ProFIT-MAP because the activities composition changes according to changes in product demand.

The validation step is a sanity check. Do the results make sense, given the realities of the shop floor? If the results don't pass this check, the methodology iterates back through the earlier steps to identify and correct the source of the discrepancy. This step relies on the experience of front-line managers to validate the results against the ground truth of operations. For example, if the station blockage and starvation dynamics do not match the way the station really works, then the parameters affecting the buffer dynamics or station failures are in question. A report or specification sheet might say that an operation can accomplish something, but if you know that's not right, you need to go back and adjust the operation's "signature" so that the parameters match reality.

If the process perspective is the only one that is of interest to the manager, then he or she can proceed directly to the "What-If?" phase and begin constructing the decision *scenarios*. This abbreviated route through the methodology applies if the business execution challenge is limited to exploring process characteristics (e.g., throughput or efficiency) without establishing their linkage to resource requirements (Phase 3) or cost considerations (Phase 4). Alternatively, the Process phase can branch to the Resources phase if these characteristics are important for management decision making. The Process phase cannot branch directly to the Finance phase (Phase 4) because the cost perspective is dependent on resource utilization. The remainder of this section provides a more detailed definition of the goals of the process analysis and required parametric information, and highlights some issues that are unique to business services.

Process Analysis Goals

The goals of the process analysis are to

- Construct the activities composition required to produce the demand in a dynamic environment. The activities composition should show the impact of downtime and nonlinear interactions between stations at an event level. An event includes the assignment of jobs to stations, station failures, quality inspection failures, and so on.
- Construct station utilization and work-in-process (WIP) buffer dynamics reports.

Parametric Information Required

Figure 8-2 gives the details of the individual parameters required. Here, we highlight some of the definitional and policy issues of this phase.

- *Line layout definition.* A line layout specifies which stations belong to the line and how they are organized into work centers.
- *Product routings.* These describe how the raw materials and information flow through the line to produce the finished product. This includes setup times and cycle times.
- *Product scheduling policies.* These may include scheduling rules, lot sizing, and real-time event handling.
- *Demand.* This describes the amounts and mix of products to be produced over the given duration.
- *General operating policies.* These provide the station, line, and site schedules and general policies, such as whether a given line is a flow line or a batch line.
- *Lot sizing policies.* What is the standard lot size for a particular product? If this is not a "pull" operation, then the lot size is defined by a policy; in a pull environment, the lot size may be defined by the demand.
- *Buffering policies.* This refers to the sizes of the buffers between stations and lot transfer policies that indicate how often units are transferred between stations and how many units are transferred at one time. In batch lines buffers would have infinite size.
- *Station failure information.* In analyzing future situations, this is the probability distribution of the frequency and duration of station failures. Whereas in validating the current or past performance this includes the actual occurrences.
- *Cycle time.* This is the time required to perform the tasks. Each task performed by a person and/or a machine has a service duration. The way you account for cycle time is critical for how the activities composition is created. Keep in mind that the overall cycle time actually contains lots of internal task durations that have a profound impact on the dynamics of the activities composition. Cycle time is not based on the machine run rate, but it depends on many factors such as product type; labor skill; loading, setup, breakdown, and unloading for each unit; and so on. It is the actual time

required to complete one complete cycle of all activities for a given product at a given station. It may depend on the individual station within the work center; all stations may not have identical capabilities. Cycle time can also be affected by quality considerations.

Implications for Business Services

The parametric information just described should be fairly intuitive if you come from a manufacturing background. The terminology may be a bit less familiar to those in a business services environment, but the process applies equally well to both contexts. The following items highlight the special considerations involved when the methodology is applied to a services environment; often, these issues reflect a lower level of complexity than for manufacturing.

- *Line layout.* There might be only one station that performs multiple tasks. It may not have a physical place that is called an operation. People can be viewed as a station, as they can get up to work at more than one location.
- *Lot sizes.* These generally default to a size of one for services because the service is provided one unit at a time. However, if an agent receives 20 audits at a time for processing, then the lot size is 20.
- *Failure statistics.* This refers to people taking breaks and includes both scheduled breaks (e.g., departmental meetings or training) and unscheduled breaks, such as if a computer server goes down, shutting down the service center.
- *Buffer designs.* These are in and out queues. A queue can build up for a person to handle. This might refer to the numbers of callers in a queue or a collection of audits piling up on an agent's desk for processing. A queue may be able to hold different types of work in various lot sizes.

We may not be accustomed to looking at a business service in the same context as a manufacturing line. However, the underlying mode of execution in both cases is via processes. With ProFIT-MAP's definition of a process as a collection of activities, services and manufacturing lines reflect similar behavior, which we illustrate with a call-center example.

In a call center, each call is a job, and jobs of the same type, such as "order tracking" or "technical support," are the product. A call center can therefore have multiple products. Let's say that a call center has 90 scripts, or caller scenarios, representing different routes that an agent could take to service a call. Each script could be treated as a product, or the scripts could be grouped into families and each family treated as a product. Every time a call comes in for a particular family, it becomes a job for that product. A job can be thought of as a repeatable quantity of the service entity, and jobs can be assigned to agents one or more at a time.

The next step is to proceed to Phase 3, Resources, or Phase 5, "What-If?" depending on the ProFIT-MAP components defined in the business execution profile in Phase 1. If the objective is only to improve throughput, then you can skip Phases 3 and 4 because you don't care about the resource requirements and finances. In this case, you proceed directly to the "what-if?" analysis in Phase 5 to create the decision options.

PROFIT-MAP PHASE 3: RESOURCES

The Resources phase identifies the resources required to execute the activities of the process. Because ProFIT-MAP is future-oriented, the resources are dependent on the activities composition of the work currently being executed or to be performed rather than the other way around. In comparison, enterprise resource planning systems ask what can be accomplished with the resources already on hand. This is an important capability, albeit for a different challenge.

The Resources phase follows the Process phase and includes capturing information about investments, labor, utilities, materials, supplies, and inventories (see Figure 8-3). The Resources steps are designed for flexibility so that you can start with whatever level of data you currently have in order to get a quick estimate of the expected resource requirements. You can then conduct a sensitivity analysis to decide what, if any, additional data to gather in order to meet your specificity requirements. ProFIT-MAP's parametric focus enables this iterative approach to cycling through the resource requirements.

Conceptually, the six categories of resources are relevant to any type of process. However, in practice, some of the categories may be more relevant to a particular business execution challenge than others. For example, capturing utilities, materials, supplies, and inventories data might not be

Figure 8-3. Phase 3: Resources

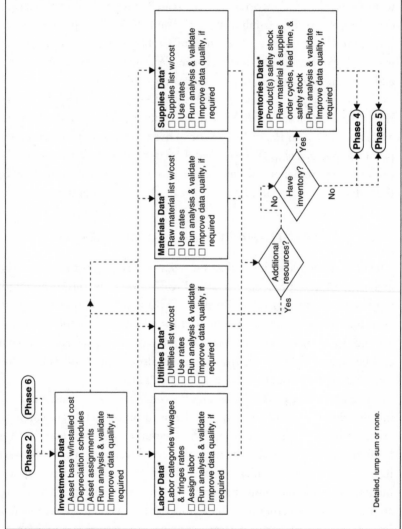

necessary for business services. For each category of resource, ProFIT-MAP requires either a detailed description at a station level or a lump-sum amount for the entire operation. Subsequent results will then be tied to the selected level of specificity. The practitioner can also elect not to provide data for a particular resource category. The ProFIT-MAP methodology simply makes this decision explicit, acknowledging a conscious choice to exclude the resource type.

We use a manufacturing example to illustrate the differential use of resources. A company is looking for a new supplier of material. This doesn't change the investment information one way or another. To conduct a competitive analysis between two suppliers simply requires a definition of the process, the materials, and the financials. In this instance, the only resource requirement was for materials. The particular resource profile one uses for any given project may not necessarily be clear-cut. For instance, the company might want to make a capital investment decision for purchasing a new station. Will the new station require a dedicated operator? The point is that the level of detail should match the manager's needs.

All of the Resources steps contain a validation component. This involves running the analysis for the particular step and then comparing the results to the realities of the shop floor. If the results raise a red flag, the manager needs to cycle through the step again to identify the source of the discrepancy and refine the inputs accordingly. After successfully iterating through this phase, the methodology then branches to the Finance phase (Phase 4) if required or directly to the "What-If?" phase (Phase 5) to create the decision options.

Resources Analysis Goals

The resources analysis goals are to match the resource requirements to the activities necessary to produce the product for the given management time frame of interest, ranging from now to any point in the future. The level of detail depends on your ability to capture and process the information in context with the activities composition developed in the previous phase.

Parametric Information Required

Figure 8-3 gives the detail for the individual parameters required. Here we highlight some of the definitional and policy issues of this phase.

- *Investments.* This is the collection of assets, such as process equipment, infrastructure equipment, buildings, and other assets.
- *Labor.* This is the shop floor direct labor, including process labor, materials handlers, schedulers, maintenance people, and so on. It doesn't include "front-office" people, such as plant managers, engineers, accounting clerks, and so on, who are not directly assigned to the line. These types of human resources are part of the SG&A in the Finance phase because their activities do not contribute to the product throughput. If such people are dedicated to specific processes, then their input must be captured here.
- *Utilities.* This is the collection of utilities sources, such as electricity, water, sewage, natural gas, and steam—but only if these data are available at the asset use rate level. Otherwise, annualized data can be used as a lump sum in overhead, similar to general plant heat and light. Knowing the activities composition from the process analysis, the goal is to find out the amount of utilities that will be required to produce the product.
- *Materials.* These are the materials that go into the product. They are also known as production goods or raw materials including subassemblies.
- *Supplies.* These are the supporting materials that are required for production but are not part of the finished product. They are also known as nonproduction goods or consumables. They can include anything from rags and gloves, to oil, cutting tools, and molds, to notepads and printer supplies.
- *Inventories.* These are the input or raw material inventories, inline inventories, WIP inventories, and finished goods inventories.

Implications for Business Services

Business services are generally less complex to model than manufacturing operations because the major focus is on labor, with little or no emphasis on utilities, materials, supplies, and inventories. These resource categories are nevertheless available should they be deemed appropriate for a business services challenge. In some cases, capital requirements can be significant. Our recommendation is to consider each item carefully before deciding on its merit. Your decision would also be contingent upon your software's ability to analyze the details.

PROFIT-MAP PHASE 4: FINANCE

The Finance phase creates the forward-looking cost and profit results based on the process throughput and the resources required to execute the activities composition of the process (see Figure 8-4). Accounting systems, in contrast, indicate what has already happened. Like the prior analysis phases, the Finance phase includes a validation component to

Figure 8-4. Phase 4: Finance

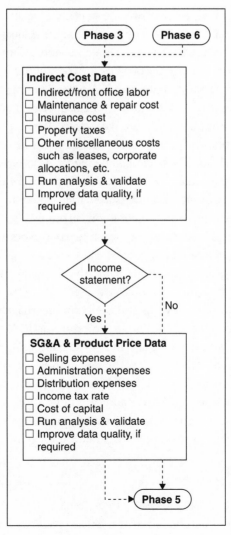

ensure that the results are consistent with the financial realities. An income statement is not necessary if you are looking only at costs, but it is required if profitability is important.

The objectives of this phase are dependent on your financial classification. Are you a cost center or a profit center? If you are a cost center, such as the information technology (IT) group, the human resources department, or a support center, you must balance costs against service levels and customer satisfaction. If your group generates revenue, then the goal is to maintain the optimal balance between profitability and customer satisfaction.

The dynamic tug-of-war between cost centers, profit centers, and customer satisfaction is being played out on the complex global stage of services and manufacturing *outsourcing*, and this will continue into the foreseeable future—at least according to the outsourcing cognoscenti. Let's explore how ProFIT-MAP applies to an outsourced IT service contract where an external vendor has taken over the entire IT management function for a company, with the exception of a few key internal management oversight positions. The company's goal is to minimize costs. The vendor's goal is to maximize profitability. These are competing interests, and the company's employees (i.e., the end customers) bear the brunt of the disconnection in the form of service quality that differs from their expectations.

ProFIT-MAP provides a common ground for managing outsourced contracts and facilitates both parties working together to rise above their competing interests for the common good of their customers and stakeholders. On one hand, the company can use ProFIT-MAP to communicate its service expectations more clearly and to highlight the specific activities and their timings that the vendor must meet. The customer can even model the vendor's profitability, if desired. This gives it a stronger hand at the bargaining table and helps it manage ongoing operations at the desired service, quality, and cost levels. On the other hand, the vendor can use ProFIT-MAP to identify and enhance its sources of profitability, and to allow it to understand how its specific activities tie directly into customer satisfaction. We would suggest that this is a win-win situation for both companies.

Finance Analysis Goals

The goal of the Finance phase is to aggregate the costs based on the activities distribution required to deliver the products. This is a product-wise collection for the line and then the site. It provides the total cost of producing the products or services, the line costs, and the site-level costs. This provides product-level cost and income statements. Without such information, it is not possible to identify which products are profitable and to what level within the considered product mix. In the "What-If?" phase, a sensitivity analysis can be developed to understand the impact of shifting market demands and trends.

Parametric Information Required

Figure 8-4 gives the details of the individual parameters required. In this section, we highlight some of the definitional and policy issues that arise in this phase. The distribution of these costs to the various products invites healthy debate. We take no sides in any such arguments, but embrace them all, with one exception: our perspective is that overhead costs cannot all be distributed judiciously based on one parameter or one rule. We therefore employ the concept of metadata, i.e., cost-specific parameters, to distribute overhead costs to individual products. For example, the cost of a loading dock cannot be properly assigned to products based on manufacturing time or production time when the products are distinctly different in size and weight. In such a situation, a similar argument can be made for the distribution costs. Products that are built under a long-term contract do not have similar selling and marketing costs to after-market products. Once again, your ability to create such differentiation depends upon your software and your analytical capabilities.

- *Indirect and front-office labor.* This is all support staff that is not directly assigned to the line.
- *Maintenance and repair costs.* These should be identified for the line and distributed to individual workstations.
- *Insurance costs.* These should be identified for the line and for individual workstations.
- *Selling and administration expenses.* If you have the appropriate metadata, you can distribute these costs to the product level, as discussed earlier.
- *Distribution expenses.* Distribution expenses must be distributed based on appropriate metadata parameters.

Implications for Business Services

In a services context, the cost of goods manufactured is equivalent to the cost of services provided at the product level. However, there may not be any distribution cost for services.

PROFIT-MAP PHASE 5: "WHAT-IF?"

The "What-If?" phase is the culmination of the Process, Resources, and/or Finance phases, in which the relevant data are gathered in order to generate an activities composition for the process at a product level. The purpose of this phase is to create the decision options that represent the scenarios that you wish to explore and quantify with ProFIT-MAP (see Figure 8-5). The candidate decision options have already been identified in Phase 1, where you specified the "what-if?" plan for investigating changes to the business execution parameters.

An advantage of the ProFIT-MAP approach is the ability to make apples-to-apples comparisons among different decision options, both within a given process and also among multiple processes. In an example of the latter situation, a senior manufacturing manager is responsible for three plants. The company is gearing up for a new product and plans to award it to one of the three sites. The manager could create a standard "base scenario" that specifies a common foundation at the same level of detail for all scenarios. For instance, the manager could frame the product, line, stations, and sites the same way and elect to skip a certain level of detail, such as utilities data.

Using the parametric capabilities, each of the three plant managers could then compete for the new product by creating a best-case decision scenario based on actual capabilities, constraints, and costs. The senior manager can then compare the various scenarios across the three sites to determine the optimal plant from a throughput, quality, and cost standpoint in which to place the new product. In this case, the specific variables to be examined are determined by the senior manager. ProFIT-MAP facilitates the decision-making process by providing a common level of analyses about expected future performance across all three sites.

"What-If?" Analysis Goals

The goal is to generate all of the scenarios that are necessary to test the various ideas for improving business execution. The structure and relevance

Figure 8-5. Phase 5: "What-If?"

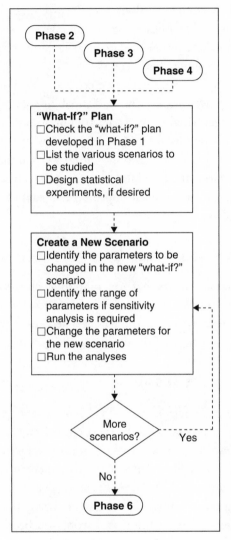

of the decision options are ultimately dependent on one's management insight, expertise, and wisdom, and specifically on how these attributes lead to developing timely and focused parametric scenarios. This is your opportunity to test and validate your ideas about how changes in business execution parameters affect business drivers and synchronize with the strategy.

We often hear from managers that they collect a lot of data, but that the quality of the data is questionable. We have seen databases that have negative cycle times, days with more than 24 hours, and, of course, a lot of omissions. Many companies don't keep records on utilities use, manufacturing supply use, and other such factors. We have also seen companies that do not have an up-to-date asset list. Our response to all of these issues is very simple: don't worry!

Based on our and their collective experience, we make initial guesses and then use the power of the "what-if?" capability of the ProFIT-MAP methodology to test whether such data are important enough to worry about. If large fluctuations in the data do not show any sensitivity in the execution objectives, then we ignore them. If we find that the sensitivity is sufficiently large, then we initiate a project to refine the data. This is truly the power of a parametric approach that cannot be matched by any other type of approach.

Parametric Information Required

This is the list of parameters that are going to be changed to create the various decision scenarios. Keep in mind that if you change the level of detail in one decision scenario, you will also need to change the related scenarios to the same level of detail to maintain parity among them.

Implications for Business Services

There are no special considerations for business services in this phase. Having said that, this is perhaps the most critical capability of ProFIT-MAP for services. Business services often do not follow a predefined sequence of operations. Data collection is also fragmented, since a large factor is human resources. This presents unique and specific challenges in implementing activities-based cost systems. Many practitioners suggest that managers estimate the cost distribution because there is no standard way of doing things.[1] We acknowledge such well-intended efforts because accounting has to have some data in order to finish the analysis. In our opinion, however, these are Band-Aids to get through the next cycle and do not help the company to advance its capabilities to do a better job in the future. We recommend using the "what-if?" capabilities along with properly identified metadata as parameters to evaluate the various different ways to do the job and then standardize on the best possible scenario based on whatever criterion the customer deems appropriate. We believe that our approach lends hope for escaping the purgatory of disarray and chaos.

TOOLS OF THE TRADE

The ProFIT-MAP Suite

In this section, we describe our ideal of an integrated software solution that complements the ProFIT-MAP methodology. It is not a trivial task to integrate all three of the management perspectives (i.e., process, resources, and finance) into a fully integrated suite. Over the years, however, we have amassed a great deal of experience and have seen the type of integration that is possible.

The ProFIT-MAP Suite integrates process simulation, resource utilization, and finance domain knowledge into an intuitive software package that provides companies with insight into their current and future capabilities, constraints, and costs. It is driven by the business needs of the organization, not by the constraints of any particular enterprise software package. Unlike MRP and ERP systems, the suite does not require the dimensions of business execution to be predefined. That is, the ProFIT-MAP Suite should automatically generate the underlying models from the functional knowledge captured in the data. The practitioner should not have to construct models, eliminating a great deal of manual effort required with other approaches.

The ProFIT-MAP Suite provides some important advantages that enable users to rapidly identify and then manage the specific set of actions and their sequencing for achieving the operational objectives set forth in their strategy. By way of a single integrated solution, the ProFIT-MAP Suite should

- Provide a common tool for use by strategic, tactical, and operational managers.
- Create the activities profile of the operational process at the product level.
- Maintain the connections between the process, resources, and finance management perspectives and the activities composition.
- Automatically update the activities profile based on changes in product demand.

- Enable apples-to-apples comparisons by enforcing a standard level of comparison among all of the management domains. The common unit of analysis can be changed as desired by management.
- Test the impact of changes to the business execution parameters according to the particular management time frame of interest, along a continuum from now to any point in the future.
- Support an iterative development of decision scenarios as desired by the manager.
- Facilitate development of the business execution roadmap.
- Enable the design of operational policies.
- Produce a variety of management outputs at the product level, including an income statement, measures of process efficiency and demand fulfillment effectiveness, resource requirements synchronized with demand, cost of goods manufactured or cost of service delivery, and profitability.
- Create an archive of the organizational knowledge developed at the strategic, tactical, and operational levels.

The ProFIT-MAP Suite should facilitate the business execution planning and management capabilities of the methodology. Next, we outline the type of functionality that must be integrated into one solution. We present a phase-by-phase description of the capabilities of the types of tools that must be applied to assist with the ProFIT-MAP methodology.

The most important requirement for any solution is that the software needs to fully integrate the capabilities underlying all three management perspectives. That is, the solution must enable complete forward and backward movement through the various components to support the iterative nature of the methodology. With the methodology, managers have the ability to branch within and between perspectives at any time, as dictated by the business requirements. The software must do this seamlessly between all modules, enabling apples-to-apples comparisons, as any "workarounds" are likely to introduce significant limitations into the system.

Process Tools Required for Phase 2

The Process phase requires four types of analytical capabilities. Each category of tool must be able to process and exchange the business execution data at the identical level of analysis to avoid creating apples-to-oranges comparisons between tools.

- Job creation
- Job dispatching
- Job scheduling
- Job execution

Resources Tools Required for Phase 3

The Resources phase captures a collection of items broadly defined as resources. Traditionally, resource analysis is generally done on a time basis. However, the ProFIT-MAP methodology's activity basis requires that it be done at an activities and product level.

- Investments
- Labor
- Materials
- Supplies
- Utilities
- Inventories

Capacity modeling tools such as those from MRP-II systems will not suffice for the ProFIT-MAP methodology because of their lack of a dynamic activities analysis capability. A key factor for success is incorporation of metadata in the analysis. Traditional SCM or MRP type tools that depend on steady-state approaches for resource requirements are grossly inadequate. We have seen managers who did not trust such tools for capacity analysis, so they wrote their own custom spreadsheets. Unfortunately, such spreadsheets suffer from the same dynamic activities analysis deficiency. Resource requirements that are not activities-based cannot be used with the ProFIT-MAP methodology.

Finance Tools Required for Phase 4

Indirect expenses that are not activities-dependent and have not previously been collected as direct costs need to be collected here. The analysis tool must be able to distribute cost to individual products based on the activities profile and the expense-appropriate metadata.

- Cost and profit

"What-If?" Tools Required for Phase 5

The "What-If?" phase involves modeling the process, resources, and finance management perspectives using all of the capabilities described earlier. It is critical that each module be capable of modeling the activities composition with the same depth as every other module. Moreover, all of the modules must connect together seamlessly and maintain synchronization to facilitate the rapid creation of decision scenarios as desired by management. It must be easy for managers to change parameters and recompute the entire decision scenario on demand.

You can think of this challenge as the equivalent of taking a generic business process modeling (BPM) tool and then integrating the domain knowledge of process simulation, resource utilization, and finance at the *product* level. This is no small challenge, to say the least. The linkages must be efficient and must support the iterative nature of management decision making.

An inherent limitation of using disparate systems is that the only way to integrate the results is sequentially in a cascading effect, with one system handing off to another. Unfortunately, such external handoffs operate by passing along aggregate data, which loses the depth and meaning of the underlying activities composition, compared to a systemically integrated approach. The old way of using spreadsheets and disparate tools is no longer adequate in today's interconnected and ever-changing business and operational environment.

MANAGEMENT BY PERSPECTIVE

The beauty of any particular management perspective is clearly in the eye of the stakeholder. Managers attend to perspectives in ways that are inextricably linked to their roles and interests. A corporate executive or a plant manager might be most interested in the financial perspective. An operational manager will have a great interest in the process perspective. Likewise, a resource manager will be most interested in the resources perspective. We don't mean to imply that managers have a one-dimensional interest in perspectives. In actuality, all perspectives are looking at the same underlying phenomenon of business execution, albeit by way of a particular filter that passes only the information that is of interest to the manager.

As we showed in this chapter, ProFIT-MAP analyzes the particular perspective that is of interest to the manager. Managers can choose to explore elements within one or more perspectives, and these elements can range from a subset of parameters within a perspective all the way up to the complete set of parameters for all perspectives. The point is that ProFIT-MAP provides a method for looking at the particular perspective(s) of interest to you, and all three perspectives are a part of the same phenomenon. You can even "walk a mile in another person's shoes" by looking at your challenge or opportunity from that person's perspective.

REFERENCES

1   Robert S. Kaplan and Steven R. Anderson, "Time-Driven Activity-Based Costing," *Harvard Business Review*, 82(11) (2004), pp. 131–38.

ProFIT-MAP Phase 6: Creating the Roadmap

Good is the enemy of great.

—Jim Collins, *Good to Great*

THE FINAL PHASE of the methodology, Choose Business Execution Option, is about selecting the best possible decision option for implementation out of the lineup of reality-driven decision alternatives, as well as building a fully aligned operational roadmap that will meet or exceed the expectations of the corporate or divisional strategy. This phase follows the "What-If?" phase, where the decision alternatives were first identified (see Figure 9-1).

PROFIT-MAP PHASE 6:
CHOOSE BUSINESS EXECUTION OPTION

The goal of this phase is to identify the best decision option, which we refer to as a *scenario*, for implementation (see Figure 9-2). For *implementation* projects, this represents the specific set of manufacturing or services actions required to achieve the business objectives. In its simplest form, this is a one-step roadmap. Building a more involved multiple-step roadmap involves cycling through the entire methodology as many times as necessary to construct the route to the operational destination. That is, each cycle through the methodology moves you one step forward and identifies a desired future operational state and the

Figure 9-1. ProFIT-MAP's Six Phases

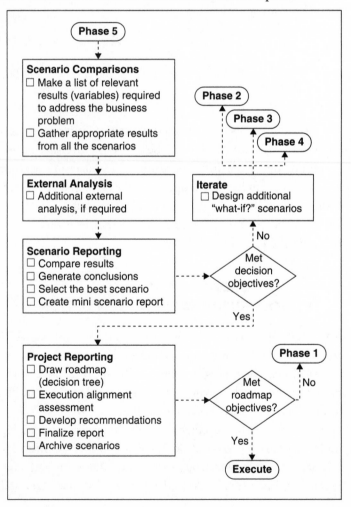

Figure 9-2. Phase 6: Choose Business Execution Option

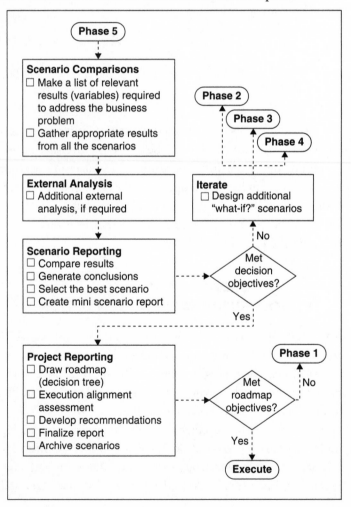

actions required to achieve that state. A roadmap is created by connecting together the successive operational destinations identified in each pass through the methodology.

In the case of *thought* projects, which are strategy development projects, the best decision option represents the particular strategy selected by the organization. Thought projects are then translated into action by converting them into *implementation* projects that are actually carried out on the shop floor. These projects are the tangible activities, where the execution occurs.

An important component of Phase 6 is a quality assurance function that ensures that the best scenario will meet the decision objectives of the project and, by association, the corporate strategy. While some decision alternatives may be good, we don't consider them to be great unless they meet or exceed the business objectives. Having a good strategy is important; successfully executing that strategy is even more important and more challenging to achieve—which is precisely where ProFIT-MAP fits into the picture.

ProFIT-MAP is always grounded in reality, including the way in which operational roadmaps are created and implemented. For example, as each step of the roadmap is implemented, each future state becomes the current state. ProFIT-MAP then uses the current-state information (which might include unforeseen changes in parameters—for instance, in demand, capabilities, or costs) to adjust the roadmap from that point forward. Thus, not only does ProFIT-MAP help create the roadmap, but it also can be used to adjust the roadmap on the fly—much as a GPS navigation system can suggest "smart" routing changes based on the conditions you encounter on the road.

Scenario Comparisons

This step involves creating a list of relevant results that will aid in decision making. You have already generated at least one scenario analysis, and possibly many, in the prior "What-If?" phase. The idea here is to collect the scenarios that meet or exceed your project's objectives or, if none of them do so, that come closest to those objectives. If, for example, you are making capital investment decisions and your company uses return on net assets (RONA) as a measurement, then you need to gather all of the relevant variables necessary to do a RONA comparison among the scenarios. If you have a nonfinancial objective, such as to reduce inventory, then you might pull out data for the average or maximum inventory, work in process, or whatever else is relevant, and then compare the scenarios. For an objective to increase line throughput, you would gather the key throughput findings, and so on.

External Analysis

There are some analyses, like economic value added, that have proprietary algorithms, and you must have a license to use them. Any such analyses therefore must be done outside or be integrated into your ProFIT-MAP Suite solution. In addition, when comparing any two scenarios, it is important to create a common basis if they involve different time periods. For example, Scenario 1 might examine a two-week period, while Scenario 2 might examine a six-week period. In this instance, you can bring the two scenarios together with a simple adjustment to create a common basis for comparison. You can also do additional statistical analyses. Let's say that you want to implement a preventive maintenance program, increasing station uptime to a desired level. An analysis could determine if the identified endpoint represents a statistically significant difference from the starting point. This is an example of a sensitivity analysis to determine in advance whether a proposed change would be worth doing.

Scenario Reporting

The goal for this step is to identify the specific decision option that best satisfies the decision objectives. You may or may not ultimately implement that particular business execution scenario, but that is a later management call. For example, a business execution thought project might use ProFIT-MAP to quantify the performance potential of several company acquisition candidates. After identifying the candidate with the greatest performance and profit potential, executive management may decide to postpone or cancel the acquisition as a result of external factors such as the economic forecast, in which case the project is not implemented. Alternatively, a plant manager might conduct a business execution implementation project to determine the optimal capital investments to make for a particular line to reach price and quality targets. After arriving at the optimal solution, executive management, in a separate action, may decide to realign company resources to another product line, leaving the plant with insufficient capital to make the desired changes. Alternatively, the plant manager's analysis may be so compelling to senior management that it decides to provide the necessary capital as a result of the demonstration of the rapid payback provided by the ProFIT-MAP methodology.

This step begins by *comparing* the results among the scenarios identified in the "What-If?" phase and formulating conclusions about the best decision option candidates for resolving the problem statement described in Phase 1. In comparing the scenario results, you will begin to *generate* conclusions about which scenarios stand out from the others in terms of their promise of a better future. After carefully examining the candidate scenarios, you then pick the *best* scenario of the lot in this step. If, for instance, five good decision options were identified, you then select the one that best satisfies the Project Objectives and create a *mini scenario report* to document the particular decision characteristics and create a management record of what was done.

Next comes a decision point, where you determine whether the best decision scenario actually satisfies the overall decision objectives. This is a reality check, where you take a step back and look at the big picture to make sure that the particular scenario would meet your performance requirements, should it be implemented.

If none of the scenarios meet the objectives, then you need to go back to the drawing board and come up with additional decision options to explore. Creating additional "what-if?" scenarios may take you back through the Process, Resources, and/or Finance phases to specify more decision options, depending on the specific needs of the project. Let's say, for example, that you have explored five decision alternatives for making some capital investments. However, while the scenarios might meet your process objectives, they did not meet your resource objectives. You decide to go back and make some changes in Phase 3 (Resources) of the methodology. You may want to explore changes in staffing or inventory policies, for example. In this instance, you do not have to return to the second phase because there are no process changes. Alternatively, you may have second thoughts about the process assumptions and go all the way back to Phase 2 (Process) to explore redesign ideas.

The process of generating the original "what-if?" decision scenarios and the capability to return to the analysis phases for further refinement illustrate ProFIT-MAP's iterative nature and how it enhances organizational learning and doing. You can easily step within and between phases as many times as necessary in order to arrive at the best possible decision option. You can also come back to the methodology and make adjustments based on what you encounter in the real world. After doing an extensive analysis, for instance, you could go back to the CEO and say that the strategy is not feasible within current organizational constraints and costs because of the lack of capabilities. "Look, we've rigorously explored these scenarios, and we still cannot do what you are asking us to do—you have a reality gap!" The flip side of this quandary is that you could go back to the CEO and say that your targets are not aggressive enough: "We can do better!" In both instances, you can then return to the methodology to explore the best possible next steps to take based on the CEO's guidance.

Project Reporting

Reporting is a fact of life for documenting and communicating the decision process and the desired outcomes. With a little foresight, reports can be integrated into an organization's way of life to facilitate knowledge sharing among all levels of management and to promote employee buy-in and support.

Draw the Business Execution Roadmap

The first activity is to draw the business execution *roadmap* representing the necessary actions that will take the organization from its current state to the desired future state selected by management. The roadmap is developed in the form of a decision tree. Figure 9-3 shows the sample execution roadmap that you have already seen in Chapter 6.

Each iteration through the ProFIT-MAP methodology is represented by one of the boxes. Let's take a closer look at the first box, starting at Time 1. The current state is shown on the left side of the box. To its immediate right are the three best scenarios or decision options that were analyzed and documented in the scenario reporting step. The lines connecting Time 1 to the three triangles represent three potential business execution

Figure 9-3. Creating a Business Execution Roadmap

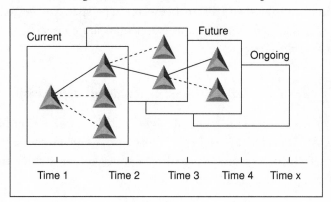

options, with the solid line representing the decision option ultimately chosen by management. In this simplest form, a roadmap describes a single-step pathway for achieving the project objectives.

Extending the roadmap further into the future, two additional scenarios were investigated in the second and third boxes (each containing two decision options), with the selected decisions again being highlighted with solid lines. Thus, the complete pathway to the desired future state that satisfies the project objectives requires three steps to achieve, as identified by the solid lines.

Once the roadmap has been implemented, the destination becomes the current state and the whole road-mapping process can begin anew, as highlighted by the Ongoing box. At this point, you can use the methodology to identify ongoing improvements, the equivalent of a single-step roadmap for each improvement. You can also refine and extend the roadmap further into the future as you make progress in implementing the original roadmap.

Execution Alignment Assessment

The ProFIT-MAP methodology is equally at home with strategy development and with managing strategy implementation. To ensure that decisions are synchronized with the strategy, we recommend that organizations create an "execution alignment" assessment that articulates a working definition of "alignment" that suits the organization's particular needs and priorities. From a strategic perspective, such a checklist ensures that the strategy meets certain achievability criteria—that it is not a pie-in-the-sky vision. From an execution perspective, the goal is to ensure that management decisions and actions are consistent with the objectives of the strategy.

Develop Recommendations (Based on Roadmap Objectives)

There are three general types of high-level decision outcomes of a ProFIT-MAP analysis. Based on a thorough and quantitative understanding of the organization's actual capabilities, its constraints, and the costs of the proposed roadmap, you can

- Conclude that the project can be done as specified.
- Conclude that the project can be done better.
- Conclude that the project can't be done within the organization's capabilities, costs, and constraints.

Each of these three high-level project outcomes can carry with it a certain amount of cultural, political, or other baggage in a company. Our purpose is not to examine such implications, but to provide the basic decision information to help managers make the best possible decisions about how to achieve desired performance and profit levels. "To execute or not?" then becomes the vital management question. ProFIT-MAP has played its role by outlining the necessary actions and the sequence in which to execute them in order to achieve the desired results. The follow-up question is, "To proactively manage business execution, or not?" as ProFIT-MAP can also be used to adjust and refine execution on an ongoing basis.

Given that businesses are always executing, managers may not have the luxury of having a fully developed roadmap in place. Some critical decisions may need to be made *now*! Perhaps a customer has dramatically increased a contract, or a critical and expensive piece of machinery has broken down. You need to know how best to quickly scale up production, or you may need to make a capital investment decision to replace the machine—or to explore alternatives for employing more labor in the short term while the current machine is being repaired.

The arrow returning to phase 1 in Figure 9-2 is there for when the current roadmap becomes obsolete, as a result of any of a number of internal or external events, or when critical or acute execution decisions need to be made in the short term before the fully developed roadmap is in place. In either instance, the manager can rapidly iterate through the ProFIT-MAP methodology to make the time-critical decisions, implement those decisions, and then incorporate the new "current-state" reality into the road-mapping process. That is, the manager uses the methodology to take action right now to realize immediate benefits, and then later adjusts the roadmap based on the new current realities. It is not atypical for managers to walk into an operational mess and have to take immediate action, yet not lose sight of the endgame. The ability to quickly navigate the trees while keeping your eyes on the forest is made possible by ProFIT-MAP's dynamic and iterative nature and its ability to tune the performance parameters based on real-world conditions.

In describing all the various possibilities with ProFIT-MAP, it may seem as if there are too many twists and turns that one has to navigate in order to reach a decision. In reality, the situation is nothing of the sort. So many options are present because there is one common methodology for many applications, ranging from strategic to operational, from thought to implementation. In practice, as you will see in the next chapter, describing case studies, the options become clear.

Finalize Report

Having a great roadmap is not of much use unless it can be communicated to those who will help execute it. It would be a bit like having a GPS navigation system in your car that computes the best route to the destination, but does not have any visual or audio output telling you how to find your way to the destination. A roadmap without a communication strategy is like the proverbial tree falling in a forest devoid of people. Does the tree make any sound if there is no one there to hear it? In a business execution context, we argue that nobody will hear it and it will have no organizational impact unless the findings are communicated through some type of reporting mechanism. This mechanism, however, must be aligned with other modes of communication within the company. Profit mapping must be a part of the organizational culture, not something extraneous. We recommend a central location, such as a portal, where anyone with appropriate authority can have access to this dynamic information. Proper communication is central to success.

Archive Scenarios

Archiving the "what-if?" scenarios to maintain a record of what was done and why is a best practice. This helps build an institutional knowledge base for the management thought processes, rationale, and outcomes. Leading organizations find a way to capitalize on this valuable repository, making vital decision-making information and knowledge available for current and future generations of managers. You can learn an awful lot from the past. History is a persistent teacher, although not a good guide.

THERE YOU HAVE IT!

We've laid out the ProFIT-MAP methodology in its full glory. The flowcharts and checklists show the requisite steps and their order, and highlight the iterative nature of the methodology. The ProFIT-MAP methodology

- Is a strategy-driven business execution management tool.
- Is easy to get started with because it leverages data that you already have.
- Complements and enhances your strategy, improvement methods, and measurement frameworks.
- Doesn't require the organization to change the way it does business, nor the way in which managers make decisions.

What clearly distinguishes the ProFIT-MAP methodology from other approaches is that it is the only one that is specifically designed from the ground up as an integrated and dynamic forward-looking management tool that helps you build the business execution roadmap based on your actual capabilities, costs, and constraints. You no longer need to rely on educated guesses and rules of thumb. It enables you to be successful before taking action, and it is ideal for refining and adjusting execution based on the realities of your internal operations and the external business environment. ProFIT-MAP is firmly anchored in the ground truth, and it facilitates synchronization between the sometimes competing priorities of strategic, tactical, and operational managers. The next chapter is intended to convince you of ProFIT-MAP's potential for solving your business execution challenges by presenting highly detailed examples of the ProFIT-MAP methodology in action.

Case Studies

Show me the money!

—Rod Tidwell in *Jerry McGuire*

If the facts don't fit the theory, change the facts.

—Albert Einstein

THERE ARE OVER 30 known applications of the ProFIT-MAP methodology (see Appendix). In this chapter, we present two highly detailed case studies. Both studies are either tactical or operational *implementation* projects. They represent decision options faced by operational managers. The cases are real, but the names of the companies have been changed to protect confidentiality. We highlight key details from the studies, balancing the need to maintain simplicity in presentation while preserving the overall spirit of each case. As you will see, the rationale, analyses, findings, recommendations, and management actions are highly sensitive and of competitive nature.

The first case examines a common dilemma of "doing no harm." That is, management actions, no matter how well intended, run the risk of harming the business, such as destroying profitability in this instance through a process "improvement" initiative. The second case illustrates ProFIT-MAP's potential to drive radical cost reductions without sacrificing quality or throughput. In this instance, ProFIT-MAP identified $500,000 in annual cost savings for a $7 million-per-year production contract.

CASE I: CONVERSION FROM A BATCH
TO A CONTINUOUS-FLOW LINE

The Company

Inmotion Manufacturing is a tier one automotive parts supplier with over $7 billion in annual revenue, serving the car, light truck, and commercial vehicle markets. Inmotion is recognized globally for the quality of its complete vehicle systems as well as its individual parts. Of the company's many manufacturing plants located around the world, the present case study examines the situation of a particular midwestern plant that supplies power train components to other plants globally. The case study represents a part of the plant that has about $25 million per year in revenues. It is an *implementation* project that sprang from a *thought* project with a larger scope.

With corporate backing, management invested heavily to upgrade shop floor processing technologies as a part of its new modernization initiative. The plant acquired new welding and metal-removing equipment to replace older and slower technologies that were experiencing quality concerns and an unacceptable amount of downtime (failures). The new technologies had the added benefit of lending flexibility to the new manufacturing process.

The new equipment was installed and the new operating procedures were validated, achieving their advertised throughput on a machine-by-machine basis. In the spirit of continuous improvement and the theory of constraints (TOC), plant management replaced several bottleneck steps with faster machines; the new machines produced at twice the rate of the previous ones, yielding lots of open capacity on certain equipment.

Despite the modernization efforts, management was nevertheless concerned because even with the new equipment, the plant still could not meet the rising demand. Quality concerns had also risen dramatically. With the older, slower equipment, operators had caught problems before a lot of work in process (WIP) accumulated. With the newer, faster machines, a lot of WIP had to be reworked because the machines produced at very high rates and the work moved downstream before the operators could catch any problems. The increase in reworking raised the overall cost of production and strained the available resources.

Inmotion's modernization plan included a corporatewide lean initiative, with this plant as the first implementation. The goal was to convert a power train component line from a batch operation to a continuous-flow line, and then apply the best practices and lessons learned to other facilities. We use the terms *batch* and *island* interchangeably in this case study to mean unrestricted processing of each operation until it runs out of work, independent of previous or following operations in the flow. The batch line was already profitable, and the goal was to reduce waste and increase profitability by converting to a continuous-flow operation.

The Problem

Inmotion had grown through mergers in recent years and now manufactured the same products at three different plants. The decision was made to consolidate production at the one plant that was deemed to have the best practices among the three sites. The plant was specifically identified for modernization, with additional investment made by the corporate office. Lean was one part of the initiative used to accomplish modernization. The line selected for the consolidated operation had recently been acquired from another company, and a significant equipment upgrade had been implemented two years prior to the acquisition at a cost of $350,000.

The current island design had very large amounts of WIP. The modus operandi was to keep machines running until they ran out of work, leading to racks and racks of output, with some buffers approaching 100 units at times. Fixing quality problems was also an expensive proposition because the large buffer inventories had to be reworked, unless an operator caught the problem early. Starvations also occurred frequently when the previous operation broke down or when there was an error in scheduling the predecessor jobs.

Management sought to reduce WIP and quality problems by converting to a continuous-flow line with limited buffers. A previous steady-state analysis—which assumed that there were no fluctuations in processing capabilities—had suggested that the flow redesign would meet the organization's objectives. The plant's executive team set a goal of 5 units maximum buffer at each station, based on the team's best judgment and lean principles. Although single piece flow is the preferred approach in lean, it however, does allow for having some buffers. Buffers do not have to be identical in size, but management wanted to standardize in order to simplify the conveyor design. The team was unsure if this was the best number for the line.

The buffer challenge was further complicated by the nature of the products. The line produced more than 250 SKUs in 24 different product families whose demand fluctuated on a daily basis. The product families dictated the processing requirements at the various stations, and the processing times were not the same for all products. The finished product was then fed to another plant (internal customer), where it was combined with other components in final assembly to form a kit supplied to an OEM.

The line had been converted to flow operation with a 5-unit buffer policy prior to implementing ProFIT-MAP. Two weeks into the redesign, it was clear that the new buffer policy wasn't working, leading to a loss of capacity and profitability over the batch design. The flow plan called for the elimination of buffer storage racks, with the 5-unit buffer residing on the conveyor between stations. Once the plan was implemented, differential station blockage and starvation dynamics yielded unpredictable line performance. The reality of the situation was that workers still maintained racks of WIP as buffers in an attempt to counter blockage and starvation problems among the stations—and capacity still dropped. Management needed to act quickly!

Phase 1: Project Objectives

Business Execution Profile

Table 10-1 shows the business execution profile for this *implementation* project.

Business Execution Profile Notes

Figure 10-1 shows the flow of material between stations. In the batch mode, the buffer size was infinite; in the flow design scenario, it was set to 5 units. In both situations, the process was divided into two parallel lines, with the lower line being reserved to process the larger-size product families that were also high-volume jobs in most situations. The two lines merged at the final assembly, and each line had its own set of support equipment.

Table 10-1. Business Execution Profile for Case 1

Dimension	Description
Roles and stakeholders	The *VP for plant modernization* was the champion for the project; he wanted to learn from this site and extend what had been learned to other sites.
	The *director of manufacturing*, the plant manager's boss, was responsible for the plant throughput and financials. He was also the customer because this plant was the feeder to another plant in his portfolio.
	The *plant manager* was responsible for the project, including on-time delivery, customer satisfaction, and financial performance. This was going to be a showcase site, and this was the first venture into modernization after the merger.
	The *engineering manager* was also the *operations manager* and had been brought in from outside the company to lead the modernization effort.
	Interested Parties
	The *senior process engineer* was responsible for implementing the modernization plan, with the engineering manager providing the oversight.
	The *materials manager* had to adapt the materials plan to the new operating plan.
	The *plant controller* was responsible for the return on investment and the profitability of the new plan.
Strategy	To assess the buffer dynamics and its impact on throughput and cost. To identify what additional capital, if any, would be required for conversion or additional design refinements.
Decision level	This was a tactical project because of the management time frame, and it had significant throughput and cost implications. It was also an operational project because of the buffer policy changes. In addition, the project had strategic implications, as it was the first foray into lean manufacturing. This was a showcase plant, and there were lessons to be learned and communicated as the company continued its modernization journey.
Assessment focus	*Reality gap:* The *business reality gap* is that the plant did not achieve the expected lean benefits from switching to a continuous-flow line. Decline in throughput required them to outsource so they could meet the demand.

(Continued)

Table 10-1. Business Execution Profile for Case 1 (*Continued*)

Dimension	Description
	The *technology reality gap* is the difference between what the steady-state analysis predicted and the real dynamics of the continuous-flow line.
	Multidimensional impact: The drop in throughput affected the customer and increased the unit cost. It also had a significant impact on cash flow as a result of significant changes in the WIP and the materials plan. This line produced multiple products with different processing times on the same stations—which had huge implications for the production scheduling for all products.
	Dynamic impact: The line dynamics caused the drop in throughput because the redesign failed to take into account the expression of the dynamic interactions. The factors dominating the dynamics changed frequently, so that the process never attained steady-state performance.
	Interaction impact: The dynamic fluctuations created extremely complex interactions, leading to blockages and starvations throughout the line.
	Financial impact: The loss of throughput converted a profitable line into an unprofitable one. Depending on the product mix on a given day, the unit costs of a given product could vary extensively. The outsourcing of products to make up the deficit in production added additional cost.
	Pathway: The goal was to develop a strong understanding of the dynamics and the various factors that control the dynamics in order to restore throughput and profitability.
ProFIT-MAP components	*Process:* This was the most important component in this scenario because of the dynamic assessment.
	Capital: An analysis of capital requirements was necessary only if a redesign was required.
	Resources: The materials requirement was directly related to the dynamics of the process. Labor and utilities would not be affected unless a redesign was considered.
	Inventory and WIP: The dynamics had a significant impact on these factors. The main goal was to reduce inventory and WIP.
	Finance: The objective was to recover financially, converting the current unprofitable operation back into a profitable one.

Table 10-1. Business Execution Profile for Case 1 (*Continued*)

Dimension	Description
Enterprise tools and data	Inmotion had an old MRP system, and the plant had devoted significant resources to update to a newer (different) MRP-II system and to clean the data. The cleaned data were used, and the plant was particularly good at maintaining data. The financials came from spreadsheets maintained by the controller. These spreadsheets enhanced the ERP financials.
Parameters	(1) Product demand. (2) Machine breakdown frequencies and time to repair. (3) Buffer sizes. If a redesign was necessary, more parameters would be explored: (4a) Additional capital, including where and how much. This would also include the first three sets of parameters. (4b) Additional resources that would be required (e.g., labor, capital, and utilities to a lesser extent).

Figure 10-1. Current Island-Type Process Flow

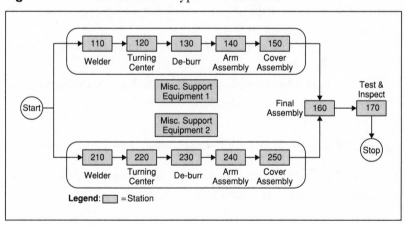

The machine processing rates and failure rates were dissimilar and depended on products, which created the need for the large buffers, and the dynamics were complicated. Some machines broke down more frequently than others. There were also some processing speed mismatches between the old and the new equipment. Stations 110, 210, 120, and 220 were new equipment.

"What-If?" Plan

The "what-if?" plan described the decision options to be quantified by ProFIT-MAP.

Challenges and Objectives

- To understand the dynamic interactions and their effects on total throughput and cost, including
  - The impact of the buffer sizes
  - The impact of product-to-station distribution—which products were processed at which machines
  - The role of preventive maintenance to reduce the breakdowns and time to repair

Approach

Analyses were conducted covering a four-week period to coincide with the corporate policy of filing financials on a monthly basis. Three studies were carried out to

- Understand the original profitable batch design, which served as the baseline model.
- Examine a range of fixed-size buffers to identify an acceptable compromise size.
- Redesign the flow line incorporating scheduling policy changes to restore performance to the desired level.

Analysis Phases (2, 3, and 4): Process, Resources, and Finance

ProFIT-MAP's three analysis phases—Process, Resources, and Finance—quantified the key management perspectives.

Batch Manufacturing Design Scenario

Figure 10-2 shows the station utilization for the original batch manufacturing design. This was the base scenario for comparison with subsequent management scenarios. The distance between the top of each *station* bar and the horizontal *available* line indicates the amount of time that the station was not utilized. Station 160 was potentially a bottleneck because it was using the most time to complete the processing of

Figure 10-2. Island Manufacturing Station Utilization

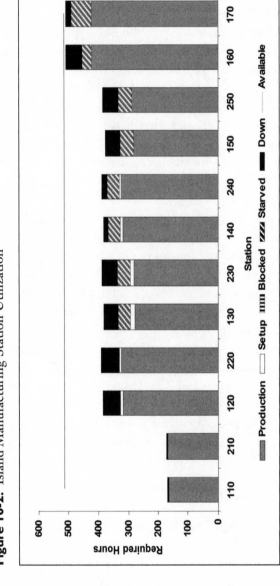

the required units. Although station 170 required roughly the same amount of processing time as station 160, it experienced more starvation time, thus pointing to station 160 as the cause. The line was already meeting capacity and profitability requirements, so management sought to improve performance by eliminating waste in the buffers.

Table 10-2 shows the island manufacturing costs. The line was fairly well optimized, as the majority of costs came from raw materials, which was better than the industry standard. That is, this line looked great on paper. The only real way to reduce costs at this point was to focus on reducing the cost of the raw materials, which was a different battle from redesigning the line. This was more of a product design and supply-chain issue. The plant could reduce material requirements though product redesign, change the inventory policies to reduce the holding cost of raw materials, or address the material costs directly in the supply chain.

Table 10-3 shows the pro forma income statement for the island design. The operating expenses were low, and the interest, which is the cost of holding the inventory, was also low. Reducing the raw material inventory would not necessarily increase the profits because the total amount was insignificant from a profitability perspective. This line provided assemblies for a finished goods line in the same facility, so there were no distribution costs.

If one views the batch design from a *process* or *resources* perspective, there seems to be an enormous opportunity for improvement by reducing the inventory levels and WIP. However, from the *financial* perspective, the extra costs of raw materials and WIP have a negligible impact on profitability. The only reason you would want to change the line at this point is if you view the challenge only from a *process* and/or *resources* perspective.

Phase 5: "What-If?"

The "What-If?" phase quantified the various decision options specified by management.

Flow Line with Operations Buffer Size of 25

A series of process analyses was conducted, starting with a buffer size of 5 and successively incrementing the buffer size upward to test the dynamics.

Table 10-2. Island Manufacturing Costs (Four-Week View)

Categories	Value	Percents
Raw material	$1,187,303	74.2%
Direct labor	$82,967	5.2%
Utilities	$27,708	1.7%
Overhead costs		
Site depreciation	$1,887	0.1%
Operation depreciation	$10,901	0.7%
Support depreciation	$570	0.0%
Supplies	$41,517	2.6%
Indirect labor	$201,340	12.6%
Maintenance and repair	$28,510	1.8%
Insurance	$2,742	0.2%
Property tax	$5,644	0.4%
Corporate allocation	$9,192	0.6%
Total overhead costs	$302,303	18.9%
Total manufacturing costs	$1,600,281	100.0%

Restricting the buffer size to 5 in the analysis confirmed the significant blockage experienced on the line. The throughput with a range of small buffer sizes was so heavily restricted that these were not feasible solutions to meet the customer's demand.

Figure 10-3 shows the representative dynamics for a buffer size of 25. The increased role of blockage, even with the larger buffer size, is clearly evident. This dynamic was not present with an unlimited buffer size in the island scenario.

Because there is no production during a blockage, one may be tempted to interpret the blockage as unused resource time, thereby not differentiating between this scenario and the previous one. The blockage time is more expensive than the unused production time, however, because all of the resources (e.g., labor and utilities) are still attached to the station, even though it is not in use.

Table 10-4 shows the increased direct labor costs ($107,815 versus $82,967) and utilities ($37,512 versus $27,708) that result because the operators are standing around waiting for the blockage to dissipate so

Table 10-3. Island Manufacturing Pro Forma Income Statement
(Four-Week View)

Categories	Value	Percents
Sales	$1,981,606	100.0%
Cost of goods sold		
Manufacturing cost	$1,600,281	80.8%
Distribution cost	$0	0.0%
Total	$1,600,281	80.8%
Gross profit	$381,325	19.2%
Operating expenses		
Selling expenses	$85,918	4.3%
General and administrative expenses	$50,788	2.6%
Total	$136,706	6.9%
Operating income	$244,619	12.3%
Interest to hold inventory	$6,821	0.3%
Income tax	$100,294	5.1%
Net income	$137,504	6.9%

that they can process more material. In the batch design, when the machines are not being used, they are shut down, and no labor is scheduled on them. In the flow design, the labor sits around idle, and the machines remain running. The trade-off between WIP in the batch design versus extra resouces such as labor and utilities in the flow design drives the cost difference. If the holding costs of the inventory and WIP could be reduced by $34,652, which represents the difference in labor ($24,848) and utilities ($9,804) costs, then this would be a profitable trade-off. Over the course of a 12-month period, the total additional labor and utilities costs for the flow design come out to about $450,476, and the line still fell below the production requirements.

Table 10-5 shows the pro forma income statement for the continuous-flow design. The interest holding costs of $5,508 are only $1,313 lower than the holding costs in the batch scenario. However, the profitability disappeared (–$9,439) compared to the positive net income in the batch scenario ($137,504). Over the course of a 12-month period,

Figure 10-3. Flow Line with Buffer Size of 25

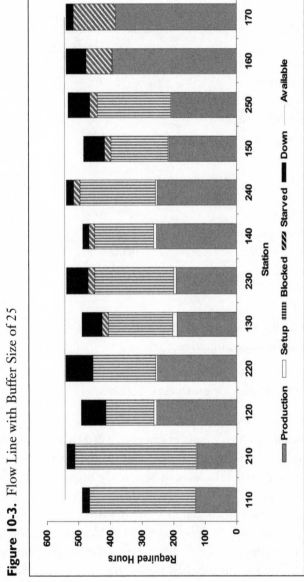

Table 10-4. Continuous-Flow Manufacturing Costs with Operation
Buffers Limited to 25

Categories	Value	Percents
Raw material	$906,915	64.1%
Direct labor	$107,815	7.6%
Utilities	$37,512	2.7%
Overhead costs		
Site depreciation	$1,972	0.1%
Operation depreciation	$11,394	0.8%
Support depreciation	$596	0.0%
Supplies	$42,180	3.0%
Indirect labor	$258,515	18.3%
Maintenance and repair	$29,799	2.1%
Insurance	$2,866	0.2%
Property tax	$5,899	0.4%
Corporate allocation	$9,607	0.7%
Total overhead costs	$362,828	25.6%
Total manufacturing costs	$1,415,070	100.0%

the batch design would yield a profit of $1,787,552 compared to a loss
of $122,707 for the continuous-flow design.

Full Throughput with Opportunistic Scheduling

The prior analyses showed that the blockage and starvation dynamics
were significant factors. Management concluded that it would be desirable to explore changing the flow design to reduce the impact of the
dynamics, bringing the throughput back to the original state, and reducing inventory and WIP.

Management surmised that merging the two lines that had identical
capabilities would soften the impact of the blockage dynamics. It was
decided to use "opportunistic" scheduling, meaning that jobs would be
assigned to stations immediately as stations became available. A buffer
size of 25 was used to facilitate comparison with the prior scenario. The
two lines were collapsed into cells for analysis, as shown in Figure 10-4.

Table 10-5. Continuous-Flow Pro Forma Income Statement with Operation Buffers Limited to 25

Categories	Value	Percents
Sales	$1,554,027	100.0%
Cost of goods sold		
Manufacturing cost	$1,415,070	91.1%
Distribution cost	$0	0.0%
Total	$1,415,070	91.1%
Gross profit	$138,957	8.9%
Operating expenses		
Selling expenses	$89,804	5.8%
General and administrative expenses	$53,084	3.4%
Total	$142,888	9.2%
Operating income	($3,931)	-0.3%
Interest to hold inventory	$5,508	0.4%
Income tax	$0	0.0%
Net income	($9,439)	-0.6%

Figure 10-4. Full Throughput with Opportunistic Scheduling

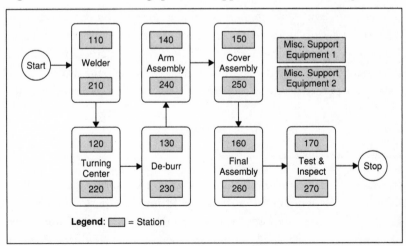

Legend: ☐ = Station

This would be easy to implement because the stations were already next to each other, so a physical move was not required. This was basically an operating policy change. The complete conversion to a fully cell-based approach also required the addition of redundant stations in Final Assembly and Test and Inspect. The cost for station 260 was $400,000, and that for station 270 was $42,000; both were factored into the analysis.

Figure 10-5 shows the station dynamics, with each "operation" being made up of two stations and work being automatically routed to the next available station for each operation. This scenario also resulted in significant line blockage throughout the various operations. The distance between each *operation* bar and the horizontal *available* line indicates some available capacity. Stations 160 and 170 were the trouble spots in the prior analysis. However, now that they are paired with the new stations, there is some flexibility or excess capacity in this scenario.

Table 10-6 shows that the total costs for this scenario are higher than those for the island design with infinite-size buffers ($1,775,833 versus $1,600,281). The direct labor cost rose because two additional people were required to run the new stations. The indirect labor cost rose because of the addition of a supervisor.

The pro forma income statement presented in Table 10-7 shows this scenario to be profitable ($27,966), but not nearly as profitable as the original island scenario ($137,504). Thus, although the opportunistic scheduling redesign was able to provide the same throughput, it was not able to recover the original profitability.

Table 10-8 presents an annualized summary of the three scenarios. The island design had a 6.9 percent profitability rate over the course of 12 months. Limiting the buffers to 25 destroyed the line's profitability (–0.6 percent). Although the final scenario met demand and was profitable (1.4 percent), it was substantially less profitable than the original design.

General Conclusions

In theory, it is reasonable to expect that conversion to a continuous-flow line with limited-size buffers would improve performance. The fact that the conversion was unsuccessful demonstrates the importance of viewing the problem from multiple perspectives. If the problem is

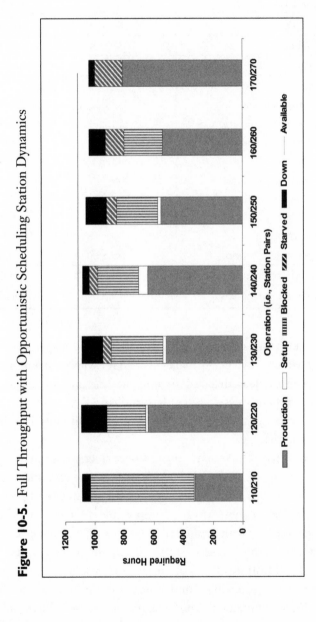

Figure 10-5. Full Throughput with Opportunistic Scheduling Station Dynamics

Table 10-6. Costs for Full Throughput with Opportunistic Scheduling

Categories	Value	Percents
Raw material	$1,187,303	66.9%
Direct labor	$133,654	7.5%
Utilities	$39,936	2.2%
Overhead costs		
Site depreciation	$2,022	0.1%
Operation depreciation	$14,754	0.8%
Support depreciation	$611	0.0%
Supplies	$42,496	2.4%
Indirect labor	$304,730	17.2%
Maintenance and repair	$30,546	1.7%
Insurance	$2,938	0.2%
Property tax	$6,994	0.4%
Corporate allocation	$9,848	0.6%
Total overhead costs	$414,939	23.4%
Total manufacturing costs	$1,775,833	100.0%

viewed solely from a *process* perspective, experience suggests that reducing WIP will improve performance. When it is viewed from the *resource* perspective, it's clear that redesigning the line and adding additional capital equipment doesn't solve the problem. The *finance* perspective closes the loop by showing the cost and profitability implications of all decision options.

The original steady-state analysis incorrectly assumed nontrivial variability in the line dynamics, which was not the case and resulted in decreased capacity. In addition, the lack of an integrated *finance* perspective in the analysis made it impossible to connect changes in process parameters with profitability. From a finance perspective, WIP is not "waste" in this instance because it actually reduces costs.

This case illustrates the types of decision trade-offs that managers face every day. If reducing a buffer size, for example, can be shown to improve throughput, then it might be reasonable to make the additional capital investment required to counterbalance the lower WIP policy, assuming that the change leads to a desired financial outcome. There are no hard and fast rules on how to make these types of decisions. The

Table 10-7. Full Throughput with Opportunistic Scheduling Pro Forma Income Statement

Categories	Value	Percents
Sales	$1,981,606	100.0%
Cost of goods sold		
Manufacturing cost	$1,775,833	89.6%
Distribution cost	$0	0.0%
Total	$1,775,833	89.6%
Gross profit	$205,773	10.4%
Operating expenses		
Selling expenses	$92,056	4.6%
General and administrative expenses	$54,416	2.7%
Total	$146,472	7.4%
Operating income	$59,301	3.0%
Interest to hold inventory	$7,022	0.4%
Income tax	$24,313	1.2%
Net income	$27,966	1.4%

Table 10-8. Annualized Summary of Scenarios

Categories	(1) Island Design		(2) Buffers = 25		(3) Opportunistic Scheduling	
Revenue	$25,760,878	100.0%	$20,202,351	100.0%	$25,760,878	100.0%
COGM	$20,803,653	80.8%	$18,395,910	91.1%	$23,085,829	89.6%
Net income	$1,787,552	6.9%	($122,707)	-0.6%	$363,558	1.4%

rationale will always be unique to the company and can vary over time depending on a multitude of factors, such as changes in strategy, customer requirements, supply-chain issues, and so on. Viewing the problem from multiple integrated perspectives provides insight that helps managers navigate their options and increase their confidence that they are taking the right actions.

Recommendations

- Return to the original batch line design, which the plant did. The original design had been refined over several years and was clearly very effective—when viewed through ProFIT-MAP. In practice, the batch design was more effective because of the dissimilar breakdown frequencies and time to recover, and dissimilar processing times for the various products.
- Invest in standardizing the work across the 24 product lines to smooth out the dynamics and improve profitability. The problem was not with the lean principles, but with their implementation. The standardization should be done on the processing design, not the buffer design. Lean calls for minimal buffers and the standardization of the tasks within processes.
- Investigate further refinement of the buffer designs. Even with the batch design, is it possible to deploy nonstandard-size buffers across station and product lines? Management unnecessarily constrained potential solutions by insisting on all buffers being the same size. The managers previously did not have a tool capable of dynamic analysis, but they recognized the need for large buffers, as they could see the dynamic effects on the shop floor. The idea is to customize the buffers for individual products and adjust them according to product demand.
- Improve the preventive maintenance practices for the older machines to improve their reliability in order to soften the transient effects on the line. The stations experience dissimilar breakdown frequencies because of the varying ages of the equipment, and the older machines break down more frequently.

Postscript

This project invigorated the company's lean initiative. It gave it a new way to execute lean. It showed the company how and where to implement lean manufacturing properly, avoiding poor implementation of lean principles. Interestingly, when the batch to continuous-flow conversion was stopped by management two weeks into the switch, operational philosophies went out the window as managers desperately searched for anything that would resolve the crisis. ProFIT-MAP quickly identified the root cause of the problem, and the solution reinforced the lean initiative by replacing rules-of-thumb application of lean principles with a systematic approach.

If Inmotion had implemented ProFIT-MAP prior to making the change to a lean flow, it would have quickly realized that the conversion would impair performance. Most importantly, it would have given Inmotion the confidence that a decision not to make the suggested change was the right decision. It can be difficult to make such a seemingly contrarian decision without the necessary facts.

The project was so successful that the company used ProFIT-MAP to shape the division's strategy. It was specifically used for plant rationalization, product rationalization, and moving equipment among plants.

CASE 2: PRODUCTION DOES NOT MEET DEMAND

The Company

Agile Manufacturing Industries is a tier one automotive supplier with revenues in excess of $4 billion. It makes vehicle interiors, lighting systems, bumpers, and other such components, using predominantly plastics, other synthetics, and fabrics for its parts. The plant at the center of the current case had $350 million in annual revenue and employed about 1,200 people. The specific line described here represented about $7 million per year in business. The new plant manager had been put in place less than six months earlier to implement lean manufacturing.

The Problem

Agile Manufacturing had an exclusive contract for an automotive tail-light. The target for sustainable production was 87 units per hour, but the actual production was 68 to 76 units per hour. The customer had decided to exercise a 15 percent over plan contractual obligation of 95 units per hour. The company was given two months to achieve the 95-unit production level.

The line was designed on lean principles, with one-piece flow in the final assembly and minimal WIP elsewhere. Andon lights controlled material and information flow, and the factory data information system kept records of all activities. The labor was cross trained, and switch-out policies ensured labor alertness without fatigue. The line operated three eight-hour shifts per day six days a week, and sometimes operated on Sunday to meet the weekly demand. The customer originally approved the line for three eight-hour shifts for five days a week after doing some onsite audits clocking cycle times that could produce throughput of 100 units per hour. This line was a part of the plant's lean manufacturing initiative and had won several awards. The plant was QS-9000 compliant.

The plant management team disagreed about the root cause of this problem. Three previous studies exploring how to improve throughput had produced conflicting results. The plant manager ordered a redundant welding station for about $400,000 on the advice of the engineering manager, based on the findings from one of the studies. This action was taken prior to implementing the ProFIT-MAP methodology, but the new station had not yet been delivered. There was some debate among management regarding whether to approach the problem as a *thought* project to explore the root cause, or to conduct an *implementation* project to fix the problem immediately. Each stakeholder viewed the project from his or her own perspective without achieving consensus.

Phase 1: Project Objectives

Business Execution Profile

Table 10-9 shows the business execution profile for this *implementation* project.

Business Execution Profile Notes

The previous three studies had been done using steady-state throughput analysis techniques with a finite-capacity algorithm based on the theory of constraints. These studies were long and expensive because they had significant data collection requirements, and each study collected its own data set. Each consulting team used its own method of data collection and did not use the existing enterprise systems.

Each of the three studies found different causes for the problem, and did not reach consensus on the identity of the bottleneck operation. All three studies nevertheless showed that reducing cycle time at the perceived bottleneck operation would increase the throughput. Imple-

Table 10-9. Business Execution Profile for Case 2

Dimension	Description
Roles and stakeholders	The *plant manager* was responsible for the project, including on-time delivery, customer satisfaction, and financial performance. He was new and his predecessor had commissioned the three previous studies, none of which had solved the problem.
	The *engineering manager* was responsible for throughput performance and line structure. He believed that the line was capable of performing at the design capacity, but that labor was being uncooperative and not performing to the required *takt* time.
	The *operations manager* was responsible for on-time delivery. She believed that labor was performing at its best and could not work at a sustainable faster pace. She believed that there was a structural problem with the line.
	Interested Parties
	The *materials manager* was responsible for the supply chain and was unable to manage materials inventory because of erratic line performance.
	The *line supervisor* was responsible for quality and performance. He was totally puzzled about why his team could not produce at the rate required when spot-checking had "shown" that it was possible.
Strategy	The project needed to develop a clear understanding of the line capabilities, constraints, and costs. From previous studies, it was evident that steady-state capacity analysis was not adequate. Therefore, a dynamic analysis to uncover the root cause of the problem was imperative.
Decision level	This was a tactical project that had direct implications for customer satisfaction and profitability. If the management could not solve the problem, then the customer had the contractual right to pull the business.
Assessment focus	*Reality gap:* The *business reality gap* was that the company had been meeting the demand by working weekends, which was not part of the design but was approved by the customer to satisfy the 15 percent over plan clause. There was no more time left in the week, however, to satisfy the over plan clause. If the company didn't meet the 95-unit-per-hour demand, it was going to lose the contract.
	The *technology reality gap* was that all of the prior studies to solve the problem had been done with steady-state throughput analysis using theory of constraints principles. The breakdown frequencies of the equipment

(Continued)

Table 10-9. Business Execution Profile for Case 2 (*Continued*)

Dimension	Description
Assessment focus (*cont.*)	were dissimilar, creating nonlinear dynamics in through put. There was no single operation that controlled the throughput *viz* a bottleneck, which violated the applicability of theory of constraints for solving the problem. The project needed to extend the best practices of a steady-state approach to a dynamic perspective.
	Multidimensional impact: Interactions among the various workstations controlled the process output. How did the equipment failure affect the throughput, the resources requirements, and the costs?
	Dynamic impact: The engineering manager wanted to reduce the cycle time of the final assembly line. Was this sustainable? How would the new dynamics of dissimilar machine failure rates and faster cycle times affect the throughput dynamics and therefore costs?
	Interaction impact: The interaction among various stations controlled the process throughput and therefore the resource requirements and financials. How would the inventory management be affected by the changed dynamics? Was one-piece flow viable?
	Financial impact: The plant manager was paying for the weekend labor and its overtime without being compensated by the customer. If, however, the company was using the weekend to perform the over plan requirements, it would be appropriately compensated by the customer as agreed in the contract.
	Pathway: The goals were (1) to understand the dynamics and their impact on the resources and financials, and (2) to identify the specific modifications to the line needed to smooth out production to meet the throughput and financial objectives.
ProFIT-MAP components	*Process:* The objectives were to (1) document the dynamics of the current situation, (2) identify where the steady-state analysis was inadequate, and (3) identify the opportunities to redesign the line to meet the throughput objectives.
	Capital: Did the line require additional capital investments for redesign? How would additional investments affect the final product cost?
	Resources: Was it a labor opposition problem? Did the line modifications require any additional labor or other resources?
	Inventory and WIP: What would be the impact on the materials inventory and WIP?

Table 10-9. Business Execution Profile for Case 2 (*Continued*)

Dimension	Description
	Finance: What was the financial burden of not meeting the design capacity? What would be the cost of goods manufactured for the redesigned line?
Enterprise tools and data	The line design and cycle-time data were available in the MRP-II system. The actual production data were available in the plant floor data collection system. The materials manager had the data for materials and supplies in the inventory management system. The accounting department had the required financial information.
Parameters	(1) Station cycle time: The engineering manager wanted to shorten the cycle time at each station in the final assembly.
	(2) Redundant capacity: The engineering manager had already added (ordered but not implemented) redundancy in the welding operation to smooth out breakdown dynamics.
	(3) Demand: The plant manager wanted to increase demand by 15 percent to reflect the over plan requirement.
	(4) Final assembly flow: A redesign of the flow through final assembly was suggested.

menting the recommendations did not produce the expected results. However, it did put greater pressure on labor, thereby increasing fatigue and injury rates, which required a change in HR policy to implement labor switch-outs more frequently. Absenteeism also rose as the flow moved closer to one-piece.

Figure 10-6 shows the process flow diagram with cycle times and buffer capacities. The buffer capacity on the figure indicates the total rack size or capability, not the number of units in the buffer. The welding station is believed to fail more frequently than other stations in the line.

"What-If?" Plan

Challenges and Objectives

- Identify the cause of the production shortfall.
- Evaluate possible solutions to resolve the production shortfall.

Figure 10-6. Process Flow Diagram

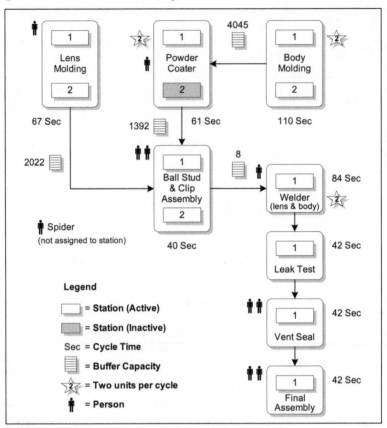

Approach

- Conduct the analyses spanning a four-week period to be consistent with corporate reporting practices.
- Study the effect of assembly cycle time on throughput, including why the original design did not meet the performance requirement. The line was currently producing a maximum of 76 units per hour. Validate the ProFIT-MAP financial analysis with current operations.
- Add the redundant capacity in the planned welding station to study its impact on throughput and financials.
- If the redundant capacity does not solve the problem, consider redesigning the flow through final assembly.
- Study the 15 percent over plan requirement with and without the redundant capacity.

Analysis Phases (2, 3, and 4): Process, Resources, and Finance

Impact of Final Assembly Cycle Time on Throughput

The dynamic analysis conducted using the ProFIT-MAP Suite showed that no improvement in throughput was possible by reducing the cycle time at the final assembly stations. The dynamic interactions among the various stations prevented any enhancement in the throughput. The line was near saturation capacity, and further reduction in cycle time had a diminishing rise in throughput. The current state, shown in Figure 10-7, is the 42-second assembly cycle time column (second from right).

Unlike the previous studies, ProFIT-MAP did not require the initiation of yet another data collection exercise. The data came from the MRP-II and enterprise data collection systems. The line was running on a one-piece flow with a *takt* time of 42 seconds. ProFIT-MAP found the upper end of the actual throughput with the 42-second cycle time. Thus, the ProFIT-MAP model was validated as required by the methodology. Either the effective average cycle time was longer than 42 seconds or there was some inconsistency in another aspect of the line, such as machine failures, time logging, and so on.

Table 10-10 shows the activities performed at each operation over a four-week period of analysis. According to the data, the Welder seems to be controlling the dynamics of the downstream processes, as suspected by the engineering manager. The significant Ball Stud & Clip blockage (304.75 hours) before the welding station led management to believe that the Welder was the source of the bottleneck. However, the process starting from the Welder and moving through Final Assembly was set up as a one-piece flow, so that these four operations collectively were behaving as one entity.

The steady-state analyses, which assumed no interactions among the stations, indicated that increasing the throughput at the bottleneck would solve the problem. Unfortunately, the blockage and starvation dynamics associated with the one-piece flow overwhelmed the assumptions. A steady-state analysis took the total available hours and deducted the failure time. The rest of the time was supposedly available, but the analysis (1) did not consider the time lost because of starvation and blockage, and (2) did not know the number of times the line went down nor the duration of the downtime. The steady-state analysis assumed that a failure at any station did not affect operations at another station.

Figure 10-7. Assembly Cycle Time

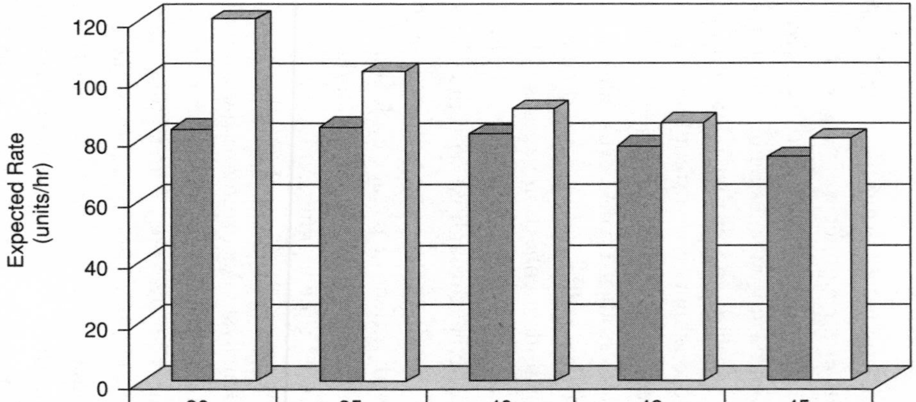

Assembly Cycle Time(sec)	30	35	40	42	45
■ ProFIT-MAP (Dynamic)	84	84	82	78	74
□ Aggregation (Steady-State)	120	103	90	86	80

Expected Rate (units/hr)

Table 10-10. Operations Activity Times (in Hours)

Operation	Available	No Job	All Ops.	Production	Setup	Blocked	Starved	Failure
Final Assembly	464.30	2.99	461.31	403.53	0.00	0.00	32.72	25.06
Vent Seal	464.30	2.99	461.31	404.61	0.00	23.26	33.45	0.00
Leak Test	464.30	3.00	461.30	404.63	0.00	22.82	23.95	9.90
Welder	464.30	3.01	461.30	404.66	0.00	31.02	3.16	22.46
Ball Stud & Clip	928.61	235.04	693.57	384.31	0.00	304.75	0.00	4.52
Lens Molding	928.61	285.57	643.04	643.04	0.00	0.00	0.00	0.00
Powder Coater	464.30	143.13	321.17	320.93	0.00	0.00	0.00	0.25
Body Molding	928.61	402.47	526.14	526.14	0.00	0.00	0.00	0.00

If there were buffers in the middle of the process, this might not be a problem, but small to no buffers interact problematically with the station dynamics. The dynamics overwhelmed the flow thereby reducing the effective throughput.

Final Assembly had the highest *failure* time, and it was comparable to the Welder *failure* time. When viewed from the end of the process moving upstream, we see that the Welder was *blocked* (31 hours) for a longer time period than the Final Assembly *failure* time (25 hours). This suggests that the Welder was not the bottleneck, as had been suspected. Rather, the problem was in the dynamics of the flow collectively from the Welder through Final Assembly.

Table 10-11 shows the WIP dynamics for the line. The *average queue* for every operation from the Welder downstream was the same. All of these operations were behaving collectively as one unit. Therefore, adding the redundant Welder capacity was unlikely to solve the problem.

Final Assembly was not viewed as the bottleneck because it was *starved* for work, whereas the Welder was not. That is, the Welder was perceived to be the bottleneck. However, the one-piece flow from the Welder to Final Assembly was collectively the bottleneck in the line. This line was an award-winning lean implementation, so reconsidering the one-piece flow was not considered an option.

Table 10-12 shows the cost of goods manufactured for the line. When the line was operated at the designed policy—the five-day operation—it produced 34,410 units over a four-week period, which was not

Table 10-11. Work-in-Process Dynamics (Output Queue)

Operation	Average Queue	Maximum Queue	Maximum Buffer Size
Body Molding	0.94	100	4,045
Powder Coater	30.83	100	1,392
Lens Molding	31.13	100	2,022
Ball Stud & Clip	0.05	3	1
Welder	0.02	2	1
Leak Test	0.02	2	1
Vent Seal	0.02	2	1
Final Assembly	1.04	100	(unlimited)

Table 10-12. Cost of Goods Manufactured (Four-Week Period)

Categories	Value	Value	Percents
Raw materials		$201,532	39.0%
Direct labor		$74,187	14.4%
Utilities		$18,871	3.7%
Overhead cost			
Facility depreciation	$444		0.1%
Work center depreciation	$10,718		2.1%
Support equipment depreciation	$229		0.0%
Manufacturing supplies	$10,077		2.0%
Maintenance and repair	$35,632		6.9%
Insurance	$3,563		0.7%
Property tax	$3,316		0.6%
700T Van Dorn Press 1 lease	$4,876		0.9%
700T Van Dorn Press 2 lease	$4,876		0.9%
275T Van Dorn Press 1 lease	$2,900		0.6%
275T Van Dorn Press 2 lease	$2,900		0.6%
Indirect labor	$142,526		27.6%
Overhead total		$222,056	43.0%
Cost of goods manufactured		$516,645	100.0%

sufficient to meet the demand. This option had a unit cost of $15.0144 ($516,645/34,410).

In order to meet the demand, a six-day operation was required to produce 41,385 units over a four-week period. This option had a unit cost of $14.2719 ($590,642/41,385). This was a validation of the current operations at throughput, resource requirements, and unit cost levels.

Management was interested only in cost management for the contract. There were also penalties for not meeting certain costs. The *pro forma* income statements were not calculated.

Phase 5: "What-If?"

The "what-if?" plan specified the decision options to be quantified by ProFIT-MAP. The results are highlighted here.

Redundant Capacity at Welding Station

- The capital investment basis increased by $400,000, by adding the redundant welding station.
- The dynamic throughput analysis showed no improvement in throughput, contrary to the prediction from the steady-state analysis.
- Because of the increase in the capital basis, a five-day operation (the design policy), which would still be insufficient to meet the original demand would increase the unit cost to $16.0890. There is less volume over five days to absorb the fixed cost.
- The line still needed to operate six days per week to meet the original demand, resulting in a unit cost of $14.9004. The increase in volume because of the sixth day of operation would spread the fixed cost lowering the unit cost. The unit cost was higher than the current operating cost because of the extra capital investment, which increased the fixed cost for the same demand volume.

Redesign the Line

- This was a follow-on scenario to the purchase of the new welding station. It was a second step in the roadmap to recover from a decision that did not solve the problem.
- The approach was to make the most of the investment (i.e., the sunk cost). This involved duplicating the portion of the line that followed the Welder to take advantage of the redundant welding capacity.
- An additional investment of $35,000 was necessary to add the extra redundancy at the other operations. Three additional people and appropriate fixtures were also added.
- The redesigned line yielded an hourly rate of 105 units.
- If the line operated at its full capacity of 105 units per hour, the unit cost would become $14.1656. The total throughput would be more than the required demand; therefore, this is an artificial number unless the customer accepts the increased production. The increased production could not be sold elsewhere because it is a captive business. If the customer agrees, then the extra production could be released into the aftermarket.
- The line capacity over a five-day period was more than the current demand per week. It was decided to operate the line for only

4.5 days per week, yielding a unit cost of $13.9302. The cost went down because the resources, which are a variable cost, were not used for half a day per week.

- This fixed both the problem of meeting current demand and the problem of meeting the 15 percent over plan clause. Furthermore, it reduced per-unit cost over the current operations by 2.4 percent, resulting in an annual savings of over one-half million dollars, a sizable savings for a business doing only $7 million per year.

Table 10-13 summarizes the unit costs for all of the management scenarios. The 4.5-Day Redesigned Line Operation not only met the over plan demand, but also had a unit cost 6.5 percent lower than that of the 6-Day Redundant Capacity Operation that was incapable of meeting the over plan requirement.

General Conclusions

- Reducing the cycle time and driving the labor harder had little or no significant advantage in terms of either throughput or financials. This supported the operations manager's intuition that the problem was with the line structure rather than with the labor.

Table 10-13. Unit Cost Summary

Scenario	Unit Cost	Result
Original design		
5-day operation	$15.0144	Did not meet current or over plan demand.
6-day operation	$14.2719	Met current demand only.
Redundant capacity		
5-day operation	$16.0890	Does not meet current demand.
6-day operation	$14.9004	Meets current demand only.
Line redesign		
5-day operation	$14.1656	Meets over plan demand with excess capacity.
4.5-day operation	$13.9302	Meets over plan demand.

- Adding a second welding station without adding redundancy in the remaining final operations did not improve the throughput in any measurable way. That is, the plant was not able to meet the over plan requirement even with the $400,000 capital investment. ProFIT-MAP showed how to recover from this investment decision by demonstrating that an additional smaller capital investment would collectively produce the desired results.
- The plant was rich in capital investment; therefore, fixed costs dominated the costs of goods manufactured, followed by material and direct labor costs. This pattern was in line with other comparable automotive facilities.
- Significant other cost-reduction opportunities still exist in reducing overhead or increasing revenues.
- The redesigned line had excess available capacity. Although it was currently a dedicated line, it is possible to convert it into a flexible line to add to the top-line revenue with similar products.
- The direct labor cost was comparatively small and therefore shows no sensitivity to using overtime labor.

Recommendations

- Invest the additional $35,000 to create the extra redundant capacity. The incremental investment increases flexibility in the line that results in over $500,000 in cost savings per year.
- Operate the line for only 4.5 days per week to meet the demand with the 15 percent over plan obligation. Dedicate the remaining half day to preventive maintenance to further reduce *failure* rates.
- The taillights were manufactured as a set of left and right units. Given the recommended parallel line for final operations, explore the possibility of reducing capital and space investments by separating them into left and right lines.
- Investigate the cost of preventive maintenance versus the station *failure* rates to determine the optimal level of maintenance to perform.

Management Postscript

Agile Manufacturing implemented ProFIT-MAP two years into a five-year contract, when management was given 60 days to correct the problem. The line had reached design capacity by the end of the first year. The three previous steady-state analyses were done over the course of the second year and resulted in investment in a new welding station. Clearly, management had its back to the wall at this late stage. It was dealing with a dissatisfied customer, bleeding money, and procuring potentially unnecessary capital equipment. The second welding station, for example, might not have been necessary if management had considered moving away from a one-piece flow to correct the bottleneck. We will never know, because management chose not to examine this issue, as they perceived it would be contrary to the spirit of the lean awards that they had received. We contend that management by facts is more effective than management by rules of thumb. Just as in the first case study, this was another misapplication of sound lean principles.

The ProFIT-MAP methodology was implemented over a four-week period, with the problem identification done almost immediately. It literally took longer to decide what management scenarios to evaluate than to crunch the numbers. Each scenario required only a few seconds of processing time on a personal computer once the parameters and the enterprise data were in place.

If ProFIT-MAP had been implemented to help design the line at the contract start-up or to refine the line shortly after setup, management would have known immediately that a problem existed and would have had the time to proactively guide the operation in the right direction. For example, if ProFIT-MAP had been deployed from day one, the company could have prevented a loss of $1 million in extra costs in the first two years, or $2.5 million over the term of the contract.

The truth of the matter was that the customer had already decided to cancel the contract. ProFIT-MAP was implemented too late in the cycle, as the customer had already lost confidence in the management team's ability to execute. This was understandable from the customer's perspective, as it felt compelled to act to mitigate the risks to its vehicle program. Don't let this happen to you!

Epilogue

Profit Mapping Your Ideal Future

Facts do not cease to exist because they are ignored.

—Aldous Huxley

A vision without execution is a hallucination.

—Proverb

PROFIT-MAP IS A strategically driven methodology for business execution with six specific intuitive steps. We designed ProFIT-MAP from the ground up to enhance an organization's ongoing initiatives and measurement frameworks. The functional knowledge embedded in the ProFIT-MAP methodology links business objectives via the three management perspectives (process, resources, and finance) to specific business execution parameters. With ProFIT-MAP, the linkages between the parameters, management perspectives, and strategy are bidirectional. Thus, the methodology is equally suitable for crafting strategy and for executing it, and it provides insight into how one affects the other. Most importantly, it firmly grounds both activities within the company's actual capabilities, constraints, and costs. In today's global economy, you no longer have the time or resources to keep firing and then aiming; you have to know that your actions will be successful before you take them.

Enterprise systems, such as ERP and MRP-II, are rich in historical performance data that help managers understand the outcomes of their past decisions. No less importantly, however, managers are concerned with making decisions that will shape the future. Ideally, this is done in a proactive and coordinated manner, and it is aided by insightful information about future performance. Unfortunately, historical data are of little value in creating the future, where the circumstances are new and different.

Until ProFIT-MAP, there was no way for managers to integrate enterprise information with functional knowledge. Thus, managers were limited to applying rules of thumb using generic tools that extrapolated historical data in ways that created an unrealistic and often incorrect view of the future. Since neither strategy making nor business execution is about optimizing past performance, managers need tools that can inform them whether their decisions will result in the expected outcomes or will in fact produce only insignificant gains, or even lead to a reduction in performance. ProFIT-MAP fills this management tool void by providing an iterative methodology for projecting execution into the future and for proactively responding and adjusting to opportunities and challenges as they arise. In addition, implementing ProFIT-MAP on top of enterprise applications and databases creates a real-time decision system unlike any that has been seen before.

ProFIT-MAP is not a reinvention of existing frameworks or process improvement philosophies. It is a new approach built on the fundamentals of systems theory in the form of a Parametric Activities-Based Framework (pABF). One of the strengths of this approach is the incredible flexibility that comes with its rigor. This flexibility has some distinct advantages. For example, the way it is applied to solve a particular business challenge is dictated by the challenge itself, not by the framework. With other improvement approaches, the particular philosophy contains inherent biases that shape how one approaches the business challenge, resulting in the exclusion of critical perspectives, which can have dire business consequences. In addition, a systems theory approach enables the system to be driven more accurately and allows you to understand the implications of your decision prior to taking action. It is the difference between navigating with printed roadmaps and navigating with a GPS navigation system. Sure, both can get you to the same destination. But the latter is a much more value-adding proposition. It can both get you to the destination more quickly and reduce the cost of getting there. Most importantly, it reduces the risk of making decisions that will take you off course, and it helps you quickly correct course when necessary.

In this book, we explored how flow dynamics provides a great opportunity to improve decision making. This is a significant advance over typical throughput models that take a static view of a process. The old adage that the only thing that is constant is change is particularly relevant here. Not only does change result from direct actions, but it also occurs in the absence of any controlling influence. That is, even without any management action, the system is always changing as a result of the effects of corporate "inertia." A healthy operational system won't stay that way forever, as the force of its own inertia (internal factors) will take it off course without any external influences. The ProFIT-MAP methodology integrates the functional knowledge about process flow dynamics to yield a unique activities composition for each management scenario that is being evaluated. It further extends this information to the resource requirements and the corresponding financials. In addition, the dynamic analysis approach underlying the pABF actually incorporates the behavior of process inertia in the activities composition, presenting a view that is much closer to reality than that given by other approaches. This helps overcome the reality gap between the expectations for strategy and the ability of the organization to execute the strategy.

BEYOND OPERATIONAL PROCESSES

ProFIT-MAP creates a business execution roadmap to help you get to where you want to go. The future is wide open for the application of ProFIT-MAP to enhance many other types of nonoperational processes. In this book, we have focused on the process of producing goods and services. But there are also other critical processes that we do not address, such as marketing and sales. These are examples of other core corporate processes that can have enormous cost and performance implications for the company.

Although the dynamic activities composition would be different for nonoperational processes, the two types of processes would nonetheless have in common an activities composition containing all of the underlying process information that could be viewed from multiple management perspectives. The extensibility of ProFIT-MAP to incorporate additional perspectives is what makes it possible to use the same methodology for nonoperational processes. ProFIT-MAP's foundation in functional knowledge as opposed to data mining makes this possible. History is a good but an imperfect teacher, and a poorer guide.

Regardless of its application to operational or nonoperational processes, using ProFIT-MAP changes your *perspective*. More specifically, it facilitates changing from the typical mindset of looking at any particular business problem from the comfort zone of one's preferred perspective, to a broader multidimensional view that acknowledges that there are other important perspectives beyond our role or discipline. It helps us see both the forest and the trees of business execution.

Appendix
The ProFIT-MAP
Methodology

USING PROFIT-MAP FOR YOUR APPLICATION

In this section, we present a number of common management questions that the ProFIT-MAP methodology can help answer prior to execution. The list is not exhaustive, but it is suggestive, and it is designed to stimulate thought about how you can apply ProFIT-MAP to your challenge. The sample questions illustrate a range from strategic to tactical and operational applications.

Sample Business Execution Questions

- How can I meet my customer's frequently changing production requirements and still hit my profit goals?
- How can I improve customer satisfaction?
- What are my low-margin products that I might want to outsource?
- How can I improve labor efficiency and reduce unacceptable overtime costs?
- How can I improve profit margins by 10 percent to hit my budget goal?
- What is the best way to alter production to build a profitable manufacturing strategy among several plants?
- What are the profit and capacity impact from converting from a batch to a continuous-flow operation?

- What is the financial return on my make-versus-outsource decision?
- How will my profits change if I alter my product mix?
- How can I achieve continuous process improvements on an ongoing basis?
- Can I scale to meet contract contingencies?
- Can I produce multiple products on the same line instead of one product per line? What is my cost in the new environment?
- How do I achieve the endgame of the strategic plan?
- Is it possible to reach our throughput and quality goals? If yes, can this be done profitably? If no, what additional capabilities and resources are required?

Sample Business Execution Projects

Table A-1 highlights eight broad applications of the ProFIT-MAP methodology. The previous questions are specific applications involving one or more of the categories listed in the table. The list covers many areas: operations, planning, optimization, real-time manage-

Table A-1. Sample Business Execution Projects

Current Operations	Real-Time Management	Plant Optimization	Operations Planning
Process, people, policy	Real-time job tracking	Line and product COGM	Production verification
Equipment modernization	Real-time costing	Line and product profitability	Labor planning
Trouble-shooting	Real-time job scheduling		Inventory planning
Asset efficiency analysis	Real-time labor scheduling		Budgeting
			Demand forecasting
			Demand fulfillment
			Line profit forecasting

Table A-1. Sample Business Execution Projects (*Continued*)

Process Redesign	Business Optimization	Product Planning	Business Planning
Product Routings	Product Rationalization	Investment Assessment	Growth Planning
Buffer designs	Supplier selection	R&D justification	Responding to RFQ
Batch sizing	Warranty cost reduction		Site selection
Hidden or idle capacity			Ramp-up strategy
			Profit forecasting

ment, redesign, and business and product planning. Although it is not exhaustive, it illustrates the breadth of applicability of the methodology. Your role in an organization will determine the types of projects that are of interest to you. Keep in mind that your interests also have interconnections with other elements of the organization.

BUSINESS EXECUTION PROFILE TEMPLATE

In this section we present the business execution profile in a template form, ready for input. The profile is first described in Chapter 6 using manufacturing and business services examples. The profile is a part of the Project Objectives phase of the methodology. It contains a statement of the problem, a description of the relevant business execution dimensions, and any additional notes.

Problem Statement
Business Execution Dimensions

Dimension	Description
1. Roles and stakeholders	
2. Strategy	
3. Decision level	

Dimension	Description
4. Assessment focus	Reality gap:
	Business reality gap:
	Technology reality gap:
	Multidimensional impact:
	Dynamic impact:
	Interaction impact:
	Financial impact:
	Pathway:
5. ProFIT-MAP components	Process:
	Capital:
	Resources:
	Inventory and WIP:
	Finances:
6. Enterprise tools and data	
7. Parameters	

Profile Notes

PROFIT-MAP'S SIX PHASES

Figures A-1 through A-6 present the phase-by-phase details of the methodology. The iterative and flexible nature of the methodology is apparent in the flow within and between phases as the practitioner navigates the business challenge with ProFIT-MAP.

Figure A-1. ProFIT-MAP Phase 1: Project Objectives

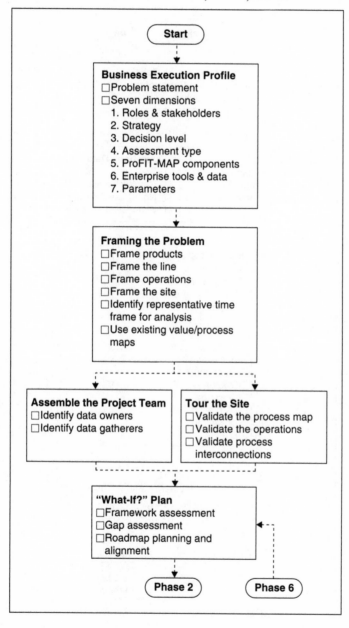

Figure A-2. ProFIT-MAP Phase 2: Process

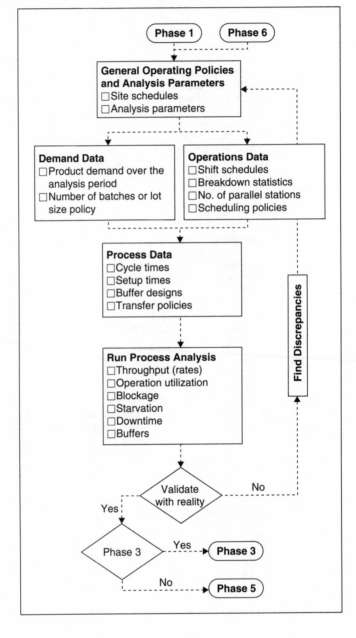

Figure A-3. ProFIT-MAP Phase 3: Resources

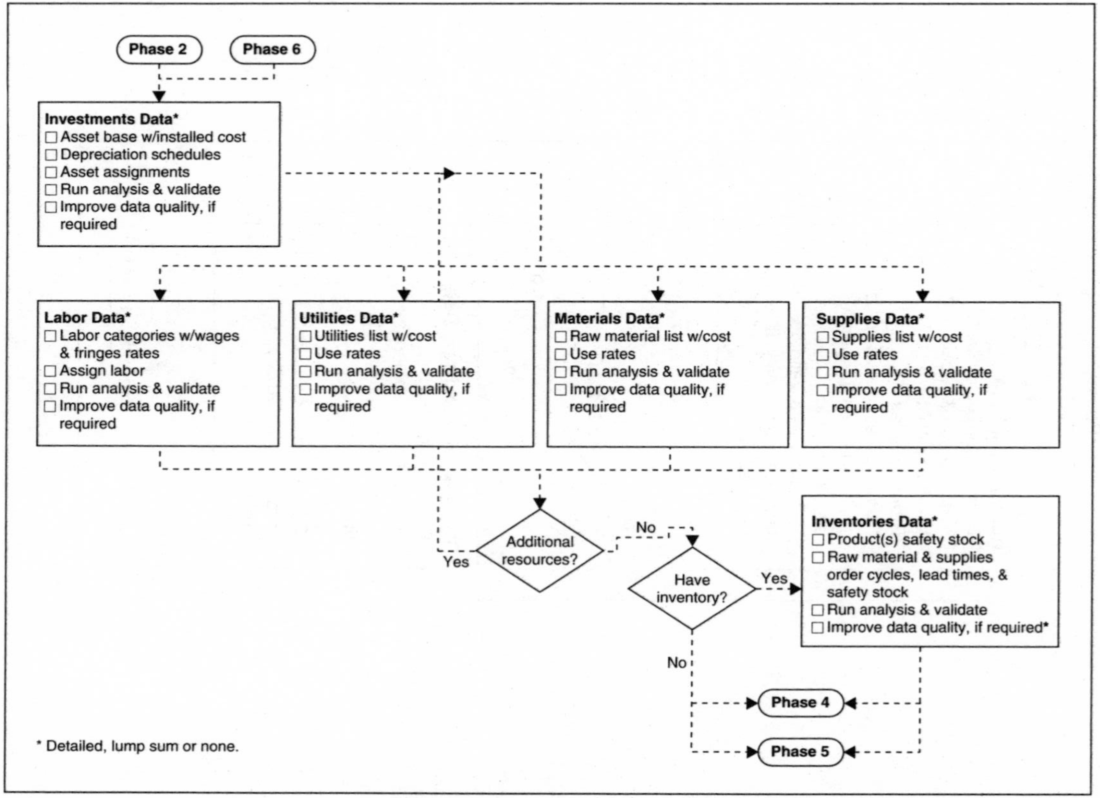

* Detailed, lump sum or none.

Figure A-4. ProFIT-MAP Phase 4: Finance

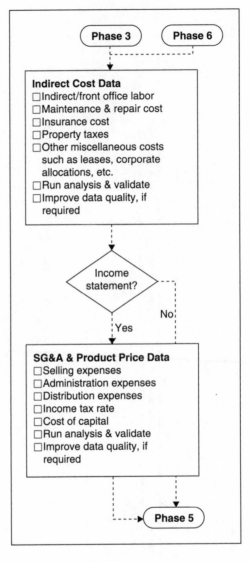

Figure A-5. ProFIT-MAP Phase 5: "What-If?"

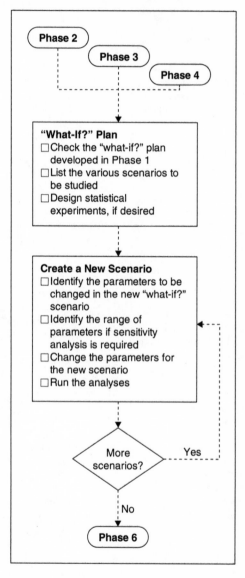

Figure A-6. ProFIT-MAP Phase 6: Choose Business Execution Option

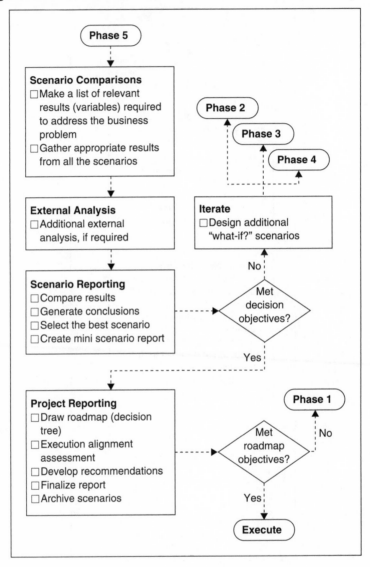

Index

ABOUT THE AUTHORS

Anil Menawat, Ph.D., the founder of Menawat & Co. (www.menawat.com), has over 20 years of experience in the manufacturing industry. As a champion of integrated process and financial analytics he has helped companies develop business and manufacturing strategies and reduce operating costs. His experience spans the automotive, industrial, aerospace, rubber, chemical, and pharmaceutical industries. Anil was a consulting engineer and senior manager for advanced manufacturing technology and new business development at Aeroquip Corp. Prior to that, he was an assistant professor at Tulane University, a visiting professor and consultant at Abbott Labs, and a process design engineer at Union Carbide. In 1994 *BusinessWeek* magazine reported on his pioneering work on nonlinear systems theory applications for decision making. He is listed in *Who's Who in Science and Engineering* and has published over 25 articles in scientific and trade journals.

Adam Garfein, Ph.D., is cofounder of Menawat & Co. (www.menawat.com). Before that, Adam founded Devane Corporation, a strategy, process, and e-business consulting and education firm. Adam has over 15 years of strategic and operational experience with both manufacturing and services companies. His experiences encompass a variety of industries including those dealing with software, the Internet, pharmaceuticals, telecommunications, automotives, construction management, higher education, and state and federal governments. He is a sought-after speaker and panelist on issues of strategy, operational execution, marketing, and e-business and has published numerous articles in scientific and trade journals. Adam was a research scientist in the field of gerontology—the study of adult development and aging—prior to entering business and technology consulting.